The International Library of Sociology

GERMAN YOUTH: BOND OR FREE

I0421424

Founded by KARL MANNHEIM

The International Library of Sociology

THE SOCIOLOGY OF
YOUTH AND ADOLESCENCE
In 12 Volumes

GERMAN YOUTH:
BOND OR FREE

by

HOWARD BECKER

Routledge
Taylor & Francis Group

LONDON AND NEW YORK

First published in 1946 by
Routledge, Trench, Trubner and Co.,Ltd

Reprinted in 1998 by
Routledge
2 Park Square, Milton Park, Abingdon, Oxon, OX14 4RN
711 Third Avenue, New York, NY 10017

Transferred to Digital Printing 2007

Routledge is an imprint of the Taylor & Francis Group, an informa business

First issued in paperback 2013

British Library Cataloguing in Publication Data
A CIP catalogue record for this book
is available from the British Library

ISBN13: 978-0-415-17667-5 (hbk)
ISBN13: 978-0-415-86351-3 (pbk)

Publisher's Note
The publisher has gone to great lengths to ensure the quality of this reprint
but points out that some imperfections in the original may be apparent

CONTENTS

First published 1946

To

MY WIFE AND CHILDREN

THIS BOOK IS PRODUCED IN
COMPLETE CONFORMITY WITH
THE AUTHORIZED STANDARDS

PREFACE

Everybody and his brother, to judge by the public prints, is now hard at work making schemes for the solution of " What to Do with Germany ? " Some of these schemes are solidly based on thorough knowledge of the motley jumble called Germany and of its kaleidoscopic changes in past and present. Certain others, however, rest only on a billowy foundation of good intentions, and might well be ignored if it were not for their superficial plausibility. Indeed, they will be ignored in the pages to follow, but only because searching examination and demolition of these jerry-built proposals would take far more room than can possibly be allotted here. Moreover, there seems little point in prying on the wrecking bar unless an alternative scheme is to be erected on the ground thereby cleared. Such a formula, programme, or what you will, is a pressing necessity, no doubt of that, but although those of us who feel the need are neither fools nor angels—or perhaps for that very reason— it seems wise to choose a new site and look it over with care before even drawing the first lines of what might be hoped to constitute a plan for a trustworthy structure.

This little book is informed by such an exploratory purpose, and that only. The eventual structure will be the work of many hands. My task is simply to sketch a rough map and make a few borings in one corner of the ground. Leaving the metaphor : One aspect of German society that seems of strategic importance is the younger generation. Offhand, nobody would contest this statement, but in order to make its remoter bearings more obvious I wish to quote a few passages from a summary expressing my convictions as they stood six years ago. This résumé was entitled " Hitler Does it with Mirrors, or The Rise and Perversion of the German Youth Movement ", and here it is :

Soon after the time we discover that there is no Santa Claus, we should be discovering that there is no magic in social and political life. Unfortunately, a great many grown-ups never learn that " it's done with mirrors " ; they think that such a thing as present-day Germany, for example, has been conjured up overnight by the mystical hocus-pocus of a mighty magician named Adolf Hitler. Well, let us go behind the footlights and see, focusing our eyes on one trick in the repertory billed as " The Creation of the Hitler Youth . . ."

Over a quarter of a century ago, a young German student and a few of his friends became what I shall call the Roamers (literal translation would give a false impression). They started a fellowship, romantic and idealistic in character, that because of its passionate championing of " the simple life " and " self-expression " set aflame the minds and hearts of adolescent Germany. Soon Karl Fischer's movement had members in every nook and corner of Germany, tramping through the woods with their guitars twanging, singing peasant songs, wearing loose, simple costume, and sending a fresh breath of naturalism through the stuffy middle-class manners of the day. . . .

But then came marching songs of another kind. The first World War revealed the true character of the Free German Youth and affiliated groups, for in spite of previous protests against the Germany of Kaiser Wilhelm, he had only to proclaim that the Fatherland was in danger to bring the whole Youth Movement thronging to the colours. In the terrible battle of Langemarck thousands of these youngsters marched singing into a hail of lead and iron from which only a handful returned alive. The life blood of the old Youth Movement was spilled in Flanders fields.

When the tragically misshapen and malnourished German Republic was born, there began a new phase in Youth Movement activities. Previously aloof from politics, German youth now rushed or were dragged into the camps of the various parties. Soon the Communists set up " youth divisions ", as did all the other parties, including the National Socialists. " Whoever wins the youth wins Germany " was the slogan, and the slogan-makers were right. Caught up in the swirl of conflicting ideologies, those who were still faithful to the old Youth Movement fought a brave but losing battle. The devotees of a youth culture, to be led by youth in the interests of youth, which was slowly to regenerate the materialistic adult world, were shouldered aside in the political stampede. Only a few insignificant hundreds, remnants of the true Youth Movement, were to be found wandering like lost children among the trampling millions of the politically regimented.

One of the " youth divisions " of the political parties was the National Socialist Youth, organized in 1924. Despised by the heirs of the old Free German Youth as politically subservient, and jeered at by the Communists and other left-wingers as reactionary, the Hitler Youth, in its beginnings, would probably have been voted as " least likely to succeed ". But under the maniacally shrewd control of a man skilled in " doing it with mirrors ", the Hitler Youth grew at a tremendous rate, and in 1933 Baldur von Schirach, Hitler's close friend and supreme leader of the Nazi youth, seized the leadership of all young Germans. Eventually (by 1936) all groups but the Hitler Youth were officially disbanded. The octopus had begun to work in real earnest. . . .

This hasty glimpse behind the scenes has given us some idea of how the trick of " The Creation of the Hitler Youth " is really worked. Now, to make the hocus-pocus still more evident, let us look at some of the specific items of the creed and ritual. Take the *Führerprinzip*, the leadership principle. This, as is well known, involves blind obedience to one's leader and entire responsibility for one's followers, a principle of which the only American examples are to be found among " party liners " and ward heelers. The general acceptance of this principle among Germans, of the younger generation in particular, has often been pointed to as the real secret of the strength of the Nazis. And now note this : The principle goes back at least as far as 1896, when Karl Fischer introduced it among the Roamers, whose unquestioned leader he was. The leader was not the elected or delegated representative of the group ; on the contrary, a man who felt himself " called " simply proclaimed himself leader, and if he had the necessary *charisma*, which we may translate as " the stuff " or even as " oomph ", he found devoted followers. All this was of no avail, however, if he was not accepted as a leader by the other leaders. It was a selective system, true enough, but the final decision was rendered by the leaders, not by the followers. . . . We can now see one of the old backdrops, can we not, that made it relatively easy for Hitler to " do it with mirrors " ? Hundreds of thousands—yes, even millions—of Germans had already been exposed, at a highly impressionable part of their lives, to the same type of domination as is now characteristic, not only of the Hitler Youth, but of German society as a whole. . . .

Once more, the drive for the union of all the Germanic peoples (which term takes in the Austrians, Dutch, the Scandinavians, the Bohemians, the Flemish, the Swiss, the Alsatians, and many others) is not new among young Germans. . . . Members of the old Youth Movement established camps or went as individuals among all the " provinces of the new and greater Germany "—not merely those " lost " by the Versailles treaty—where they zealously propagandized their cause. Beyond doubt many of the Fifth Columnists in these regions were men who as youngsters had been won over to " good-will " toward all things German. Was this Hitler's magic, or did he simply " do it with mirrors " ?

Again, anti-Semitism is not a Nazi innovation. True it is that among some of the sects of the old Youth Movement a few Jews were to be found, but in general they had to form their own organizations in the post-War period under religious or political auspices. The Jews, in the thinking of the old Youth Movement, were largely identified with crafty money-getting, mechanized philosophy, scheming rationalism, cold-blooded intellectuality. As a city people they were held to be for ever incapable of absorption in the holy cult of " Blood and Soil ", of acquiring the Germanic virtues of the simple, unspoiled peasant. The latent anti-Semitism of the old Youth Movement, therefore, needed only a powerful stimulus, such as that furnished by Hitler, to become fanatical hatred of all things Jewish.

Finally, the great ritual symbols of the Nazis, the shout of " Heil ! " and the extended right arm, were not originally Nazi at all. " Heil ! " was a greeting carried over from the Middle Ages, and used well over thirty years ago by the Roamers, and in 1923 there were several Youth Movement sects in which the ramrod arm was a standard gesture. Reflections, reflections every one.

Now, could readers ask questions, I am sure that many of you would say something like this : " What has become of your contention that ' Hitler does it with mirrors ' ?   If so many of these things were already in existence, no reflection was necessary.   The Hitler Youth was not a creation in a vacuum, we grant that, but neither was it the product of a trickster's skill.   We see no real difference between the old Youth Movement and Hitler's regimented youngsters, except for the greater numbers of the Führer's cohorts.   You have proved your point so well that you have destroyed your most important conclusion."

Taking into account only what I have said so far, the objections of my readers are sound.   But one thing has not been mentioned, and on that one thing the whole trick depends.   We have overlooked the mirrors themselves !   Have you ever visited a carnival or a side-show, and stepped into " The Crazy House"?   There, cleverly placed, you find mirrors that make you seem to be treading on air, mirrors that transmute the erect, soldierly man into a hunch-backed, club-footed changeling—mirrors, mirrors, mirrors, and not one of them yielding a true image !   Something like this has given Hitler his power.   With all its faults, the spirit of the old Youth Movement was something entirely different from that which now animates the distorted, perverted, terribly powerful, and yet pathetic-ally misguided Hitler youth.   Love of things German has become hatred of everything non-German ;   romantic idealism has become contempt for thought ;   allegiance to the values close at hand has become scorn of the values held by the rest of mankind ;   sturdy independence has become swash-buckling, truculent aggression ; loyalty to the chosen leader has become blind subservience to a despot ;   reverence for the sound body has become the avowed anti-rationality of " We think with our blood " ;   devotion to children as the bearers of the future German spirit has become the breeding of cannon-fodder.   Yes, Hitler has done it with mirrors, with mirrors patterned after his own warped and twisted soul.

What is the future of Germany, with its youth thus completely perverted and dominated by the illusions which they think to be the only images of the good and true ?   I fear that there is but one answer to this question.   From lads in the junior Hitler Youth at the age of eight to regular *Hitler Jugend* at fourteen, to labour service at eighteen, to compulsory military training for two years, to the Brown Shirts and the Black Shirts for the rest of their lives—if those lives have not been snuffed out at a far earlier age in the war that is to " make Germany supreme for the next thousand years "—German youth never once has the chance to escape from the encircling, distorting mirrors.   To smash the " Crazy House " will require a defeat and a revolution of such terrific proportions that even the anti-Nazis within Germany itself sometimes shrink at the prospect of the blood and tears it will inevitably entail.   But who can doubt that *we* dare not shrink ?[1]

---

[1] Revised and abridged rom a radio speech delivered over the N.B.C. Blue Network, San Francisco, California, August, 1940.

Since this was written further research and reflection have led to shifts in emphasis. Specimen : I would no longer assert that the connection between the Roamers and the Hitler Youth is quite so direct. Another : The undertone of approval of the Roamers and their methods would be eliminated. Still another : Much more attention should be given to what may be called youth tutelage organizations, as well as to the so-called alliance youth. These and similar transitional bodies considerably altered the ways in which, as I hope to show in the book proper, " perversion by the Führer's grace " was finally brought about. In broad outline, however, my 1940 statements still seem to have had fairly substantial warrant.

The lapse of six years would certainly have led to much more radical alteration had it not been for the exceptionally careful preliminary study conducted by Robert C. Schmid. As indicated above, Dr. Schmid was a graduate student at the University of Wisconsin who, in his capacity as my research assistant, did extensive field work in Germany on youth movement problems. At earlier periods I had myself studied these problems, and I did supervise both Schmid's field work and the writing of the report on which his dissertation, " German Youth Movements : A Typological Study ", was based. I should be less than straightforward, however, if I were to intimate that Schmid's work had not been of much help in the documentation of the present book. The footnotes here and there bear witness, however inadequately, to this fact. Dr. Schmid has been for several years a member of the armed forces, and in his military capacity is prohibited from any participation in publications such as this. Consequently, I have made use of his 1939 dissertation *only,* in spite of the fact that he has perhaps worked since that time along lines which would greatly expand and qualify his evidence and hypotheses. When and if he returns to civilian life and thus becomes able to speak in his own name, it is entirely possible that he will bring out an independent youth movement study in published form, but until then I must rest content with saying that on the basis of his 1939 work alone his part in this book deserves prominent acknowledgement.

Acknowledgement should also be made to my research assistant for 1943–4, Hugh Engelmann, who has done much both in the uncovering of highly significant data with which I was not previously familiar, and in suggestions for modification of the hypotheses which I have tentatively formulated. His primary function, however, was the collection and analysis of materials bearing on Austrian youth movements, particularly among the working classes. Unfortunately, I shall be unable to make much direct reference to his interesting and meaningful results. At some date not too far in the future it may be possible to publish the gist of Mr. Engelmann's conclusions.

Thanks are also due to the Research Committee of the Graduate School of the University of Wisconsin, which through its generous underwriting of research assistants and summer leave made the researches of Schmid, Engelmann, and myself possible. For my own earlier investigations, mention should be made of George Pratt, Jr., who financed my National Student Forum field study of German youth movements in 1923, to the Institute of International Education, instrumental in securing my research fellowship in Cologne for 1926–7, and to the Social Science Research Council, responsible for my post-doctoral fellowship in France and Germany during 1934–5. The library staffs of Smith College and the University of Wisconsin gave efficient aid, but second only to their assistance was that provided by many other librarians at institutions all over the United States—too many, much to my regret, to list.

Further, I wish to express my gratitude to the many refugee scholars who have provided documents, personal reminiscences, and counsel. Some of them, even now, feel that their chances of getting along with a minimum of friction if they should return to Germany would be greater if their names were not mentioned here, and I yield to their wishes. Others, however, have no such misgivings ; I mention Drs. Hans Ebeling, H. H. Gerth, Paul Honigsheim, Hans Rehfisch, and Svend Riemer.

Naturally, I also wish to thank the editor of the International Library of Sociology and Social Reconstruction, Dr. Karl Mannheim, for the considerate attention he gave to the manuscript at a time when V-1's and V-2's occasionally seemed of overwhelmingly greater importance than anything else. A debt is also felt with regard to Herbert Read, one of contemporary Britain's most eminent writers, critics, and social analysts, who patiently read the entire manuscript—but who is in no way responsible, I hasten to add, for flaws in style or shortcomings in content.

The fact that I was a member of the Office of Strategic Services during the latter part of World War II is noted on the title page. This organization, as is now generally known, was the American equivalent of the British Political Intelligence Division of the Foreign Office and of the Secret Operations Executive as well. As explained in the Epilogue and its notes, however, the acknowledgement due to OSS is, for *this* book, of general character only. The tenses used in Chapters VIII and IX make it clear that the book as such was completed *before* I had any access to secret sources of information. Even in the Epilogue, added just before publication, no " personal experiences of a military character " are recounted ; I have simply brought the exoteric phases up to date. Consequently I have not submitted the manuscript for security check. At the same time, the opportunity to deal with things German during wartime, and to enter Germany, has been of much indirect value, and I hereby express my appreciation.

Finally, mention should be made of Elisabeth Settlage, whose efficient secretarial services lightened the burden at a crucial time, and of my son, Christopher Bennett Becker, who did yeoman work on the Index.

HOWARD BECKER

MADISON, WISCONSIN
February 1, 1946

PART ONE

CHAPTER I

MYTH : THE LINDEN TREE

> Am Brunnen vor dem Tore
> da steht ein Lindenbaum :
> ich träumt in seinem Schatten
> so manchen süssen Traum.*
> —Müller, " Der Lindenbaum ".

Man lives by myth. Animal among other animals, yes—
but animal of altogether peculiar kind, for on his long and
toilsome path of development he has acquired " the gift of
tongues ". Man talks, and talking, he weaves a network of
symbols that simultaneously helps him to master some aspects of
the world about him and to create, in what we loosely call
imagination, Golden Ages of past, present, or future. In those
brief moments when he escapes from the ruts of routine, when
for fleeting instants he ceases to respond automatically to the
pushes and pulls of every day, he is gripped by fancies of which
he is himself the creator. The realm that we call real fades ;
the vistas of myth shimmer and glow. " If men define situations
as real, they are real in their consequences."

No one can understand the rise of the German youth movement, its unhappy fate, and its uncertain future, unless he
succeeds in projecting himself, however imperfectly, into the
myth-inspired minds of the boys and girls, men and women, who
strove to realize what they held to be an ideal Germany. The
revolt of Karl Fischer and his successors is meaningless unless we
too catch the appealing vision of The Linden Tree through the
haze of The Dear Dead Days, and see how that vision helped to
engender the appalling image of Rimmon's House. We must
grope our way back to the Biedermeier time, the era from 1815
to 1845, and immerse ourselves in the little world of Friedl and
Bärbele :

No snow was on the ground, and the firs lining the path to
grandfather's tiny retreat stood there in their dark green uniforms

---

* At the wellspring by the village gate
There stands a linden tree :
In the leafy shade beneath its boughs
Sweet dreams oft came to me.

The Linden Tree.

like stern but friendly soldiers. The linden leaves had fallen, of course, and just outside the primly raked little dooryard the ground was covered with them, but still their silvery glow in the moonlight could seem like footing for the reindeer only to the wide-eyed children. Perhaps Nikolaus first began to make his early December visit farther to the north, but what of that? Here in Suabia he was welcome, you may be sure, and neither Friedl nor Bärbele ever thought of asking how he came. For almost a month he could be counted on : hiding in the old clothespress or high up in the smoky rafters among the sausages ; scuttling hastily out of sight when he and the long-bearded dwarfs who helped him were taken by surprise ; petting the purring cat, quieting the yelping dog, and stroking the clucking chickens on the roost ; tapping busily in the cellar and the shed—making everything ready for the Christ Child who would bring the nuts and apples or alas ! the hazel switches.

Jockel was too little to share in the twittering excitement, and even squalled when Friedl, tired of the task of rocking him, gave the cradle a hasty push and scurried to the door in the hope that he would be safely out of sight before Vaterl and Mutterl could realize how he had shirked his duty. Lisel, Rudolf, and the rest of the older children began to grumble a little, for they knew that one of them would have to supply the gentle to-and-fro, but still there were compensations : Friedl could be reminded of the hazel switches, or better—and this is what did happen, *Juchhe !*— Mutterl would hale him back by the slack of his shiny leather breeches. After a few brisk taps on the appropriate spot, she told a story—one of the *Ach !* so many stories—about the witch who puts changelings in neglected cradles. Grandfather had often regaled his numerous progeny with the same folktale, but on this occasion he did not need to refresh Mutterl's memory, although he did add a few horrifying details that sent delicious shivers through even big Konrad, who as a nineteen-year-old had for several years thought of himself as among the grownups.

But Konrad kept those shivers very much to himself, for sixteen-year-old Annele was sitting beside him on the bench, and her round apple-red face was turned archly toward him, toward Konrad Baumann himself. No betrothal yet, but it couldn't be far away ; of all the village lads he was the only one to whom her window ever opened now. She too had a swarm of brothers and sisters, but they weren't underfoot any longer. All the Hoebel girls had married and the brothers were scattered far and wide. Two were in faraway America, but from the one letter they had jointly written about their pleasant Pennsylvania farms it was clear that they would never come back to claim patches of the ten-acre Suabian hillside, and the other two had fallen when Napoleon bestrode their little world. Odd that one had fought for him and one against! But politics was bad for simple folk, *nicht wahr?* The lucky chap who married Annele would have the whole ten acres, and two of the pieces lay side by side— only one three-acre strip was separate, and that was but a brisk quarter-hour's walk away.

More, Annele's solid arms and broad back promised good hoeing and easy childbirth, and already she had been spinning and weaving the towels and sheets and shirtcloth. By two more Christmases, at the most, she would have enough so that four or five washings a year would carry them through, and after all only the daughters of fifty-acre peasants could possibly fill chests good for the times from harvest to Easter and from Easter to harvest. Her father and mother seemed to think that he was a good worker too; at least at the last parish fair they had gone out of their way to give fat chunks of roast goose to his parents. Perhaps it was already arranged. Hadn't Annele been coming over a lot lately, and hadn't Vaterl chucked her under the chin, and hadn't Mutterl given her the recipe for marrow dumplings that had come down from great-grandmother?

Soon, perhaps Annele's father would ask him to go to the village schoolmaster and draw up the agreement about how much food and fuel Konrad would provide after he and Annele had taken over the two-room house with the three bed niches. The other, the little one-room dwelling where the old folks would live out the rest of their days, needed a new roof, and panes were missing from each of the two windows, but perhaps the schoolmaster would see that Konrad didn't get the worst of the bargain; after all, every one of his whole four years of school had been under the kindly eye of the old fellow. He thrashed a good deal, but that was expected, and he gave fair warning, after all—" Du kriegst Schläge!" He told famous stories, too, but usually out of school hours; when you were in school there was no time for pleasant little asides. But the stories were not like Mutterl's; they were different as befits a learned man, a real *Gelehrter*. Odd that he should have drifted into a Suabian village school— all his learning! Why, he might have become a professor, maybe even at Tübingen. With that queer light in his eyes, he would tell all about the Spartans and the Athenians and the Romans, and the wayfaring scholars of old times and beweaponed knights and Siegfried's sword-winning and how that wicked old French Louis—which one was it ?—had burned and slaughtered everywhere up and down Father Rhine. How could he know so much ? After all, though, your betters always know so much. . . .

Maybe the schoolmaster's help wouldn't be so necessary ; the Hoebels were shrewd, as good peasants should be, but they were proud and probably would prefer to wear out rather than rust out. Just like the old clock up there, ticking away, with the glow of the fire on its face. Yes, in Horb, just a few miles away, there was a place where you could sell those hand-carved clock cases that Grandfather Hoebel was already turning out when the weather kept him indoors. Too, Grandmother Hoebel—and it wouldn't be long until they would really be grandparents—was a needlewoman renowned for miles around ; she'd have things to sell. They might even leave a little nest-egg. Already there were jokes about the stockingful of coins under the loose brick in the hearth. No, it wouldn't be a hard bargain.

After the schoolmaster, then the priest—but quite a while after. A year or two, perhaps ? It would be fine if Annele was well along in the family way before the wedding ; she looked healthy—*ein saftiges Mädele*—but sometimes women were barren. The priest would make them do a little penance, and Mutterl would shake a reproving finger, but Vaterl would know how it was. Well, maybe not, maybe not. What would the Hoebels think ? And the worthies from the Schnitzelbank tavern—would they scatter straw at the wedding ? It might be a little risky. But anyway, with luck there would be plenty of strong youngsters to weed, glean, tend the geese and pigs, pick up wood when the watchful eye of the forester was turned aside, and run little errands for the old folks—that would be good. And always to see merry faces at the *Fest*, blood of your blood, flesh of your flesh, who would never let the homestead pass on to strangers. The boys might get into a brawl now and then, of course—those villagers beyond the hill, with their odd twang and noisy ways, sometimes had to be set back on their heels—but knifeplay needn't be feared if you had a little skill. Konrad felt the scar on his wrist, and grinned to himself.

The girls would be harder to handle, but Annele could watch them, and loose women were rare. Let's see, there were only the daughters of that cooper in Horb, and they'd be moving on soon, anyway. The one with the brown hair looked *appetitlich*, but it would be best not to think about her—trash was trash. Yes, Annele's daughters would be safe. She was a good picker of the sober lads, those who meant no nonsense. Of course, tinkers and the rest of the footloose *Gesindel* weren't a real problem. You could tell what they were as soon as you saw them coming. True, a really good-looking girl might strike the fancy of some nobleman, especially if she went to work at a *château*, but somehow you needn't worry much about that. When such girls came back home nobody asked impertinent questions if they didn't give themselves too many airs, and occasionally they could help out with their own dowries.

Nobles were a queer lot, always travelling around or going to the wars. Elegant, too, even though Frenchified. Count Hohentwiel was one of the best of them ; even before the land went back to the peasants you had to work on his estate only for about two weeks a year, and nowadays he never asked for more than was his due. All this talk of getting rid of him was well enough in its way, but God had put bits in some people's mouths and gave the reins to others. As long as he didn't take the parish lads and hire them out for soldiers, the way they did in Vaterl's time up there in Hessia, things weren't too bad. Let those greasy fellows in Stuttgart talk about red caps and trees of liberty if they wanted to ; Vaterl had heard the same story forty years ago and, just as he said, no good ever came of that nonsense. Count Hohentwiel wasn't like the Junkers up in Mecklenburg with all those hired hands they had made out of their serfs. *Pfui*, they were serfs anyway. Let well enough alone ; those who didn't like what they had could always go to some outlandish country.

Besides, hadn't Father Hauer said that God had set everybody in his proper place ? Maybe the good priest was too thick with the nobility and their hangers-on, but he was himself the son of a peasant who didn't even have a span of oxen. Surely he knew what was best for this world and the next. When you went to confession he seemed to know what you were going to say even before you'd thought of it yourself, and how impressively he could chant all those long words in the mass ! Yes, he was a real holy man ; everybody said that he stopped to say a " Hail Mary " or an " Our Father " at all the crossroads shrines. Sometimes he blessed the fields or prayed for rain even though his bishop thought he shouldn't. " Württemberg isn't Bavaria ! "

Bishop Kern had said. But Father Hauer did what he thought God would want him to do for his peasants, and although there were bad crops and droughts, maybe someone in the parish was sinning in secret. If the hard-hearted wouldn't confess, not even Father Hauer could fix things up. No question but that he knew the right saints.

It was good, too, that the priest always backed up the old folks. Annele had never been undutiful and neither had he, but it was just as well to hear those words about obeying parents and living long in the land. What was that other saying: " Whoso looketh upon father or mother with an angry eye shall die the death " ? That was pretty hard, but when you were thinking about starting your own family it had a different ring. No, it was only right that Vaterl should lay down the law, mildly if possible, sternly if need be.

Mutterl had to obey Vaterl too, but she had her own little ways of getting what she wanted. It was all well enough, but Annele had better not try any of those tricks. If she cried in order to get her own way that would be too bad, but women were like that anyway. " The wife should not crow like the cock." Just let her flap her wings a little when she told the children that her good Konrad was always right and that he had always done what his father had told him. That wouldn't be a lie, either, for Vaterl had always made it clear that if you were going to be a man you had to learn everything that Vaterl had learned from his father, and so on back. The almanac wasn't enough. What chance would you ever have if you were for ever grumbling and balking ? Sons and fathers should always stick together ; " clashing pots are soon broken ".

Konrad's musings came to a sudden end as Annele jogged him with her plump elbow. Didn't they have an honoured guest ? Sure enough, the old schoolmaster had been there all the time, and now he was smiling indulgently at the boy who forgot to pull at his forelock and bob a bow. The flush on Konrad's face ran around to the back of his neck and up into his close-cropped black hair, and he stammered something about Nikolaus and the babies, and then added : " Too bad, Frau Lehrer isn't here." It was all meant for an apology, but it had an overly familiar tone—if Frau Lehrer had come it would have been just a little too much social intermingling—and the schoolmaster visibly drew his dignity about him.

These good people meant well, but they had to be reminded that their superiors condescended only when they met with appropriate humility. Herr Lehrer Bertram's own father had been a privy councillor in Oldenburg, and had provided a fine education for his oldest son. Only think : in the *Gymnasium* he had read Horace and all the other great writers, and at Heidelberg, Göttingen, and Tübingen he had made a special study of the Homeric Hymns. Fate had placed him in a little Suabian school, although Tübingen had also had a hand in it, but that was no reason why he should ever forget the responsibilities of his station in life. Moreover, these peasants were a little too easy-going ; they needed a stern schoolmaster to keep them properly respectful and mindful of discipline. One should deal kindly with these grown-up children, but kindness had to be tempered with firmness—how else would they learn to order themselves lowly and reverently to all their betters ?

It was just as well that those two Hoebel boys in America didn't intend to return ; there were too many ideas about natural rights and the rest of that romantic nonsense floating about. Even Goethe had come to realize that ; he might have written *Götz* as a young fellow, but when he got older he steadied down—for a while he even did the work of an honest official up in Weimar. That companion of his, Schiller, had received a medal from those odious French revolutionaries, and he had never got rid of his frothiness ; " The Robbers " could have done a lot of damage if it had seeped out among the common people. Even as it was these feverish little knots and clusters of students who banded together in those Young Fellows' Clubs, those absurd *Burschenschaften*, chattered about Karl Moor, and in Giessen and other places they were causing enough political trouble to make it necessary to suppress them ; right here in Suabia you heard something about them occasionally.

In spite of that, though, they seemed to be good Germans ; certainly they despised the French Bourbons. . . . Most of their fractiousness came from their longing to stop the squabbles between the pocket-sized principalities and dukedoms, and if they had their way they might succeed in getting enough union to shake a hard German fist under the nose of that conceited French king. Napoleon was a great man, after all, but a petty Bourbon. . . . How refreshing it would be to give him a good knocking about ! After all, a loose sort of union might be possible ; the Germans from Königsberg to Freiburg could understand each other easily if they mixed a little high German with their dialects, and that argued that the same blood flowed through their veins. To be sure, lots of these Suabians weren't blond, and Annele would be as dumpy as her mother when her hair grew grey, but the language must be in the blood. If only those fellows who followed old Jahn could be a little more discreet! Those *Turnvereine* where they swung on parallel bars and turned hand-springs and the glee clubs in which they performed with such gusto were really political ; one couldn't help being uneasy about them. Good Germans were never like new brooms ; what looked like feudal rubbish was really necessary if honest folk weren't to be like those delirious Frenchmen—revolutions and tyrannies and restorations and nothing settled.

Old Fritz knew what he was about ; he had really made Prussia amount to something. Naturally, no loyal *Untertan* of another state would want to see the Prussians get too strong, for they might overpower Württemberg and the other neat, orderly little *Länder*, but something could be learned from the example, just the same. The big thing was to keep the older and cooler heads in control. Young fellows might run fast but they finally got out of breath. *Gott sei Dank*, the *Burschenschaften* didn't have any real influence among the solid burghers, and of course the peasants had never heard of them. Even at the universities lots of the students were indifferent ; good Rhine wine and the land-lady's daughter rightly proved more attractive than for ever bellowing songs about German freedom.

The landlady's daughter . . . H'm : " Vivant omnes vir-gines, faciles accessu . . ." The old schoolmaster relaxed per-ceptibly, and Annele ventured a fleeting smile. Aha, that Annele was a fine match for Konrad ; she'd more than make up for his lubberliness. Yes, Frau Lehrer Bertram had always said that Annele had her head screwed on the right way. Somehow she brought back memories . . . " Vivant omnes virgines . . ." Those days in Göttingen had been happy, but no son of a privy councillor would ever think of marrying so far beneath him. What would happen to society if honoured burghers and the lower orders married back and forth ? Romantic slush could cause nothing but trouble—and in spite of the Vulpius, who took any stock in Goethe's *Elective Affinities* ? Good it was that Schlegel's *Lucinde* was *verboten* ; an old married man could read it without harm, but no telling how it might have befuddled youngsters. His own father had been a wise man ; he had suspected—nay, known—what was going on in Göttingen, with its aristocratic morals. Twenty marks extra on the monthly allowance and fifty for a nice silk dress when it finally came time to say "Adieu". Father knew that old Behrens was looking for a husband for his Else, and that although she was the youngest of all the daughters she would have a nice little dowry. A Hanover sugar merchant wasn't quite the equal of a privy councillor, granted, but he had a White Star of the Fourth Order. And what was more, Father had said that he would keep things going until a steady income was assured, and he had kept his word. Else had made an impressive, dignified scholar's wife, for all her skill as a *Hausfrau*, and four daughters and two sons was all that anyone had a right to expect. Marriage was an excellent thing; "it is not good for man to live alone". Hadn't Saint Paul said, "It is better to marry than to burn"? H'm, it wasn't as bad as that—sounded almost like Schopenhauer, that *Hagestolz*, that disquieting cynic! Nobody knew much about him, and he had few readers—good, good.

Luther was a heartier fellow; he believed that marriage was necessary and right, and he practised what he preached. A little dose of Luther would help to stiffen up these Catholic Suabians. Anyone could see that the Lutheran Suabians were of sterner stuff. Yet Goodman Baumann wasn't putty, by any means; he had already put in his word about the roof on the house the old Hoebels would occupy when Konrad took over. Just as well, though, to get everything arranged; let the young folks think they are running things, but see that they don't get themselves snarled up. When Konrad came with Goodman Hoebel to sign the paper, he'd have his Vaterl behind him without knowing it. No respecting of persons, true enough, but one couldn't ignore the customs either.

Luther stuck pretty close to the customs, in spite of some of the things his followers did. Hadn't he said that "God Almighty hath made our princes mad, but mad or sane, they must reign"? The sermon in Horb last Sunday was just what was needed, for although everything seemed to be quiet one could never tell what notions might get into people's heads. It was a good text, too: "The powers that be are ordained of God, and whoso resisteth the power, receiveth unto himself damnation." That was the pure doctrine; something ought to be done about those wild-eyed Silesian sectarians who were talking about the end of the world and the community of goods. They'd wind up like

the Anabaptists in Münster a couple of hundred years ago—
community of women, that's what. Such fanatics were well out
of the country. The Pietists were not like that—quiet, sober
folk, they were. But uncanny, uncanny. Let them all go to
America, and good riddance. He didn't envy the Hoebel boys,
hobnobbing with offscourings like that. But look here, one must
be sociable ; day-dreaming in the midst of Nikolaus festivities
was hardly what these peasants expected of a learned guest.

Schoolmaster Bertram once more sat bolt upright in his chair,
the best in the house, and looked inquiringly at Goodman
Baumann.

" How were the crops this year ? "

Old Baumann hushed Lisel's prattle and gently put her off his
knee.

" Oh, none too good. Ever since that bad year in 1817 the
potatoes have been poor, and the turnips were only fair. That
one strip on the edge of the commons is in its second year. After
it rests for a season it will be back in shape again. The three-
field system was good enough for father and it's good enough
for me ; all these new fancy crops and planting-times will lead
to no good. And our old village bull is all right. That Alsatian
Jewish cattle buyer in Horb keeps telling me about the new
breeds they're raising in England now. But let him mind his
own Jewish business ! Of course I don't care much about his
Jewishness ; it's his Frenchiness that I don't like. He came
trailing along in Napoleon's time. Him and his offers to lend
us money for a new bull ! Him and his interest ! We need a
little cash money once in a while, but we can get that by selling
a calf now and then. And if we did drain the soil to raise big
crops, the Jew would buy our potatoes and turnips too. Are we
going to worry and sweat and smash all the customs just to help
a Frenchified Jew to get fatter ? "

" Well, that may be," rejoined the schoolmaster, " but they're
talking about a railroad all the way from Kehl to Stuttgart.
Down in Austria they're building one from Linz to Budweis now.
Maybe you could sell your crops and livestock to an honest
German if you could send them farther than Horb."

" Bosh ! I mean—saving your respected presence, sir—we'll
only get smoke and dirt and squashed geese and a kettle of
travelling scum. Here we have lived for many generations, and
we want to be let alone. Let the Britishers have their railways

and steamboats and newfangled farming. They're a gadabout people, anyway. When they fought the French, where would they have been without the Germans?"

"Yes, yes," answered the schoolmaster, "the Germans are the salt of the earth. But I'm astonished to hear you talk about 'the Germans'. You sound like one of those *Burschenschaftler*. Most of us just say Pomeranians or Saxons or whatever. Old Blücher was a Mecklenburger, but he scattered that French chaff like the north wind. Some of your people in Württemberg here liked Napoleon, though. I think he was a great man myself. Too bad he had such rabble for soldiers. . . . Just the same, we'll have to feed those city workers who make our guns and bayonets, and it would be too bad to bring in foreign meat and grain. If the Stuttgarters can't get all the food they need from Württemberg, at least they ought to buy it from the Bavarians. Our toll roads and all these local duties make everything so high that the sooty mechanics keep yelling for more wages. They make too much now ; let's give them cheaper bread instead. Maybe this talk about wiping out the special imposts and establishing a Customs Union has something in it. That fellow List has good ideas."

Goodman Hoebel chimed in, wiping the foam off his moustache and setting down his stein. The face of his *Frau*, hitherto beaming, flashed a warning signal, for she knew how tactless he was, but the old man ploughed straight ahead.

"I beg for the pardon of the honoured sir, but I—I—we all think that politics is too high for us. Our good princes have let us have the land, and they look upon us with fatherly eyes. Sometimes the *Fürstendiener* try to squeeze more out of us than *honest servants of our masters should, and some of them are Jews,* and I never liked this paying taxes in money, but all these things ought to be left to our superiors, to the *Obrigkeit*. We can talk around and around but they know what's best. Herr Doktor, I know you're not one of the *Burschenschaft* hotheads, but there are some of them who come out from Tübingen and talk to the merchants—I overheard one in the Schnitzelbank tavern. You're not like them, even if you did go to the university, but you know yourself that we can't understand all the things you could tell us, so I say that we just ought to go along our well-trodden paths and let our superiors arrange matters for our good. I do hope, though, that they won't try to make us move too fast ; I like to think of "—and here he dropped his voice to what he thought was a whisper—" Konrad and Annele over there in our old house making merry with our grandchildren thirty years from now, when the good wife and I are resting in holy ground alongside of those who have gone before us. Baumann, look at your Jockel there sucking his thumb and drowsing away through all this hubbub we're making. And then think of Annele's young ones—and Konrad's too, of course—when the Nikolaus-time comes a few years from now. Why should they have to bother their heads about affairs of state and the councils of wise men ? I think that our old oxen can teach us something ; they wear

their heavy yokes and pull the carts and ploughs, but we're good to them. Why, I heap straw around Crumple when the nights get cold and he lows contentedly and munches away. We can't do that, but here comes Frau Baumann with the roast pig and the rye bread, and even if the mouth is full a song can struggle through. Get your fiddle, Konrad, and we'll strike up ' Joseph, lieber Joseph mein '. Let the women start off. The men can do their brum-brum-brum in the second verse."

Just then Friedl broke in excitedly, " Look, everybody, there's a dash of snow on the window-pane ! Now we know that Nikolaus has brought it with him. He must be here now, Bärbele. Sing, like a good girl, for he tells the Christ Child everything, and you want pepper-nuts instead of switches on Christmas morning."

The first thin notes of the violin knifed gently through the room ; the real Nikolaus-time was under way at last. The warm light of the candles and the flickering fire shone through the window out of which Konrad gazed as he played and sang, and he could see the snow falling lightly through the starlit air. Slowly the black outlines of the old linden near the village well-spring were picked out in white along the upper sides of the sturdy branches. There it stood while generations came and went, came and went. Annele leaned closer as young and old chorused the last lines :

> " Dasz Gott müsse dein Lohner sein,
> Im Himmelreich der Jungfrau Sohn Maria." *

NOTES

Given the character of this opening chapter, footnotes for specific passages would clearly be nonsensical. Elaborate documentation could be offered for every least turn of thought imputed to the persons involved, but to do this would destroy the illusion of fiction for the engendering of which the chapter was given its somewhat unusual form.

Yes, the *illusion* of fiction . . . Strictly speaking, the chapter presents sober truth—or at least, truth as nearly as it can be determined by a sociologist who cherishes a belief in his own sobriety. Under the sway of this belief, I assert with some confidence that others having access to the same evidence would sketch a picture very much like that presented here.

Why then has there been an effort to conjure up the semblance of fiction ? Is there not the danger of producing a sterile hybrid, neither good science nor good literature ? Unquestionably. My aim is scientific, but this chapter may be only the start of a bad novel. If so, I can only say that I intended otherwise. Further, there is the danger of not being taken seriously. Truth disguised in fictional garb seems, for the moment at least, to be less austere and more attractive, but in dispensing with austerity one runs the risk of inviting that familiarity which breeds contempt. Nevertheless, I have knowingly run this risk, believing as I do that even the reader of markedly scientific and scholarly bent will value the allusive, evocative qualities attributable to the fictional disguise. Why ? Because such disguise affords one way of bringing out certain " subjective " nuances, overtones, or emotional tinges basic to that sense of wholeness without which analytic exposition is often so peculiarly flat—and, it may be added, often so peculiarly unreliable.

The sense of wholeness to which I refer derives from the fact that even the most everyday social action has at least two aspects : one as viewed by the observer in question, and the other as viewed by the acting personality

---

* God will give thee thy reward
In the heavenly realm of the Son of the Virgin Mary.

(the subject). Unless there is some attempt at " definition of the situation " from the standpoint of a given type of subject, there is no way of telling what he is likely to do next. It is the vague awareness of this fact—an awareness which we all possess at one time or another—which makes us uneasy when fanatical " objectivists " refuse to consider the subject's account of his own actions. Surely, such an account may be the sheerest falsification or delusion, but it is essential evidence, and cannot be ignored or set aside without grievous damage to the scientific interpretation of the conduct with which it is integrally related. (I do not wish to dwell further on this point, for obvious reasons ; the interested reader is referred to my essay, " Interpretive Sociology and Constructive Typology ", and to its accompanying bibliography in the volume edited by Gurvitch and Moore, *Twentieth-century Sociology*, New York, 1945.)

It is of course true that no *complete* account precisely defining the given situation and drawing directly from any of the subjects entering into the personalities constructed as typical is to be found in the documents utilized in the chapter. Letters, diaries, traveller's tales, parish records, discursive observations by worthies such as Garve, proverbs, old songs, surviving folk-ways, stories told to children, local art, present-day treatises on contemporary German family life, and scores of other sources provide bits and pieces here woven into something like a coherent, interpretable whole. In other words, there has been condensation and construction ; types of personality and conduct are outlined which seem adequate to the interpretive task and which in one way or another derive from the available data. Here again there is only the illusion of fiction. This illusion has another aspect of which account must be taken ; namely, that it is one of the few ways in which both myth and the materials of which myth is made can be simultaneously presented.

For those who wish to see what the same store of details can yield when worked up without primary regard to their allusive, evocative properties, the second chapter may be instanced. " Nostalgia : Once in the Dear Dead Days " treats many of the themes of " Myth : The Linden Tree " in the fashion generally approved—with the addition, naturally enough, of its own special evidence and emphasis.

Returning now to the present chapter . . . Even though the reader may provisionally grant that specific references are out of place in any presentation that attempts to maintain " the fictional illusion ", he certainly wants to know what the chief sources of the disguised truth are, and I therefore list them :

First, personal experience : Suabia was chosen because I know it better than any other part of Germany, with the possible exceptions of the Hunsrück and the northern Rhineland. Several long Suabian " roamings ", one of them from the Neckar bend east of Heidelberg all the way to Lake Constance, were undertaken with youth movement groups. Later my wife and I cycled over a large part of Lower Suabia, finally reaching higher ground on our departure by way of Freudenstadt. Peasant accommodations were chosen whenever possible ; " tourism " was sedulously avoided. I should not care to dignify these excursions with the much-used and -abused title of " field work ". Properly so called, the field work which I have done has been in the Hunsrück, a region different from Suabia in some important respects. Nevertheless, I can say that through my Suabian roamings I gained a few insights that have notably supplemented my library research.

Second, conversations in the United States : I have discussed the themes of this chapter with many first-generation Suabians, both ordinary immigrants and refugees.

Third, participation in second- and third-generation life of Americans of

German descent as my name might indicate. My grandparents on the paternal side (maternal, Scottish) came from Baden as children in 1835, but they escaped being born in Suabia by a mere twenty miles.

Fourth, attention while in college and university, both here and abroad, to German literature, art, music, and social studies. Among the teachers to whom I feel deeply indebted even for this chapter are James Taft Hatfield, Hans Kurath, George Curme, Wilhelm Bernstorff, Paul Honigsheim, Leopold von Wiese, Max Scheler, and Robert E. Park.

Fifth, the inescapable *general* books (a minimum list) :

Gustav Freytag, *Bilder aus der deutschen Vergangenheit,* in the translation by Mrs. Malcolm, *Pictures of German Life in the XVIIIth and XIXth Centuries,* second series (London, 1863).

Hans F. K. Günther, *Das Bauerntum als Lebens- und Gemeinschaftsform* (Leipzig, 1939).

Walther Hofstaetter and Ulrich Peters, eds., *Sachwörterbuch der Deutschkunde,* 2 vols. (Leipzig, 1930).

Gerhardt Lüdtke and Lutz Mackensen, eds., *Deutscher Kulturatlas* (Berlin, 1928–38), esp. vol. V, 1938.

Georg Steinhausen, *Geschichte der deutschen Kultur,* 3rd ed. (Leipzig, 1929).

Ferdinand Tönnies, *Gemeinschaft und Gesellschaft,* 8th ed. (Leipzig, 1935). The translation by Charles P. Loomis, *Fundamental Concepts of Sociology* (New York, 1940) may be mentioned, but for some purposes the German original is indispensable.

Martin Wähler, ed., *Der deutsche Volkscharakter* (Jena, 1937), esp. chapter by August Lämmle, " Die Schwaben ".

A minor matter, but one which might lead to charges of inaccuracy, had best be mentioned : the passage beginning " Vivant omnes virgines ", etc., placed in the mouth of the old schoolmaster, comes from a *variant* version of the famous student song, " Gaudeamus igitur ", as sung in Jena and Göttingen from about 1750 to 1810. See Arthur Kopp, *Deutsches Volks- und Studenten-Lied in vorklassischer Zeit* (Berlin, 1899), p. 205.

CHAPTER II

NOSTALGIA : "ONCE IN THE DEAR DEAD DAYS"

> Mir träumt', ich ruhte wieder
>   vor meines Vaters Haus,
> und schaute fröhlich nieder
>   ins alte Tal hinaus ;
> die Luft mit lindem Spielen
>   ging durch das Frühlingslaub,
> und Blütenflocken fielen
>   mir über Brust und Haupt.*
>   —EICHENDORFF, " Wanderlied ".

Children in any land live in a vivid world of " occasions " and " sites " rather than in an abstract framework of " time " and " space ". The seasonal festivals, the birthdays, the night when father imitated a monkey, the day when the paring knife slipped and mother cut her finger so badly, the long weeks in bed with that hacking cough and the spread that unravelled when you picked at the fringes, the tree under which you day-dreamed, the jolly old pump with the tin cups hanging from the clattering chains, the ditch where your first toy sailboat tipped over and was never seen again—all these form the texture of experience before clocks, steel rails, telephone wires, and those confusing shiny disks begin to twist into taut, metallic cables fencing off the grownups' world.[1]

For German children whose start in life was a decade or so after the Franco-Prussian War, a great deal of what was really vivid came from an earlier Germany of bucolic simplicity and family warmth. No one would contend that in the first and second quarters of the nineteenth century—the Biedermeier time, let us say—the lives of German burghers and peasants were free from petty cares, jealous bickering, or tragic narrowness ; we must always remember that the Garden of Eden was somewhere in Mesopotamia. Nevertheless, the parents of the Germany after 1870 still told the folk-tales of bygone days, saw to it that

---

* Thus did I dream : I rested
    My father's house before,
And joyfully gazed downward
    On the valley as of yore ;
The breezes gently sported
    The springtime leaves among,
And scented, flutt'ring petals
    On my breast and brow were flung.

17

Nikolaus went tap-tapping about the city house or apartment, sang songs of Grandmother Bärbele's time, and unweariedly repeated the maxims of honesty, sobriety, thrift and reverence. Furthermore—and this is of the highest importance—this early nineteenth-century German world was defined by many of the writers, artists, and musicians of the later Germany in terms of sentimental homesickness, of longing for the " dear dead days beyond recall ", of a Golden Age of unspoiled, unaffected natural virtue, of communion with nature and with fellowmen.[2]

Altogether apart, however, from fantasies of an Age of Innocence, no matter how fatefully meaningful these fantasies later came to be, there does seem to have been very substantial warrant, given the contrasting conditions evident in Germany after 1870, for a relatively idyllic picture of the Germany of Konrad and Annele.

No question, the pace of social change just after the Wars of Liberation was very sluggish.[3]   In all but the largest cities the artisan plied his craft either in his home or but a stone's throw away.   Father taught son to swing adze, hammer horseshoe, or pierce leather, or if this was not possible, master, journeymen, and apprentices worked together under the same roof.   True, the journeyman might grumble at the master's closefistedness, and the little apprentices, when they dared to say anything, might complain of their hard beds and niggardly fare.   Still, the road was open, and with bundle slung on stick the journeyman who had abandoned hope of marrying the master's daughter could trudge his way over the hills to kindlier folk.   The apprentice, too, was not a helpless cog in a great machine, for although a runaway could be brought back if he was caught before he got beyond the petty political boundary, journeymen who remembered their own struggles might take his part.   They knew him ; he knew them.   Officials, teachers, priests, and pastors sided with the master more often than not, but at least you could appeal to them in person and on the way out get a *Butterbrot* or a glass of small beer from the sympathetic serving girl.

Even where mass unrest existed among the journeymen and apprentices—and there were swirls and eddies here and there even in the first quarter of the nineteenth century—it had not yet deposited crystals of definite organization.   A shoemaker might get the notion that all men should be brothers withholding nothing from each other, and his cheaply-printed little pamphlets might be scattered here and there by his disciples, but the results were virtually indistinguishable from those achieved by roaming religious sectarians. Little clumps and clusters formed and broke up continually, but at the most they merely prepared a saturated solution for the Communist Manifesto two or three decades later. Marx and Engels themselves had nothing but contempt for Utopians such as Weitling, for example; his visions of the time when the lion would lie down with the lamb bore more than superficial resemblance to those of Isaiah. In most cases the economic crisis of the 'twenties, which brought so many peasants face to face with starvation and threw so many artisans out of work, simply swelled the stream of emigration; as the Suabian popular song of that day had it, " Gloria, Gloria, we journey to America ".[4]

As far as the religious sects were concerned they had almost none of the Calvinistic passion for the establishment of a Kingdom of God on earth; there was no ideology upon which a people's army of Cromwellian type could be based. Instead of Ironsides, whose charges scattered even the hard-bitten cavalry of Rupert of the Rhine, there were only—after the shortlived flareup of the Anabaptists—occasional prophets of the Second Coming and, in particular, the little communities of *die Stillen im Lande*,[5] i.e., the Pietists, and those were in some sense their successors. These Pietists, as we may call them, kept to themselves, enduring and suffering all things from the lords of this world, in the unshakable trust of a glorious resurrection. They too fed the currents of emigration, but when they remained, as many of them did, they were obstacles not only to tax-collecting officials and conscription sergeants, but also to the wandering Utopian apostles. " The world is evil," said these quiet, seclusive folk; " our task it is to keep our little communions of the faithful unspotted from this world and to prepare for the next." Scorned by both Lutherans and Catholics, they maintained what might be called " Christian ghettoes " in the remoter nooks of the countryside, where the powers that be wore themselves out in the vain effort either to command or punish people so completely and lethargically limp. Left largely to their own devices, the tiny Pietist fellowships remained, all through the first three-quarters of the nineteenth century and even thereafter, as centres where old-fashioned folkways and folklore were preserved like flies in amber.

Hastening to add : The Pietists were by no means the only museum exhibits. Coached by Friedrich Schlegel, Madame de Staël, writing in 1804, described the ordinary German as a sort

Once in the Dear Dead Days.

of good-humoured, simple-minded sleepwalker, and a little later Jean Paul Richter did the same thing. Richter's characterizations, in particular, were spread far and wide beyond the German boundaries, and through the enthusiastic sponsorship of Carlyle, his Scottish admirer, set a stereotype in the English-speaking world that endured until well toward the close of Victoria's reign. Both De Staël and Carlyle were carried back to Germany ; their translated writings tremendously sharpened the developing outlines of the German Michel.

With his homely, honest features, stocking-cap and slippers, lean, gangling build, and dropped lower jaw (leaving his mouth half open in an expression of dreamy stupidity), he was an idealized caricature of a German for whom one could feel the same amused affection as might be evoked by an old, loose-jointed, faithful sheepdog.[6]

In spite of evident distortion, these lovingly humorous sketches contained a large amount of close observation, selective though it was, for many other contemporary writers choosing their data on a different basis incidentally provide evidence of the same sort. These and many other kinds of information were drawn upon by Gustav Freytag in his *Pictures of the German Past* ; in these *genre* studies surprising continuity between the Germany of even the sixteenth century and as late as the middle nineteenth are clearly apparent. The drawings of Ludwig Richter and the paintings of Moritz von Schwind and Karl Spitzweg likewise captured the spirit of parochial, bucolic intimacy ; virtues and vices are those of a " little world " drowsily unaware of the bustle and stir going on in many other parts of Europe.[7] Goethe's *Hermann und Dorothea*, for all its idyllic flavour, also seems to be a fairly accurate representation of the same state of affairs. The hero is quite content to remain bound to his native landscape and neighbourhood circle ; wars and rumours of wars resound far away like the rumbling of distant thunder and Hermann feels no concern. Only when foreign troops actually set foot on the soil of his little homeland is he roused to action, and even then immediate liberation is all that the future holds in store. Of grandiose conceptions of a German mission to spread *Kultur* abroad there are none.

In fact, very little of the *Kultur* of that day was specifically German. Polite society was still governed by French etiquette in the south-west, and in Hanover and its neighbouring states the English gentleman was the model. Goethe bemoaned the

fact that the language in which he wrote represented the " trashi-
est stuff " in all of Europe, and French and English words dotted
his contemporaries' pages. Legal patterns ranged all the way
from adaptations of the Napoleonic code to the so-called " common German law " ; it was not until the Thibaut-Savigny controversy got under way that distinctively German codifications
began to emerge.

Within the confines of the numerous petty states, common law
and custom resisted centralizing tendencies with great tenacity.
Toll roads and like imposts created a snarl of restrictions far more
hampering to local trade than were the fluctuating frontier
tariffs. In part because of this, and for other reasons as well,
inland commerce was still in the pack-pedlar, wagon, and river-
boat stage, and of all the rivers the Rhine was the only one that
really tied the crazy quilt together at all. Specialized office staffs
were virtually non-existent ; the famous " white collar worker "
had not as yet separated himself from his " menial " fellows—
the counting room shared in the dust of the warehouse. High
stools, goose-quills, and sprinkled sand provided the setting for the
cumbrous ledgers, and the young burgher who lorded it over the
errand boy and clerk was a man of the world only in the sense
that he had studied a little commercial arithmetic and book-
keeping and occasionally journeyed a full hundred miles from
home.

Trade beyond the seas languished ; the old Hanseatic towns
were no longer flourishing. Hamburg was of course an exception, but its inflows of pepper and cotton and tobacco and herring
represented only a trifling proportion of world market dealings.
Outward-bound commerce was insignificant ; the cutlery of
Remscheid offered no serious competition to that of Sheffield.
" Export or die " was not yet the watchword, and the Britisher
did not yet refer derisively and defensively to the Leipzig bag-
man with his samples of the " cheap and nasty ".[8]

Part of the backwardness of trade and commerce undoubtedly
resulted from the absence of national unity ; foreign merchants
found it almost impossible to thread their way among conflicting
economic and political policies. Another part, and a very large
one it was, came from the subsistence economy practised by the
greater number of German peasants. There might be an extra
calf or a few surplus bushels of rye now and again, but in general
the Hoebels and Baumanns ate up and wore out what they produced. When the seasons were favourable they were fat and

warmly clad ; when they were not, potato-peeling soup and feet wound with rags were taken as all in the day's work.

Still another part in the absence of economic " progress " was borne by the religious factor. The scattering of Pietists we have mentioned were largely self-sufficing, but the same was true of Lutherans and Catholics.

The Catholics retained the medieval preference for home consumption and, at the most, barter ; cash crops, the buying and selling of land, and money dealings generally smacked of the sin of avarice. Good Catholics would lay up treasure in heaven and let Jews and Calvinists damn themselves even more thoroughly than God had already done. If there were extras such as a few fat geese and a little wheat flour to make *Kuchen*, there were always neighbourly visits, the feast days of the saints' calendar, betrothals, weddings, and funerals to take care of them. To borrow money from a usurer was a sin almost as great as that of usury itself, and although not all the moneylenders were Jews, by any means, their share in the traffic of gold and silver lent an unhallowed air to the whole nefarious business. Money for taxes, needles, spices to help keep the sausage through the long summer months, little comforts in old age, Peter's pence, and a handful of coins for dowries and token legacies, yes ; beyond that, " moth and rust corrupt, and thieves break through and steal ".

The Lutherans were not much different, for the break with Rome was not profound. Luther denounced the universities, called reason the devil's most seductive harlot, filled his *Table Talk* with tales of demons and witches, and was the first important European to condemn the Copernican theory shoving God's footstool out of its central place in the universe. He despised commercial activity, hated the Jews, and demanded that the peasants humbly submit themselves to the inscrutable decrees of their princely overlords.[9]

After the wave of the Peasants' Revolt (which Luther helped to put down), many of the peasants so effectively practised submission that the overlords were sometimes frustrated by the success of their own efforts. There was no initiative, no self-improvement, no accumulation of surplus that would make increases in traditional levies—rendered urgent by rising standards of living among the aristocracy—other than very difficult to bring about. Passive resistance to change, sometimes sullen but frequently good-humoured, came to be the order of the day.

Even at a time far later than that now under view, the supine character of the peasantry cropped up in the most unexpected places :

In the latter part of the nineteenth century a *Landrat* conceived the rather startling notion of installing a water and sewage system in the village of which he was still, in a certain sense, the feudal lord. Having perhaps been infected by the liberal doctrines of the *Paulskirche*, he decided to allow the village to decide whether or not it should be installed, and accordingly called a town meeting so that the decision might be rendered in true democratic fashion. To his great surprise, however, the peasants and burghers refused, almost to a man, even so much as to attend a meeting ; there had never been one before and they were suspicious of the innovation. By dint of much persuasion, however, the meeting was held, but the proposal to install the improvements was unanimously rejected. Disgusted with the Ingratitude of Man, the *Landrat* removed himself to one of the stuffy little duodecimo courts and perhaps forgot his dreams of reform. Years later, when on a chance visit to the town, he was fiercely reproached by a villager as follows : " Here we are without a water or sewage system," he cried, " while all the other villages near by have them ! You have been neglectful of the people whom the Lord gave into your care ! " When the good *Landrat* mildly expostulated that he had tried to persuade them to take the very course of action which he was reproached for having neglected, the peasant snorted contemptuously. " Überzeugen ? Sie hätten uns einfach zwingen müssen ! " (" Persuade ? You should simply have compelled us, forced us ! ") [10]

This feeling that the overlord ought to induce the peasant to act for his own good by exercising traditional princely prerogatives has its comic aspects, but the sullenness already mentioned was occasionally evident. Sometimes this arose because the old Roman law, which in south-western Germany had tended to favour the peasant, was here and there superseded by modifications of the Napoleonic code, and sometimes because the Napoleonic code was set aside in favour of legal principles drawn from highly centralized Prussia. Whatever the specific occasions, violations of traditional rights led the peasants to intensify their habitual passivity. Otherwise put : They " went into a dumb sulk " when " progress " became too irksome.

Still more deeply rooted was passivity of directly defensive character. Owing to the agelong particularism of Germany, its complex history, and peculiar position in central Europe, the German peasant has perhaps been exposed to more strife than the peasant of any other country. With so many different masters, so many voices shouting " Do this " and " Do that ", his only salvation lay in doing, as nearly as possible, nothing at all. In scuffles between schoolboys many a lad has discovered that the most effective resistance against the combined attacks of the others is complete relaxation ; one must be carried off the playground like a spineless dummy. The scuffles of the peasant with his various overlords in the seventeenth and eighteenth centuries, let us say, were of rather more earnest, not to say serious nature, but the technique was the same. When a company of soldiers sallies out of the courtyard in the train of the tax-collector, pay your taxes when they have plodded toilsomely to your village, but not before. When the lord of the manor calls for his stint of feudal labour, well and good ! Do what he compels you to do, and let that be all. When soldiers are foraging for rations, hide everything and quietly allow them to search until they are blue in the face, but give them nothing short of threats of a firing squad or torture. Garve put it thus :

> One circumstance has great influence on the character of the peasantry : they hang much together. They live far more sociably one with another than do the common burghers in the cities. They see each other every day at their farm work ; in the summer in the fields, in the winter in the barns and spinning-rooms. They associate like soldiers, and thus get an *esprit de corps*. . . . They seldom see or hear the judgments, conceptions, and examples of the higher orders, and only for a brief space. I have long studied the special signification of the word *tückisch*, which I have never heard so frequently as when the talk has been of peasants. It denotes, without doubt, a mixture of childish character, of simplicity, and weakness, with spite and cunning. . . . One may add, as an ingredient or as a consequence of the " *tückischen* " nature, a certain amount of stubbornness which distinguishes the peasant when his mind is agitated, or when a prejudice is once rooted in him. His soul in this case appears to become stiff, like his body and his limbs. He is then deaf to all representations, however obvious they may be, or however capable he might be, in an impartial state of mind, of seeing their justice. . . . Sometimes whole communities become thus addle-headed.[11]

In the early nineteenth century all this had of course receded into the haze of the past, but some of the basic attitudes had been passed on from one generation to the next. Many of the princes were revered as fatherly masters, but not even a father should make you abandon too many of the ways hallowed by fatherly tradition.

Enough : It seems fairly evident that under such conditions economic changes could win their way only with extreme slowness ; practices so apparently self-justifying as rotation of crops, use of green fertilizers, and improvement of breeding stock were hard to introduce. Consequence : The peasant was industrious but he was never afflicted with " busy-ness ", and he preserved his ancient ways with a considerable degree of success. In particular, fathers and sons remained on a reasonably harmonious footing, for the fathers did not have to hold back impetuous youngsters determined to get rid of " old-fogyish notions ", and sons were on the whole content to draw from the well of paternal wisdom.[12]

This relative absence of family tension was also manifest in other than economic matters. Take erotic practices, for example : The survival of bundling, betrothal familiarity, and early marriage made for smooth and easy transition from adolescent to adult life. The traditional standard of living was accepted ; children did not crave for advantages unknown to their parents. Slowpaced but diligent labour almost from cradle to grave appalled no one. Numerous children were actively desired, for they were distinct assets in the household economy. Holidays were frequent and were spent within the parish. There was no reading matter that would excite errant inclinations : devotional books, handbills and broadsides, and an occasional newspaper (sometimes one subscription for a whole village) covered the range. The three R's were taught, but schooling was short, and there were no laws making it difficult to use children as fieldhands or home-helpers throughout the larger part of the year. Peasant girls received very little schooling, and in most instances that little was soon forgotten when baking, hoeing, and childbirth began to bear down with full weight. Divorce, to speak in paradox that is only apparent, was usually both unknown and impossible ; once married, partners got along as best they could. Fathers and mothers naturally had their trials, but their sons and daughters had little reason to be restive except in ways that an occasional brawl, spree, dance, window-visit,[13] or *Fest* would appease.

In the ranks of the burghers conditions were in many respects similar, although here and there a son who had been exposed to the rationalism of the university kicked over the traces. When he did, it often took the form of refusal to follow the paternal calling ; after the 'twenties, for instance, the heirs of tradesmen often tried to become state officials. Too much, however, can easily be made of this tendency. Most middle-class young men, particularly when they were elder sons, slipped into father's harness and tugged loyally at the traces.

In most instances, bourgeois fathers felt the obligation to finance the sons, even though married, in the early stages of their careers. In addition, dowries were taken very much as a matter of course, and because of the fact that individual choice did not enter into the selection of marriage partners to an overwhelming degree—parents frequently arranged things—neither husbands nor wives thought of their unions as being "marriages of convenience". Women were on the whole satisfied with their traditional roles as bearers of children, housewives, exponents of charity under religious auspices, and representatives of their husbands' dignified status. If husbands were unfaithful or unkind, wives meekly resigned themselves to their lot; divorce did not offer itself as a solution. The unmarried burgher could readily exploit serving maids and other girls of the humbler walks of life without becoming a victim of intense moral conflict or resolving that conflict by a cynical adjustment. To "sow wild oats" was accepted as the way of the world made inevitable by man's originally sinful nature. Even the taking of a mistress after marriage, although rare outside aristocratic circles, was regarded by burghers with similar resignation. Prostitution of course existed, but it was not widespread or specialized, and was readily fitted into the burgher's world-view as part of the static order of original sin.

It is therefore possible to say that in family matters German "doctor, lawyer, and merchant chief" jogged along well-worn roads like sedate livery stable nags, occasionally balking or shying, but never running away. "When the old dog gapes the puppy yawns"; fathers and sons lived in essentially similar familial worlds and consequently understood one another.

Politically, it must be granted, young burghers and old frequently did not present a solid front. To-day most of us know the *Turnvereine* only as rather old-fashioned Teutonic combinations of gymnastic exercises, choral singing, and beer-drinking, but for the burghers who were growing into manhood after the War of Liberation they represented somewhat radical societies designed by their founder, Turnfather Jahn, to overturn the rickety feudal structures of the petty states and replace them by constitutional monarchies having up-to-date parliamentary and bureaucratic machinery.[14] As a result, many members of the *Turnvereine* were arrested by the conservative régimes and were confronted

Turnfather Jahn.

with choice between moral surrender, flight, expulsion, or crushing fine. In order to avoid such consequences the *Turnvereine* went underground with their political activities, as it were, leaving to public view only the innocuous features we now know. After national unity had been achieved, there of course seemed little if any reason for continuing with " subversive " politics, and the *Turnvereine* became thoroughly respectable in all their aspects.

Somewhat like Turnfather Jahn's gatherings were the *Burschenschaften* (previously although inadequately translated as " Young Fellows' Clubs "), but these had their largest clientele in university circles. From the 'twenties onward they were centres of nationalistic zeal combined with economic and political liberalism, occasionally spiced with a dash of philosophical and religious rationalism. In particular, the young Hegelians were numerous in the *Burschenschaften*, and they bent their efforts towards the creating of a Germany that could take its place with the great powers of Europe.[15] This brought them into opposition to the political credos of their fathers' generation, and " Disinherited ! " and " Never darken my door again ! " were frequent utterances. Nevertheless, the conflict was basically political ; there was no conception of a revolt of youth for the sake of youth against a total social order presumably " perpetrated by a corrupt older generation ".[16] Similarly, the merits of youth as youth rather than as preparation for adulthood were nowhere expounded— which is to say, the antagonisms peculiar to the youth movement as such were not in evidence.[17]

Once the victories over Denmark, Austria and France had come about, the repugnance and opposition once evoked by the *Burschenschaften* were speedily forgotten and they were assimilated to the conservative tradition. Student fraternities or corporations oftentimes took over the names of one or another of the old *Burschenschaften*, and with their ceremonials, duelling, and so on, thoroughly obscured the earlier significance of their predecessors. To the German boy or girl of the 'eighties, then, the burgher students of grandfather's day rayed forth brotherliness, conviviality, joy of life, and national loyalty. They too entered into the glories of the " dear dead days beyond recall ".

But to return to the actual life of the early Biedermeier period in the effort to see how the aristocracy fitted into the picture : It had been stripped of many of its ancient privileges, but after weathering the storms of Napoleonic times it sailed with Metternich as pilot into a harbour at least temporarily safe. The

Karlsbad decrees did much to implement the Austrian demand for the suppression of constitutionalism and liberalism, and in many parts of Germany this or that Serene Highness reclaimed a part of his ancestral privileges. The march of social change could not be stopped, but it was checked for a time just long enough to prevent the peasants and the lower ranks of the burghers from catching up with the procession. Changes in ideas, to take only one species of social change, may take a long time to spread from their centres of origin to the remoter margins of a populace, and the outer ripples of the splash-rings started by the French Revolution had just begun to lap their way into the placid pools of the petty German states when the Peace of Vienna stopped the process. With this time-lag working in their favour the German aristocrats were able to maintain their prestige until the advent of the era of Bismarck gave them another shelter from equalitarian assaults. They were oftentimes quite sincere in their protestations of paternal intent towards their subjects, but even when they clearly protested too much their claims were taken at face value by the great majority. In other words, they were permitted to rebuild their régimes to suit the altered times, but at a rate slow enough to avoid the collapse of the upper stories. Laws were modified, economic liberalism gently pushed along convenient lines, limited suffrage introduced, parliamentary bodies set up, all without detracting notably from " the divinity that doth hedge a king ".

This astonishing result was achieved, in many cases, through a shrewd policy of playing liberals off against conservatives. To the conservatives the nobles presented themselves as defenders of time-honoured customs and differentiations of rank, but to the liberals the very same aristocrats posed as indispensable aides in coaxing their own backward followers to the watering-trough of progress and inducing them to drink a little. The peasants, in particular, often appealed to their traditional overlords as their defenders against the exactions of the rising bureaucracies. The old *Fürstendiener* or " servants of the princes " had previously enjoyed no great esteem among the lower orders, but they had at least known how to personalize their dealings with them. The new class of *Beamten* or officials were the bearers of the newer political rationalism, and in the rigid application of the rule of " no respecting of persons " they often rubbed fur the wrong way, and rubbed it hard. Most of the nobles reluctantly conceded the necessity of this sort of thing, but then saw to it that they garnered whatever credit was to be had by discreetly stroking their outraged subjects in the right direction.

Their success was greatest in the smaller towns and villages, for in the larger cities the ravages of industrial capitalism, although as yet only nibbles when compared with the voracious crunchings going on in Britain, were beginning to pile up " proletarian refuse ". Rebellious spirits raised their unhallowed voices in songs such as " Blood Must Flow ", with its catchlines of " Kick the concubine out of the noble's bed " and " Smear the guillotine with the fat of tyrants ".[18] Good burghers and peasants were so frightened by such savage outcries, however, that even the direful year of 1848 saw no such successful upheavals in Germany as those which caused thrones to totter or collapse in other European countries regarded at that time as backward by the Germans themselves. The stereotypes of " city rabble ", " misfit intellectuals ", " impulsive idealists ", and " dreamy fanatics " sprang into being, and with the judicious application of a little force here and there the nobles and their conservative retainers stayed on top. For at least ten years before the flight of the Forty-Eighters to more hospitable lands an intermittent stream of the disgruntled, disaffected, and dispossessed spurted out of the various German states, and with the last great burst of 1848, the revolutionary fever subsided in considerable measure.

As late as the 'twenties and 'thirties, the nobles had taken little pains to conceal their differing way of life. For example, erotic exploits among admiring females of underling status called forth little resentment ; attentions by condescending " betters " sometimes held an element of flattery not altogether unappreciated. Moreover, even the deeply antagonistic husband or father oftentimes passively acknowledged the superiority of noble blood, and the " natural offspring " of the great were not always cast out of the nest. As the winds of political democracy began to blow more strongly, however, the aristocrats dexterously trimmed their sails. Still following the tradition with which we have become familiar through " The Student Prince ", the nobles nevertheless pointed with pride to their model wives and large families, which they placed on display whenever opportunity offered. In fact, they cleverly saw to it that such opportunities were created with increasing frequency, and institutionalized them with appropriate ceremonials. The surplus claimants to Serene Highnesshood thereby brought into the world were sent to serve as princely consorts, queens, or kings in many other parts

The failure of the 1848 Revolt.

of Europe—Prince Albert was by no means the only exported product. The monopoly on regal personnel formerly enjoyed by the Hapsburgs was threatened, and long before the beginning of World War I " my esteemed cousin " was a familiar mode of address among the crowned heads of Europe.

On top of all this, the tradition of a specifically German kind of nobility was rescued from the French and English overgrowths that had threatened to smother it earlier in the century. Germanic heraldry, Germanic armour, lances, and swords, and Germanic knight-errantry experienced a boom toward the end of the Biedermeier period. In the popular mind the noble came to be more and more idealized as a splendid mań on horseback rescuing damsels in distress and standing guard between overbearing, greedy seneschals and helpless, honest toilers. He was still the father of his people, their strong shield and defender, but with a dash of adventurous romance and sacrificial gallantry added. Once more the " dear dead days beyond recall " had brought forth an entrancing vision.

Finally, it can be said that even the few dark spirits who found nothing idyllic in the Napoleonic period and the Biedermeier time, who felt that the family warmth of the peasantry was disgustingly sweaty and the solid good sense of burgher life merely thickheaded and obsequious, helped in their own way to create another fateful myth. Kleist, Hölderlin, Lenau, and their like despaired, and in their despair they took refuge in a remote and faraway world of freedom. Wandering scholars, roving tinkers, peasant equivalents of Robin Hood, noble savages, orgiastically adventurous Greeks, and devil-may-care gypsies thronged through their imaginations. " Thoughts are free " was their admitted maxim, and they roamed hither and yon in the realm of fancy, bringing back novels, poems, and plays that expressed deep dissatisfaction with their surroundings and passionate longing for untrammelled lives of word and deed.[19] Fleeting popularity a few of them did enjoy, but for the greater number obscurity in their own day weighed heavily upon them. Two of the three we have named went mad, and the other chose suicide as the way out,[20] but their fervid writings remained, and among the disillusioned liberals who had chosen moral surrender rather than flight, and to the romantic conservatives who despised even the slightest concessions to constitutionalism and reform, they were martyrs. Continuing the metaphor, their blood was the seed of a new church, a church of primitive freedom, of liberty from the here and now. More will be said about these "primitivists", "hard" or "soft" as the case may be, in later pages ; at this point it is enough to indicate their ambivalence and the way in which that very reversal of the standards they despised set up still other "days beyond recall" that were to enter into the myth of a Golden Age.

NOTES

1. The background of this paragraph is provided by the French school of social psychology and sociology. I merely mention Durkheim, Halbwachs, Granet, *et al.* For detail, see Harry Elmer Barnes and Howard Becker, *Social Thought from Lore to Science* (Boston, 1938), II, pp. 824–48.

2. Jethro Bithell, *Germany : A Companion to German Studies* (London, 1932), pp. 220–324 *et passim.*

3. Georg Steinhausen, *Geschichte der deutschen Kultur*, 3rd ed. (Leipzig, 1929), p. 631.

4. Ernst Meier, *Schwäbische Volkslieder* (Berlin, 1855), pp. 257–8.

5. Gustav Freytag, *Pictures of German Life in the XVIIIth and XIXth Centuries*, translated by Mrs. Malcolm, 2nd series (London, 1863), I, pp. 211–67.

6. Among the countless cartoons of the *Deutscher Michel* is an exceptionally amusing one in Hans Blum, *Die deutsche Revolution 1848–49* (Florence and Leipzig, 1898), p. 466.

7. Steinhausen, *op. cit.*, p. 632.

8. *Ibid.*, p. 631.

9. James Harvey Robinson, *The New History* (New York, 1927), pp. 117–18.

10. Howard Becker, " Sargasso Iceberg : A Study in Cultural Lag and Institutional Disintegration " (report of field study of the Hunsrück peasantry), *American Journal of Sociology*, 34, 3 (Nov., 1928), pp. 492–506.

11. Freytag, *op. cit.*, pp. 66–70. The passage quoted is from Christian Garve, *Upon the Character of the Peasants* (Breslau, 1786).

12. Steinhausen, *op. cit.*, p. 633.

13. Hans F. K. Günther, *Das Bauerntum als Lebens- und Gemeinschaftsform* (Leipzig, 1939), pp. 500, 504.

14. Emmett A. Rice, " Physical Education " in *Encyclopedia of the Social Sciences*, 12, p. 130.

15. Blum, *op. cit.*, pp. 12–20.

16. Charlotte Lütkens, *Die deutsche Jugendbewegung* (Frankfurt a. M., 1925), pp. 131–3.

17. Ignaz Jastrow, *Geschichte des deutschen Einheitstraumes und seine Erfüllung* (Berlin, 1885), p. 133.

18. Blum, *op. cit.*, offers splendid documentation in this connection.

19. Bithell, *loc. cit.*

20. *Ibid.*, pp. 222, 224, 227, and *Der grosse Brockhaus*, respective articles.

CHAPTER III

REVULSION : IN RIMMON'S HOUSE

Wherefore with knees that feign to quake—
Bent head and shaded brow—
To this dead dog, for my father's sake,
In Rimmon's house I bow !

—KIPLING, " Rimmon ".

Taking a cue from the poem that heads this chapter, let us try to see how German youth in the late nineteenth century came to feel that their fathers' idols had feet of clay and how their enforced worship at the old shrines brought revulsion ;

Until we entered to hale him out,
And found no more than an old
Uncleanly image girded about
The loins with scarlet and gold.

To begin with, note this : The web of childhood experience is woven out of strands spun by forerunners, young and old, and the personality patterns that slowly take form have their models, at least, in the surrounding society. Among these models those that are most important, that most strongly shape the child's personality, have to do with conduct labelled good and bad, right and wrong, proper and improper. Technically put : The construction of a system of social norms is a universal process, beginning afresh in every generation but always guided by the example of the elders. Ranging over the whole world we can nowhere find a society that does not develop some kind of basic agreement about alternative ways of acting. A " fact " of social life in any society, however small and however " primitive ", is the defining of approved and disapproved modes of conduct. Usually only certain members of a society are responsible for setting the models of good conduct, and their choices are made in the light of what they think or feel to be for the best interests of all concerned. Beyond doubt they make mistakes, but so great is man's capacity for self-justification that these mistakes are rarely admitted ; instead, they are enveloped in the same normative halo that surrounds genuinely beneficial decisions. Depending on the foresight, special privileges, and dispassionateness of the controlling minority, the limits of what is thought to be for the good of all may be broad or narrow. Nevertheless, however greatly such limits may favour those who have staked them off, with the lapse of time the favouritism is obscured, and the " boy as he should be " and " girl as she should be ", to name no other members of the society, become so sharply outlined that they seem to have endured from all eternity.

. In the folksay of all peoples there are proverbs equivalent to our " As the twig is bent, the tree's inclined ". In effect, this signifies that the immature and helpless are freighted with the full burden of the society's heap of norms. Ceaselessly pressing down is the weight of what is right and what is wrong, what should and should not be done ; " education " of this kind begins in the cradle and never stops. Among the elders of many if not all societies, parents are the special agents who must place the moral knapsacks on the children's shoulders and pile them full. Even if these parents, speaking in " average " terms, had any coherent notions about the sources, implications, and meaning of the baggage, they would find themselves almost wholly unable to pass such notions on at the time when little backs must begin to carry the load. Until the child's self expands to the point where he takes in others as others rather than as parts of himself, he cannot absorb ideas about " It's best for everybody ", or " Duty tells us that we ought to take heed of the other fellow too ". Dimly realizing this, most parents quite rightly do not try to explain why some things are sanctioned and others are tabooed, but simply say " Good children always play quietly " —or eat without greediness, refrain from pulling up the neighbour's flowers, say prayers with folded hands, or are seen and not heard.[1]

Thus indoctrinated, the child takes for granted almost any maxim or practice passed on to him. If he should run across inconsistencies, he is told that " When you get bigger you'll understand that ", and he readily falls into the habit of giving himself the blame for the discrepancies he discovers—if he thinks about them at all.

When he does get bigger, however, and especially when the first stirrings of adolescence appear, his position in the social order slowly alters. He is expected to justify his decisions, to be " responsible " for what he does. No longer an innocent by-stander, adults ask him to reel off the rules of the game and say why they are rules. When he tries to do this, he can no longer avoid the task of untangling the snarls which he at first thought were only intricate knots. Then he becomes distressingly aware

of the fact that not even his revered elders can unravel the skein—
in fact, he may find that their hesitant efforts only make things
worse. There often follows the effort to jerk the tangle straight,
i.e., the stage of " idealism " appears :

> The young . . . are idealists, partly because they take working
> ideals literally, and partly because they acquire ideals not fully
> operative in the social organization. Those in authority over children
> are obligated . . . to inculcate ideals as part of the official . . .
> [norms of the society]. The children are receptive because they
> have had little social experience—experience systematically kept
> from them . . . consequently young people possess little ballast for
> their acquired ideals, which therefore soar to the sky.[2]

This lack of ballast is the outcome of the child's lack of
experience with the inevitable contradictions of any social
organization of which we have knowledge, and more especially
with those of a social order undergoing rapid change. The
elders pass on their images of the " days beyond recall ", and then
the young, unchecked by the adult habit of keeping things in
mutually exclusive divisions, try to realize them with rigorous
consistency. What happens ? The older generation bemoans
the " hot-headed ", " impractical ", " flighty ", or " impious "
schemes of youth for pulling " the sorry scheme of things entire "
apart and rearranging it in ways which gratify youth's ideals.[3]

Beyond question youth frequently is thoroughly " impractical ", largely because of the complexity of our society, which in
turn makes necessary a great deal of formal education before the
younger generation can step into the highly specialized tasks of
adults. During the educational period, there has been a sharp
separation of " school " from " life ", with the result that youngsters possessing considerably more information than their elders
nevertheless have no familiarity with the white lies, evasions, and
even downright deceit by means of which adults reconcile, with
more or less success, the conflicting standards of their world.

In the later stages of school experience, however, the younger
folk slowly acquire knowledge of the ways in which their elders
succeed in " adjusting ", and the battlefield for a great struggle
between the world as it exists for most adults, on the one hand,
and the ideal demands which youth has learned to formulate,
on the other, begins to be mapped out. Basic contradictions between the ideal conduct ceaselessly recommended by parents and
teachers and the real behaviour which those same mentors themselves practise are discovered, and the revolt of youth begins.

That is to say, in one way or another the world turns out to be hard and ruthless, and youth movements represent only one of the many kinds of rebellion observable when the stage of disillusion sets in.

Under the stress of such disillusion youth's ideals are definitely seen to be poorly adapted to actual situations, or *vice versa*, and adolescents begin furiously to think. In Housman's phrase, the youth is " a stranger and afraid in a world he never made " ; he had known for a long time that cheating, lying, theft, fornication, drunkenness, and gluttony existed, but he had thought of those giving way to such practices as utterly beyond the pale of ordinary society. Now he finds out that these appalling vices and sins are scattered generously through the ranks of the people he has been brought up to admire and revere, and it can occasion small wonder when he becomes thoroughly upset, intellectually and emotionally. In a few cases—happily few, be it said—he must wrestle with the dark suspicion that even the members of his family circle are not all that he has thought they were.

Clearly, extreme disillusionment is the lot of only a handful of the younger generation in most societies, for if the experience were universal the study of youthful revolt would not be so esoteric a matter—except for chitchat and ponderously inconclusive " research " about " juvenile delinquency "—as it usually is. By separating out the differing ways in which youth responds to the " adjustment " process we may be able to see why attention to the basic problem has been lacking.

First of all, the discrepancy between the real and the ideal does not arise in exaggerated form for many young people, inasmuch as they have never been exposed to the conditions that would have made idealists of them. " Dead end kids " and other slum youngsters from poverty-stricken, uneducated neighbourhoods are not likely to be burdened with an excess of idealism. The same is true of the mentally retarded, whatever their walk of life. Added to these are many children from upper-crust families whose training has been so neglected by socialite mothers and club-dwelling fathers that their horizons are almost as limited as those of children from the slums. Assuming agreement here, this point can be dropped with the simple statement that many children know little or nothing of highly developed systems of value ; they are essentially unidealistic.

Taking less extreme instances, it is probably true that young people not at the slum level, but from families definitely low in the income scale—the famous " ill-fed, ill-housed, and ill-clothed lower third "—receive fairly heavy injections of morals and the like from home, church, and school.   Granting this, it is still true that when the efforts of virtually everyone in the family must be bent toward the getting of the barest necessities, little time or energy is left over for worry about the oftentimes startling gaps between precept and practice.   When such concern does appear, it most often takes the form of general resentment against a social order regarded as unfair and unjust ; proletarian youth movements may then arise, but usually in alliance with a labour $v.$ capital struggle in which elders sharing one's own hard lot make common front against the enemy.   Reference will later be made to German youth movements of " political auxiliary " character, and among these the specifically proletarian youth movements will be placed.   Nevertheless, it must be said that in most cases the latter do not manifest many of the signs of late adolescent rebellion now under consideration ; they are unidealistic *in our special sense*, although in that only.

Poles apart from unidealistic youngsters are those aflame with noble ideals and depressed by the discovery of flagrant contradiction, but who dissipate the resulting tension by flight into fantasy.   In effect :

> They cannot ever rightly tell—
> Nor are they anxious overmuch—
> Whether this world in which they dwell
> Is real or crumbles at a touch.

These are the personalities—poets, romancers, artists, aesthetes—who shape in imagination a private realm in which discords are resolved in a higher harmony.   Flying in the face of the evidence, they succeed in preserving their belief in the Nikolaus-time—but with the ultimate fate of these escapists it is not necessary for us to deal at length.   Suffice it to say that where youth movements are concerned they are ordinarily only wistful hangers-on ; rarely if ever do they become active participants.   If they do, even a youth movement incorporates too many hard realities to command their continuing loyalty, and they sooner or later retreat into the more satisfying domain of " innerliness ".

Still another way out is afforded by cynicism.   Many a callow youth has a teething spell of this kind, but the greater number pass out of it with reasonable speed.   Those who do not, finally abandon all ideals or even jeer at them in an ostentatious way throughout their whole lives.   When this occurs you have the deeply pessimistic, hypercritical, and generally unpopular personality of the professional cynic. It need hardly be said that such types have little relevance for youth movements.

Once more, it is possible to find many young persons who avoid the collapse into cynicism because their faith in the adult world is preserved by their own families. No matter how great may be the confusion and moral abandonment of society at large, youth of this type finds that its ideals are not out of joint with its own home life. Of course, when the shelter of the family can no longer be forthcoming such youngsters may undergo veritable agony in fitting into a harsh, remorseless world, but memories of the genuine warmth and moral uprightness of parental examples may make it possible to endure. Here again few if any recruits for youth movements are to be found.

Now at last we come to that part of the younger generation which has traits making participation in genuine youth activities possible. Neither dulled, escapist, cynical, nor shielded, in the face of the chasm between real and ideal they attempt to span it by definite action. In brief: They try to bring about actual situations in which the ideals they cherish can be put into effect. Differently stated : Youth movements arise when the effort is made to remould the world so that it fits the ideals.[4]

" Hm-m ! " is a quite natural rejoinder. " It may be that a youth movement is made up of youth on the move, as it were, but you have given no real answer to the crucial question : ' Why do some young people who would be entirely eligible as youth movers fail to participate, whereas others throw themselves heart and soul into the remoulding effort ? How do you discriminate between those who meet all your requirements and still remain aloof, and those who try to span the chasm ? ' "

The objection is well taken, and can be met, if at all, only by anticipating the next chapter, " He Spoke as One Having Authority ", wherein the emergence of German youth movement leaders is described and analysed. The second part of what I hope will be regarded as an answer will be offered in the chapter following the one on leadership, " Come Ye out from among Them and Be Ye Separate ". As the title somewhat vaguely indicates, this has to do with that tendency to form little clusters of the like-minded so frequently apparent not merely among youngsters but in all ranks of society. Using terms hitherto applied only in the study of religious groupings, it can be said that like-mindedness resulting from dissent, from rejection of adult standards, gave rise in Germany to little conventicles which later fused into sects. If a boy or girl had developed a personality making association on the basis of like-mindedness congenial, it was then possible for him or her to join forces with other rebels against a despised adult way of life. I wish explicitly to disavow any reliance on a so-called instinct of gregariousness in presenting such an explanation ; it will be noted that I have said : " *If* a boy or girl had *developed* a personality making association on the basis of like-mindedness congenial . . ." There is some similarity here to the phenomenon of " ganging " described by Thrasher, and I do not wish to deny that there may be some common-human or personal-social basis for the resemblance.[5] Be that as it may, however, I simply assert here that the differential response indicated in the " Hm-m " question is to be explained on the basis of leadership and congenial association ; corroboration must come later.

Proviso : Of the two factors indicated, it is my conviction that leadership of a certain kind is more important in the rise of youth movements than is " ganging " and related activities; as we all know there are many cliques, coteries, or bands of youngsters who are in no sense youth movement participants. Like-minded clustering, then, is a necessary factor, but the sufficient factor resides in the leader.

Turning now towards the contradictions between the real and ideal which played so important a part in the German youth movement, let us remind the reader of " The Linden Tree " and " Once in the Dear Dead Days ". The children who were born in the 'eighties and onwards were surrounded by a Germany rapidly casting off a great many of the stabilizing influences of the Biedermeier time, but within their homes the old virtues were still imparted. Given the mentality of the generation which founded families after 1870, examples of these virtues were found in a German past just far enough away to have the roseate tint of " the good old days ". When you add to this the fact that the good old days really did have many aspects strikingly different from those of a present which, no matter how glorious, still lacked the halo which hovered about Grandfather Friedl's boyhood, it is easy to see why youngsters were told, quite sincerely, that to be good German men and women they need only look back to and faithfully follow the example of their ancestors. Had not the virtuous Germans of bygone days lived sober, responsible, God-fearing lives ? Were they not loyal to church and state ?

Did they not honour their parents and therefore live long in the land ?   Only those means sanctioned by the leaders whom God had set in authority, whether spiritual or temporal, should ever be chosen by good little boys and girls who hoped to grow up into men and women of whom papa and mamma could be proud. Even if the " Do's " and " Don'ts " were not always clearly mapped by God's earthly representatives, they could always be found by looking for the footsteps of the departed and by listening to the tales of their loyal, pious, and kindly deeds.

Not only this : Word of mouth was rendered ever more insistent and penetrating by the almost bodily transplantation of the " occasions " and " sites " of Grandfather Friedl's time into the nursery and kindergarten.   Stories, songs, pictures, and other vivid devices for " traditioning " the child were abundantly available, and among the middle classes were almost universally used.   Further, seasonal merrymaking of every description preserved many features of olden times—indeed, the increasing scope of communication made it possible to draw from the festivities of a great number of German regions.   The child was almost overwhelmed by a wealth of varying impressions which nevertheless gave unity in diversity—a unity of brightly-coloured, warm, sympathetic expectations of a world that, so to speak, would prove to be a perpetual Nikolaus-time.

The elders who provided these expectations for their children, however, were themselves living in surroundings of radically altered stamp.   After the threatened overturns of 1848 there came changes which permitted the streams of commerce and industry to flow more freely :

The triumph of reactionary principles . . . seemed to herald a period of internal peace.   The whole country . . . flung itself . . . upon the conquest of material prosperity and wealth.   The spirit of enterprise and the love of speculation were not confined, as they had been at the beginning of the century, to a small fraction of the public, but invaded the lowest layers of the nation, and once for all took possession of the business world.   During the twenty years which separated . . . 1848–49 from the Franco-German War, modern capitalistic Germany was formed. . . .   The years inaugurating the second half of the century formed the first lap in the marvellous economic development which was to place Germany at the head of the industrial nations of Europe. . . .[6]

This break with the Biedermeier time would in itself have done much to produce a Germany in violent contrast with The Dear Dead Days.   Then came the easy wins over Denmark and Austria, and the consolidation of a German empire which could boast of victory over a France that little more than a half a century earlier had been virtual master of the European continent. The Swiss-like ingenuity of German craftsmen and technicians had borne fruit in the needle-gun and other successful weapons, but with imperial consolidation, the fruits of the French indemnity, and the example provided by heavily industrialized predecessors such as Britain, Germany burst into an age of economic activity and prosperity comparable only to the mushrooming of Japan after the Meiji restoration. Essen, Berlin, Leipzig, and scores of other cities became great centres of industry and commerce almost overnight, and ports like Hamburg, Bremen, and Duisburg experienced unbelievably rapid growth.

The four years following the war of 1870 are known in the economic history of Germany by the name of . . . [founders' years]. The fructifying rain of wealth due to the millions of the war indemnity produced a luxuriant and disordered crop of capitalistic enterprises. A veritable debauch of speculation filled Germany. The economic phenomena which had followed . . . 1848 appeared once more, but exaggerated beyond all bounds. There was a formidable inundation of economic activity in all quarters and a headlong rush for fortune. It is sufficient to quote one figure to illustrate the extraordinary intensity of this movement. The twenty years between 1851 and 1871 . . . had seen the birth of 205 joint-stock companies. . . . The four years between 1870 . . . and 1874 witnessed the sprouting of 857 . . . [a twenty-fold rate of increase].[7]

Accompanying this was a shift in occupations leading to a complete reversal of rural-urban distribution, for while in 1800 at least four Germans out of five were engaged in agriculture, in 1900 four out of five were following pursuits other than the tilling of the soil.[8]

In this transformation Germany possessed a tremendous advantage precisely because its modernization had been so long delayed. Equipment could be of the very latest and most efficient kind, whereas neighbouring nations felt it necessary to tinker up the old machinery and thereby adjust in piecemeal, halting fashion to the accelerated pace of international competition.

Moreover, the emergence of the King of Prussia as German Emperor brought about the spread of an efficient bureaucratic network, hitherto exemplified on a less complex scale in Prussia, over all the new empire. During Bismarck's time the bureaucracy came to control, sometimes behind the scenes, sometimes openly, the policies of the monarchy and the futile negative activities of what passed for a parliament.

Progress was the watchword not only in what may be called the technological and control phases of German society, but also in the realms of expression. Architecture became flamboyant, grandiose, and banal ; music brassily pompous ; graphic and plastic arts, in their more popular forms, cheaply sentimental, chauvinistic, or both ; scholarship and science steadily more specialized—production lines for the *Doktorat* ; and scepticism, relativism, and positivism flourished.[9] In adult life, then, The Linden Tree was left farther and farther behind :

> Die kalten Winde bliesen
>   mir grad ins Angesicht,
> der Hut flog mir vom Kopfe,
>   ich wendete mich nicht.*

Elaborating and adding : Family life, master-servant relations, political inclinations, religion, and education suffered serious upheavals.

Family : The peasants who drifted to the cities or whose little villages and towns were sucked into urban whirlpools soon found that too many Jockels and Bärbeles were not a blessing, economic or otherwise. Social welfare legislation designed to draw " milk from contented cows " did not yet favour large families, and lengthened compulsory school attendance, plus other devices of the Bismarckian state, made it very hard for the working-class father to provide the needed supply of cabbage, coal, and clothing.

Younger men and women of rural background found their family lives thwarted by the fact that the old bundling, betrothal, and marriage customs proved impossible to transfer to urban life. Among the burghers family tension previously latent, perhaps, but largely unrealized, now took on the openly threatening character of a bent bow or a cocked trigger. In the Biedermeier time many of the lads who left the callings of their fathers behind them did so out of patriotic conviction, and those who did not dutifully followed parental pursuits. Rarely was there an arbitrary break with the hereditary occupation merely because it was hereditary or because of the son's conception of his own narrowly defined interests. During the imperial boom, however, the vogue of progress and the rapidly increasing number and

---

* The icy winds roared loudly,
    Straight in my face they blew ;
 Away my hat went soaring—
    But I sought no backward view.

range of economic opportunities led to a wholesale abandonment of traditional vocations. Frequently this meant that the father no longer felt the obligation to support the son while his career was getting under way; wounded pride opened rifts in the family lute. When a son did slip into the groove worn by his father, it was no longer with the feeling that " At last I'm doing what Vaterl did ", but rather that the groove was a rut. Consequent self-justification quite often led to boastful exaggeration of the rut's importance and to escape from boredom in the commercialized " amusements " of the great cities, with their pandering to all vices.

Flush living in competition with business and professional associates made it more and more difficult for fathers to provide dowries for their daughters, more especially as these daughters came to expect education in a finishing school or similar establishment. Even when the dowry system did not fall into the discard, changes in dwelling-place, neighbours, and ideas of the socially praiseworthy not only gave more scope to individual choice but also meant that bride and bridegroom began to contrast " marriage for love " and " marriage for convenience " in a way unknown to earlier generations. This, added to the ethical questions raised by the existence of the prostitute and the mistress, provided material for literary men like Sudermann, Heyse, and a host of others; tension and unrest were thereby increased.

The strenuously competitive character of the professions led to ever greater deferment of marriage, with the usual result. Because, as hitherto noted, so many of the delayed marriages were regarded as " marriages of convenience ", the double standard carried over from the wild-oats stage into the life of the married man. The German woman, except when she joined the ranks of prostitutes and mistresses, did not follow suit to any significant extent, but she began to absorb doctrines of natural rights and ethical consistency; a woman's movement, although on a much smaller scale than that which appeared in some other countries of Europe, notably Britain and Sweden, began to get under way. In spite of the ostracism with which divorce was visited it greatly increased in frequency among the middle classes, and thereby brought the moral contradictions in which it had its source into ever greater prominence.

Master-servant : For all of the niggardliness, downright exploitation, and even cruelty shown by masters in the Biedermeier time, the personal character of their relations with workers at least gave some focus for feelings of resentment—somebody could be blamed. In the new Germany, impersonal clerical machines kept employer and employee far apart; thwarted rage found no satisfying vent as it had among workers of the kind depicted in Hauptmann's *Weavers*. Before 1848, many left-wing ideologies were random and structureless, and even after that time they were kept alive and more tightly organized chiefly by refugees living in Switzerland, France, or England. But as masses of human beings having no ownership of the means of production began to pile up in the larger cities, and as the passionless inhumanity of a new and raw capitalism began to wreak havoc, the gospels of Marx and Engels, Lassalle and Bebel, became intensely appealing. " Class conflict " and " recognition " were slogans that spread like wildfire, and after 1870, in spite of the heavy demand for labour, emigration of floodlike volume poured out of Germany. Pressure was relieved to some extent, but even the repeal of the laws against Social Democracy in the 'nineties failed to reclaim the vanished loyalty of the proletariat. " Fellows without a Fatherland " held forth in every city tavern. When devotion to " the good prince, father of his people ", was incautiously expressed by some relic of the past, jeers or even blows and kicks were promptly forthcoming.

Politics : Of course, the claims of the monarchy to rule by the grace of God sometimes evoked an indulgent smile from the bourgeois *Untertan*. But as an alternative to a republic—of which France presumably provided a horrible example—even the flighty Wilhelm II received unswerving allegiance, or at the very least was held to be an indispensable figurehead. Yet though the monarchy as an institution was not always worshipped without question, the bureaucracy indubitably was. The clamour for a kind of liberty which would make national solidarity possible, once shouted forth by the *Burschenschaften* and *Turnvereine*, had become pointless in view of the unifying web of bureaucratic administration. " There must be discipline ", " Order is the first duty of the citizen ", and " The welfare of Germany as a whole is more important than the prejudices of its parts " [10] were visibly embodied in the regulations of staid officialdom. Except among the workers, politics dwindled in relative importance, for the ordinary middle-class German, if his own economic interests were not obviously involved, was content to leave crucial decisions to experts. He gloried in the smooth running of an elaborate administrative machine that apparently foresaw every contingency, provided for every exception, regulated everything from buttons to battleships, and incidentally furnished the pattern by which the German army, always to be victorious, mobilized, manœuvred, paraded, and appropriately impressed foreign observers. Efficiency, probity, calculability— *was will man mehr*?

Religion : Supernaturalism, especially Roman Catholicism, retained its hold on the peasantry, but as we have seen, the proportion of peasants in the German population rapidly dwindled. Once the walls of the parish, whether Catholic or Lutheran, were breached by strange ways and strange people, all but those in sheltered nooks and corners felt the chilling blasts of doubt. In the swollen ranks of the urban proletariat the coldness of official religion and its identification with a despised political régime led to ready acceptance of competing ideologies in the form of Marxism and the like.

The middle classes in earlier days had weakened in religious allegiance because of the vogue of Hegelianism and the pantheism of figures such as Goethe, but there was nevertheless no widespread defection from orthodox belief, nor indeed any great loss in whatever effectiveness that belief may have had in the control of conduct. After 1870 the middle classes waxed fat, and with their fatness came conviction that this world is not a vale of tears in preparation for a better, but rather an Abbey of Thelema. Evolutionism and the higher criticism found hearing outside the treatise and the lecture room, and the notion that " religion is an opiate of the people " was tacitly accepted even by those persons who had most to gain if the continued administration of the opiate were assured. That is to say, many eminently respectable people came to feel that religion is a good thing because it keeps otherwise troublesome people contented. Further, the Sunday morning promenade to church with *paterfamilias* in the van still carried a halo of solid social position ; only *vaterlandslose Gesellen*, viz., social, political and economic malcontents, ignored the comfortable duties of pew-warmers. Again, few churchgoers forgot the legal and other disabilities which failure to keep up membership in the official churches entailed. Profitable hypocrisy is rarely painful ; hence, although orthodox belief steadily waned in influence, church membership and attendance notably diminished only where the " dangerous thoughts " of Social Democracy had wreaked havoc.[11]

Education : Schools provide only one of the many kinds of training through which the young are brought up " in the way they should go ". Family, neighbourhood, and hosts of other formative influences are probably of much more importance. Where parents were concerned, maturing children not only became slowly aware of parental insincerity or uncertainty, but in addition were expected to become little replicas of conventionally stylish adults, while at the same time it was thought *artig, niedlich* or " cute " for them to be Jockels and Bärbeles in the presence of near relatives and friends. The dual role thus forced upon youngsters brought premature sophistication ; lads of fourteen tried to drink, smoke, and engage in amorous exploits when temporarily released from supervision, and girls of even more tender age chattered about the delights of being the beloved of an officer. Observing these *Pennäler* and *Backfisch* manifestations,[12] fathers and mothers were often assailed by doubt, but they could do little to overcome the consequences of their own double standard. It might even be said that the extent to which parents had departed from what earlier generations had taken for granted was inversely proportional to their demands for the semblance of childish innocence, on the one hand, and on the other in direct ratio to their insistence upon the child's precocious adaptation to a new world in which " progress " in all departments of life had become fashionable.

In the domain of formal education the clamour for applied science, the increasing use of modern languages in salesmanship, and a host of other developments led to a rapid expansion of the school system designed for middle-class youngsters. The old humanistic training, à la Schoolmaster Bertram's Homeric Hymns, became more and more unsuited to the needs of the day, and schools offering combinations of mathematics, science, modern languages, and commercial subjects in varying admixture were established or expanded by legislative enactment in all parts of Germany.[13] Many Germans recognized the liabilities incurred in this process, but little was done to remedy matters :

A onesidedness which only esteems material values and an increasing control over nature is destructive in its influence. . . . We Germans have ceased to be the nation of thinkers, of poets, and dreamers, we aim now only at the domination and exploitation of nature. . . . Have we Germans kept a harmonious balance between the economic and the moral side of our development, as was once the case with the Greeks ? No ; with the enormous increase of wealth dark shadows have fallen on our national life. In the nation as in the individual we see with the increase of wealth the decrease of moral feeling and moral power.[14]

Even more drastically :

Inasmuch as genuine values were disappearing there was an effort to devise substitutes. The Wilhelmian Age, with its Victory Esplanade and false marble statues, decorations, and façades on even the cheapest tenements, began to get under way. In place of quiet devotion to the past of living tradition appeared an epoch of " historizing ", with its accompanying museums and literary evocations. Instead of the deeply felt standards about which a people need not speak there came the blatancy of cheap toploftical phrases. Instead of firmly grounded personalities came *poseurs*, obscurantists, advocates of conceited caste divisions. Essential worth was pushed aside in favour of " front ", and rank, title, diplomas, " society " connections, " pull ", and wealth oftentimes acquired decisive significance.[15]

Certainly education was deeply affected by these general tendencies. Herrle complains that the introduction of dozens of specialized courses in the schools made it virtually impossible for the student to have anything but a smattering of knowledge in any field.[16] The old practice of releasing the student from classes in the afternoon in order to make it possible for him to do independent work and round out his knowledge—and strange as it may seem, a goodly proportion had once done just this— was abandoned ; a very heavy schedule of cut-and-dried lectures and recitations was set up. The stuff of learning was thoroughly predigested and then presented in take-it-or-leave-it fashion, with severe penalties for those who left it. The impersonality of the process, the absence of discussion, and the pedantic authoritarianism was neatly expressed by one educator thus : " We must find the path to the hearts of our students, but we must go armed with constant watchfulness and a goodly share of sound, sceptical distrust." [17]

As might be expected, .whatever school spirit appeared was in the solidarity of students as opposed to their teachers. A school morality which not only permitted trickery and deceit in examinations but actually approved of such methods soon flourished. " Cramming joints " of all kinds sprang into being, and given the character of the official examinations, it must be said that the ordinary student was almost forced to hire the services of the professional *Pauker*, the crammer.[18] There were no sports ; physical exercise was limited to two hours weekly of apparatus work in the gymnasium, although in the 'nineties, at the special request of Wilhelm II, this was raised to three. Shortsighted eyes, narrow chests and hunched shoulders, flat feet, and flabby muscles were avoided only by the fortunate few.

With the educational machine grinding away like this, the older generation need hardly have been astonished at the indifference with which their flatulent preachments were received by students. As early as 1885 even a conservative like Paul de Lagarde cried out in protest :

> I do not complain because our youth is lacking in idealism, but I do make the accusation that adults, especially those in political control, do not offer youth the genuine ideals out of which alone the latent idealism of youth can grow. . . . I believe in German youth. I believe in the future of our Fatherland, but I do not believe in the fitness of the system now dominant, nor in the capacities of the men who want to satisfy the longings and needs of their offspring with the outworn relics . . . that remain in their hands.[19]

As if this were not enough, the disastrous effects of the rigid separation of the sexes during adolescence, especially under the conditions peculiar to Germany at that time, had long been apparent and were increasing in scope. Not only were school classes segregated in the higher grades but also in the lower. In addition, smaller families, lack of nearby kindred of comparable age, the greater extent to which girls were educated outside the home, growing formality and impersonality of social relations, *und dergleichen mehr*, led to barriers between the sexes during the 'teens and early twenties to an extent far greater than had previously been in evidence among the middle classes—even though Germany has long been a land in which the division between the realms proper to man and woman has been sharply marked. After twelve or thirteen boys saw very little of their former girl playmates, and when they did see them it was usually only on Sunday afternoon visits or at parties presided over by hawk-eyed chaperones. Nevertheless, novel literature was saturated with gushy romantic love at the very time when the demands of education, both informal and formal, made it almost impossible for youngsters to form individual attachments with those of the opposite sex. Girls associated chiefly with girls and boys with boys ; " crushes " become more and more prevalent. As the younger generation grew older, Paragraph 175 of the German Criminal Code (STGB) * began to seep into the

---

* This is the law dealing with the punishment of male homosexuality.

" humorous " journals, and in cities like Berlin " high-class " establishments catering to adults of doubtful gender or " unusual " proclivities plied their specialized business.

Now comes the crux of all this : What did the sons and daughters of the middle classes, especially the sons who were at least potential idealists, think of the brave new world their fathers had acquired and were ready to bequeath ? The older generation had lived through the triumphs of the 'sixties and 'seventies, the upward zoom of Germany as a first-rate industrial as well as military power in the 'eighties, and the plush-upholstered comfort and respectability of the 'nineties. Were the youngsters grateful for the warmth of Germany's place in the sun ? To put it mildly, they thought that the brave new world was brassy and that the brass was badly tarnished, that the warmth was not the warmth of sunshine but the enervating stuffiness of overheated, tawdrily furnished apartments filled with the reek of stale beer and the acrid fumes of cigar stubs. Specifically, they thought that parental religion was largely sham, politics boastful and trivial, economics unscrupulous and deceitful, education stereotyped and lifeless, art trashy and sentimental, literature spurious and commercialized, the drama tawdry and mechanical, the dance cheaply titillating or excessively formal, family life repressive and insincere, and the relations of the sexes, in marriage or out, shot through with hypocrisy.[20]

The times were ripe and overripe for a revolt of youth ; Rimmon's house was seen to be a flimsy shelter for a false god, and the idol was thrown from its pedestal :

> By the picket pins that the dogs defile,
> In the dung and the dust He lay,
> Till the priests ran out and chattered awhile
> And wiped Him and took Him away.

One thing only was lacking for the founding of a new faith : namely, the indispensable leadership. Who ?

NOTES

1. A whole heap of references might be given for this hasty sketch of the child in society, but a few summary treatments alone will be cited :

Read Bain, " Personality Development and Marriage " in Howard Becker and Reuben Hill, eds., *Marriage and the Family* (Boston, 1942), pp. 121–52.

Katherine Whiteside Taylor, " Parent-Child Interaction " in *op. cit.*, pp. 441–68.

George H. Mead, *Mind, Self, and Society* (Chicago, 1934), pp. 42–81, 117–76, 192–213, 245–80, 311–16, 328–36.

2. Kingsley Davis, " The Sociology of Parent-Youth Conflict ", *American Sociological Review*, 5, 4 (Aug., 1940), p. 526.

3. As used in this book, " ideal " and " real " are taken in their popular senses. No epistemological implications should be read into them.

4. The classification of the different ways in which youth may respond is taken from the dissertation by Robert C. Schmid mentioned in the Preface, *German Youth Movements ; A Typological Study* (unpublished, University of Wisconsin, 1941), pp. 15–19.

5. Frederick M. Thrasher, *The Gang* (Chicago, 1927), pp. 26–44.

6. Henri Lichtenberger, *Germany and Its Evolution in Modern Times* (New York, 1913), pp. 10–12.

7. *Ibid.*, pp. 12–13.

8. *Deutschlands Wirtschaft, Währung, und Finanzen* (government report, Berlin, 1924), *passim*, quoted in Schmid, *op. cit.*, p. 23.

9. Charlotte Lütkens, *Die deutsche Jugendbewegung* (Frankfurt a. M., 1925), pp. 24–54 ; Theo Herrle, *Die deutsche Jugendbewegung* (Gotha-Stuttgart, 1924), pp. 1–9 ; Günther Ehrenthal, *Die deutsche Jugendbünde* (Berlin, 1929), pp. 9–10.

10. This is the real meaning of " Deutschland über Alles ".

11. For everything between this and the previous footnote, a minimum list is :

Georg Steinhausen, *Geschichte der deutschen Kultur* (Leipzig, 1929), pp. 543–672 *passim* ; W. H. Dawson, *The Evolution of Modern Germany* (New York, n.d., but probably a reprint of the 1908 ed.), Chaps. 1, 3, 5, 23 *et passim*.

12. Ehrenthal, *op. cit.*, pp. 6–7.

13. Dawson, *op. cit.*, Chap. 6 ; Lichtenberger, *op. cit.*, pp. 362–78.

14. Rein, quoted in Dawson, *op. cit.*, p. 8.

15. Ehrenthal, *op. cit.*, p. 11.

16. Herrle, *op. cit.*, p. 4.

17. Quoted (no author given) in *ibid.*, p. 5.

18. *Ibid.*, p. 6.

19. Quoted in Lütkens, *op. cit.*, p. 24.

20. Ehrenthal, *op. cit.*, pp. 14–15, is but one witness among the hundreds who might be brought to testify to this mood of German youth.

CHAPTER IV

PROCLAMATION: "HE SPOKE AS ONE HAVING AUTHORITY"

> The peace of shocked Foundations flew
>   Before his ribald questionings.
> He broke the oracles in two,
>   And bared the paltry wires and strings.
> He headed desert wanderings;
>   He led his soul, his cause, his clan
> A little from the ruck of Things.
> "Once on a time there was a Man."
>   —KIPLING, "Things and the Man".

"Who is to lead us?" can never be answered if the shout resounds in empty space; there must be the time, the place, and the man.

The time was 1896, the very peak of the dizzy climb to the supposed glories of the brave new world.

The place was at the centre of the empire of Wilhelm II—Steglitz, a fat, contented, upper-middle-class suburb of Berlin.

Steglitz lay on the rail-route which led from Berlin to Potsdam, and thence to the four corners of the world. This was decisive, for it awakened from its bucolic slumber by the rumbling of the rails; the men who lived in Steglitz could not avoid noticing that there existed a great, wide world outside . . . and who can make such a discovery without being swept away by its implications? [1]

Within this small city many of the contradictions between the Biedermeier time and the Wilhelmian era were visible in startling contrast. Witness:

. . . immediately beside the city hall . . . there already stood examples of elegant metropolitan life . . . the Kaiser's coffee house and the Hotel Albrechtshof . . . but the gleaming white sparks of the village blacksmith [still shot forth across the street] . . . and you could hear the sharp cling-clang of iron in the midst of the bustle of the city. [2]

The complacent burghers probably smiled tolerantly at the sooty smithy, thinking that it would soon be torn down to make way for real elegance, but their contemptuous calm was ruffled when they heard another kind of cling-clang issuing from the doors of their fondly-admired high school, their elegant *Gymnasium*. A certain professor, Ludwig Gurlitt by name, had dared to say that everything was not for the best in the best of all possible worlds. He had openly challenged the prevailing bourgeois standards of education ; subversive phrases such as " school reform " and " independence in thought and deed " were perpetually on his lips. He had actually said that the prevailing system was stultifying and insincere, and that parents should not impose their adult standards on the personality of the growing youngster. Horrible and dangerous ideas ! Gurlitt was dismissed just as promptly as bureaucratic routine permitted, and it was hoped that the infection for which he was responsible would soon be cured.[3]

The searing brand of purifying dismissal, however, had touched only Gurlitt ; his pupils still remained. Among them was Karl Fischer, called " Crazy Fischer " by the solid citizens of Steglitz, so extraordinary a personality that his fellows began to fall under his sway :

. . . everyone who had any dealings with Karl Fischer, or who enjoyed his friendship, invariably had this experience : Here stands someone who has highly unusual capacities.[4]

[He is] . . . a romantic rebel of the type of Karl Moor [the hero of Schiller's " The Robbers "] . . . who is conscious of ideals which he thinks better than those which society imposes and who devotes his life to winning respect for them in the face of social antagonism . . .

Fischer was an absolute monarch in his way, and tolerated no opposition.[5]

Here there emerges what I shall henceforth call the charismatic leader, a term which has won a secure place in the vocabulary of the modern social scientist. *Charisma* is a New Testament word meaning " grace ", but it has been stripped of its narrower theological meaning and now denotes simply the possession of extraordinary qualities.[6] These qualities may be many and varied ; Mohammed owed a large part of his grip on Abu Bekr and other early disciples through his terrifying ability to " throw fits " and recount the visions he had seen while out of the flesh. Joseph Smith was a prey to hallucinations which he took for reality, and these *plus* his oratorical powers dragged in his train men such as Brigham Young, whose sober good sense in other matters is abundantly attested.

The extraordinary qualities of the early youth movement

leaders certainly did not pass so far beyond the limits of the
" normal " as did those of the supernaturalistic mouthpieces just
mentioned ; in Karl Fischer's case it seems to have been primarily
the *charisma* of virility, recklessness, and intellectual force which
attracted adherents. In spite of Blüher's contention that any
leader of the Roamers was necessarily a " masculine hero " of
" inverted type ", i.e., someone whose erotic potentialities or
practices brought flocking about him a kind of male harem, it
seems highly unlikely that such a diagnosis is adequate to account
for men like Fischer, however plausible or even probable it may
be in other connections. It must always be remembered that in
spite of the segregation of the sexes and the widespread phenomenon of the male-male or female-female " crush ", a great many
young Germans remained basically heterosexual in inclination.
What they wanted was someone capable of Promethean defiance :

> May the coming generation of our people finally succeed in
> creating something that will blaze before us with the compelling
> power of an ideal . . . that in the Middle Ages was incorporated
> in the knight or, as in our time, by the English gentleman ! . . .
> But in both of these something is lacking ; what we seek seems to
> lie in the words " personality " and " robust fellow " (*Kerl*). Here
> too, however, we encounter difficulties ; the first is too artificial,
> abstract, and trite, whereas the other is too crude. . . . Perhaps
> we should simply bring back, as an honorific term, the word *man*.
> Our people needs whole *men* and not fragments such as notaries,
> party hacks, scholars, officials, and courtiers. In the word " man "
> there lies force and character ; it has an upright, specific, and
> essentially German essence. . . . Perhaps our longing will be
> fulfilled and . . . finally all Germans, . . . particularly our uni-
> versity-trained leaders, will set far above official titles and orders of
> merit or nobility the final encomium, " He is a man ! " [7]

A sorry state of affairs it was, beyond question, which could
make so deeply felt an appeal necessary, but there is no doubt
that men of Fischer's type were rare—so rare, in fact, that it was
virtually impossible for the ordinary German youngster to avoid
the feeling that such persons were in some way superhuman.
Result, *charisma* :

> . . . " When we shoot, he makes the most points ; when we
> march, his endurance far surpasses ours ; when we laugh, his example
> is the most infectious ; when we talk, he talks the best . . ."
> Readily apparent in these comments from a circular letter is the
> decisive power of common-human personal superiority, more generous
> " dimensions ", higher merit. Not only this : Many other comments
> show that over and above this the leader was held to possess some-

thing of "unfathomable background", of the "superpersonal", of the "irrational" that veiled him in mystery, that made him seem like someone possessed by and possessing a Socratic *daemon*. Better expressed : These qualities give him secure standing in a higher, superpersonal, and thereby superhuman complex of values.[8]

In the German setting the consequence was that the Roamer's " Heil ! " and extended right arm—both of them revived on the basis of medieval example—were virtually religious in meaning, if we take " religion " in a sense sufficiently broad. On the basis of direct contact with youth movement groups, as well as through close study of their literature, I am convinced that such an interpretation of their attitudes is eminently warranted. Many a time I have heard youngsters chorus forth, " Leader, we follow thee and shout ' Yea ! ' " with a passionate intensity that reminded me of camp-meeting revivals.

But even the revival must have more in its total setting than the charismatic preacher, and the same holds for the appeal of any charismatic leader whatsoever. No matter how extraordinary or uncanny the men, they never present a wholly novel message ; they ordinarily assert, to choose a familiar example, that they come " not to destroy the law but to fulfil it "—meaning thereby that old traditions are accepted but infused with new meaning. Against such a background as this, they can then safely proclaim : " Ye have heard it said by them of old time, but I say unto you . . ."

Returning to the example of Joseph Smith : Without a Biblical tradition and Protestant sectarianism he is simply unimaginable, but given these and like essentials, the Book of Mormon found its martyrs and its triumphs. Eventually, to be sure, all-powerful routine makes sedate ceremonial out of ecstatic deliverance, and tradition, temporarily set in second place, resumes its ancient sway, changed in outward seeming but inwardly much the same.

But I anticipate the day when Baldur von Schirach donned the mantle of Karl Fischer. . . . My task now is to present more clearly the way in which the charismatic leader of pristine stamp gains and holds his power. To begin with, he boldly attacks the problem that faces him—even though that problem may be but dimly envisaged—and seeks a following obedient to him and appropriate to his mission. If his " call " to leadership is regarded as spurious by potential devotees, or meets with indifference, his claims collapse. But if they do recognize him, then he is their master as long as his personality and deeds continue to command their submissive allegiance. Frequently, of course, the leader who feels a call regards himself as independent of any particular body of followers, and his unshaken self-assurance oftentimes overcomes all aloofness and suspicion :

. . . I do not know *whose* leader I am ; but I do know *that* I am a leader, even if I were not chosen to lead by anyone. How do I know this ? [As a Chinese sage might say, from the innermost essence of all things.] [9]

This reference to principles over and above ordinary life is not jocular but serious, and the utter confidence with which it is made points to the basic trait of " him who hath received assurance of grace ". Karl Fischer recruited his followers directly ; they were not voted into membership. He stalked about among his fellow-students, estimating their potentialities, their zeal and devotion, and then chose those whom he thought worthy of him and his cause. The cause, as will be shown later, was not much more than the right of youth to live its own life in accordance with its own standards, and it was visibly embodied in the practice of " roaming " hither and yon in freedom from the cramping routines of school and home. It seems entirely possible, however, that Fischer's leadership gifts were of such outstanding sort that he could have gathered disciples for almost any scheme that released the tensions so rapidly building up to the breaking point among the potentially idealistic German youth of that day.

However this may be, he soon gathered about him a group of fellow-students, announced himself as their leader, and told them of his plans for escaping from the " culture of the sofa " to a kind of life " where youth could regain its birthright ". Not only charismatic but also sensitive and intelligent, he was followed eagerly, and his example set off a veritable prairie fire of youthful rebellion throughout all of Germany. At the beginning, to be sure, the flames blazed only through the eastern part of Brandenburg and adjacent regions of Prussia,[10] but they soon kindled among the youngsters of Upper Saxony, Bavaria, and the southwest.

Success so immediate and sweeping would have emboldened anyone, and certainly Fischer steadily intensified his challenge and defiance. Nevertheless, it is altogether likely that a personality of such colour—perhaps tinged with Messianic delusions

A Roamer (*Wandervogel*) as idealized in " Pluck-Fiddle Jack ".

—would steadily expand its claims regardless of outward events. In any case, Fischer's insistence on recognition as the kingpin of the rapidly increasing throng of Roamers grew more and more pronounced. Subordinate leaders appeared, but they were kept under his rule with all the force—and that was not a little !— at his command. His self-assumed titles grew steadily more grandiose : First, *Bachant* (a term derived from the Latin *vagantes*) ; * next *Oberbachant* ; and finally *Grossbachant*—positive, comparative, superlative !

It might be thought that this assumption of supreme power on the part of a leader would immediately call forth strenuous opposition among his entourage, but at the beginning Fischer seems to have had things all his own way. Many of the youth whom he recruited were so firmly held in his grip that he could have done almost anything with them. For some the readiness to submit was never put into words, but a few of those who could speak more freely brought forth astounding testimony of their longing for an unquestioned leader and their willingness to obey his decisions to the letter. Their utterances ran thus :

Leaders. Leadership, that is our need, and obedience, and great wordless activity. . . . We must waste no more effort on discussion and controversy. . . . The discussion can be left to the leaders round the council fire. . . . The new religion must be inarticulate . . . convictions should be sealed in the dark . . .

I believe . . . in the wheel of the stars and the rhythmic cycles of birth and death and of the seasons, which preserve the exquisite freshness of life from ever staling . . . I want the fight and man naked and unashamed, with his sword in his hand, and behind, the stars sweeping westward, and before, the wind in the grass. It is enough, Brothers. Action ! The word is spoken.[11]

Such lust for action for its own sake, coupled with fanatically tinged devotion to the leader, is approached in recent times only by a handful of the followers of Mussolini and Hitler. Unlike the Fascists and Nazis, however, the bands of devotees following in the train of Fischer and similar leaders by the grace of " the innermost essence of all things "—which I am tempted to paraphrase as " the Limitless Whichness and All the Works "—did occasionally put their masters' claims to the test. There was no formal procedure, for that would have been damned as parliamentary, bureaucratic, rationalistic, and cold-bloodedly mechanical, but there was a tacit expectation that the leader

* " Hearty fellow " or " boon companion " ; it is apparently not derived from the Greek, and hence is not analogous to our Bacchant.

would every now and again give evidence of his extraordinary or
" superman " qualities.

Technically : In the earlier stages of charismatic leadership,
" the gift of grace " is regarded as valid only as long as its presence
is attested by actions to which the disciples yield complete
obedience. The moment that the slightest reluctance appears,
doubt has been cast on the genuineness of the *charisma*.
Ordinarily these doubts are personified ; some disciple begins to
feel that he himself is charismatic, and he puts forth his claim
by a direct demand for the reins of power. He is then a
" belittler " or *Verschmäher*, but if he should succeed in winning
adherents, he too heads a discipleship or, more frequently,
deprives the former leader of all his following. This state of

Roamers, from " Pluck-Fiddle Jack ".

affairs is graphically depicted in a passage from an early youth
movement magazine :

Roland, the time has come when you must give me the group.
I want to lead. I can no longer stand by and see you carry out
my plans half-heartedly. Night and day as we roamed in the open
I have been your follower. Now I shall lead . . . A year ago, at
the summer solstice ceremony, I wanted to take over. Then you
laughed. Now you have stolen a year from me. A year out of my
life. Now I will wait no longer. What ? Of course I have experience ! I know exactly how I shall do everything. . . . You know
that they would sooner listen to me than to you. Oh, you ! You
led the group for five years and it has never amounted to anything.
Get to the devil out of here ! Everyone here listens to me ! From
to-day on I am the leader ! Anyone who doesn't like it can get out.[12]

And nobody went but Roland. . . .

In many such cases, the deposed despot eventually managed to get together a new cluster of the faithful, with the result that the old group and the new despised each other with all the fervour of religious sects. In the long run, of course, the progressive splitting up led to a slackening of the antagonism, for when you have fifty or a hundred rival followings, it is impossible to bestow an amount of dislike on each of them equal to that which could be discharged on one. In the next chapter, " Come Ye out from among Them and Be Ye Separate ", it will be possible to show something of the way in which these schismatic tendencies worked themselves out.

Going back to Karl Fischer : His eventual fall from power came about in a way about like that described. For all his sensitivity and intelligence, he finally proved unable to see that a number of the Roamers were becoming dissatisfied. Before long his failure to interpret properly the numerous intentional and unintentional hints let drop by his followers brought on an open break. The successful belittler was Siegfried Copalle. A close friend of Fischer's, he was nevertheless dismayed by the rough-and-tumble conduct of some of the Roamers :

Copalle was more refined in manner than the others, and experienced the romanticism of youth in forms less gross. Fond of art, music, and the writing of poetry, he must have become disgusted at the way in which Fischer's lofty ideas were spoiled in the hands of rough, insensitive deputies and followers. . . . Nevertheless, he did not completely cut himself off from the Roamers, for he foresaw that the time and the personalities would arrive for which his ideas would be more suitable and acceptable.[13]

Copalle was right, for he began to become the centre of a group of youngsters representing the Steglitz " pseudo-nobility " ; they possessed the wherewithal to commune with nature a little more comfortably than the programme of the original Roamers called for :

" Scenery ", Copalle insisted, " cannot be properly enjoyed by the dusty wayfarer. The best method, always, is by carriage, for from a carriage you have the advantage of a higher point of view. The trees and fields are spread out before you. This bumming (*Bummeln*) on foot is quite barbaric. Fontane [the great novelist of the German countryside] invariably travelled by carriage." [14]

The example set by Copalle and his cohorts soon led to partial crumbling of the " hard primitivism " which until that time had characterized the Roamers. In fact, the comradely spirit of

" one for all, all for one " began to break down. Initially the practice so common among charismatic discipleships, that of throwing all resources into a common pool, had been followed ; " share and share alike " was the rule. But now clefts opened with startling suddenness :

> It turned out that on Copalle's trips the wealthier . . . gentlemen regaled themselves with roast meat and wine while the others, looking on enviously, gnawed at their hunks of hard sausage.[15]

The strain on the comradely tie, as might well be imagined, became rather great ; the " boon companions " or *Bachanten* began to feel that things were getting " close to the end of the limit ". The latent quarrel came into the open when Copalle's " soft primitivists " began to undertake roamings on their own initiative ; Fischer and his deputies were not consulted. Outraged, Fischer wrote a brusque condemnation of such perfidy in the Roamers' magazine, accusing the Copalle clique of " deception " and " breach of faith ". A piercing light is thrown on the whole affair by the fact that the denunciation did not bear on the obvious failure to observe the most elementary expectations of comradeship, but rather on the breaking of the oath in which every Roamer, on being admitted to the *Bund* or alliance, had sworn eternal allegiance to him, Karl Fischer !

His *charisma* thus corroded, Fischer made the fatal mistake of resorting to political manipulation and discussion. No charismatic leader can ever do this and still retain his hold ; so it proved with the Roamers. A sort of Council of Charter Members among the disciples had informally existed for some time, and now, the matter being laid before it, the council resorted to the typical parliamentary device of compromise. As is usually the case in small bodies of this kind, the compromise solved nothing, for the issues were rooted in basic antitheses of temperament and conviction. There could be no dodging the fact that the Roamers had given birth to a heretical sect under Copalle's leadership, and Fischer's ill-advised politics, coupled with what may well have been a defensive accentuation of his monarchical manner, did the rest. He had tried to use the Council of Charter Members as a tool, but Copalle's sectarians turned the tables by insisting that the real Roamers were those qualified to sit in the council, and not merely those who enjoyed Fischer's continuing favour. Thus shrewdly flattered, the council pondered the affair, and although the record is not quite clear, apparently decided in

favour of Copalle's group. " The old Roamer alliance is dead,"
proclaimed the rebels. " Now we shall set up an entirely new
Roamer group built along quite different lines." [16]

As it seems, Fischer realized his mistake in submitting his
decrees to the council, and his kingly poise returned :

If it please you, gentlemen, you can dissolve the council and
with what remains of it form a new group, but you cannot dissolve
the Roamers. The Roamers are the *Bachanten* [who are still loyal
to me], and we *Bachanten* will close ranks and hold high the old
tradition. [17]

In saying this, however, Fischer had tacitly admitted that
Copalle the belittler had won his way, and that as far as the
total body of Roamers was concerned, the king had been deposed.
Still, he snatched partial victory from the ruins of his realm, for
the oldest and most famous of his deputies, Wolfgang Kirchbach,
remained loyal, together with a few other " boon companions ".
Two bands of Roamers thus came into being : The little circle
centring about Fischer, which bore the title of the old or " Original
Roamers ", and the " Roamers, Incorporated " (1908), the name
assumed by what had initially been Copalle's group. Fischer
was by no means disposed of as a leader of German youth. In
a few years he was to reach heights even loftier than those from
which he had fallen, but for the time being at least even his best
friends could not gloss over his failure. Moreover, in spite of
his later expansion of domain, his career was chequered with
ups and downs, all of them apparently attributable to the traits
which had initially made it possible for him successfully to ruffle
the dovecotes of Steglitz :

The headstrong, restless egotism and dictatorial rigorousness of
Karl Fischer, and his blunt, rough-and-tough attitude, led to tension
with even his most intimate companions [18] . . . the very intensity
of his inner convictions led him to discount the views of others. [19]

Granting all this, it still remains true that without Karl Fischer
the revolt of German youth might have worked itself out in
different channels. In all likelihood, those channels would have
meandered in a fashion just about as aimless, so far as clearcut,
definite goals are concerned, as did those of the early Roamers.
But I am certainly not prepared to say that any outspoken,
vigorous youngster could have done what Karl Fischer demonstrably did. In this context we are dealing with unique events

and time-series, not with what have been called "constructed types". To be sure, any "type" of German youth leadership that might be devised for the provisional explanation of the early revolt would necessarily incorporate many of the features so markedly exemplified by Karl Fischer, but still and all the empirical world is one thing and scientific devices for bringing order into the helterskelter are something else.[20] I am not presenting a "great man" theory of history, but I am unqualifiedly asserting that at the empirical level there is no escape from the crucial significance of personalities at least relatively unique.

This much said, attention should now be directed toward those phases of the early Roamers which have been interpreted in psychoanalytic terms by the notorious Hans Blüher. In his history of the Roamers, published in 1912, he had given many broad hints about the character of the bond uniting leaders and followers, but it was not until the 1917 appearance of the first volume of his general study of male eroticism that these hints were expanded and thoroughly systematized.

Blüher drew on a fairly extensive collection of evidence for his 1917 treatise ; it was by no means confined to the Roamers, although its focus was unquestionably on this aspect of the German youth movement. Following a number of ethnographers and social historians, Blüher dealt with the homosexual pairs exemplified by Spartiate military figures, the sacred Seven Hundred of Thebes, Epaminondas and Pelopidas, Damon and Pythias, squires and knights of chivalric times, the Templars, some of the Freemasons, and of course any number of so-called "savage" or "primitive" societies.

In all of these Blüher held that the social bonds were basically of sexual character even though an elaborate superstructure oftentimes camouflaged the fact. Such male societies, he said, were built around one or a number of "masculine heroes", all of whom represented the *typus inversus*—the "inverted type" to which reference has already been made. If the male society in question is at all complex it has a number of deputies or sub-leaders, also inverts, who are or have been favourite companions of the "hero". Essentially, however, the society begins with a particular pair-relation ; there is the leader and the first favourite (*erste Liebling*). After a while friends of one or another of the first two are admitted, and eventually the whilom favourite is brushed aside in the push toward a new lover. The rejected favourite may nevertheless remain within the circle, organizing for himself a cluster of acolytes and following the pattern initially set.[21] By a process of conjugation, fission, and addition of new cells, as it were, the cluster undergoes considerable expansion and internal differentiation, and in most cases finally splits into two or more distinct groupings.

The inverted type, according to Blüher, is drawn from among those who are sexually attracted only (or primarily) to members of the same sex. Like Freud, Blüher is not very clear as to the basis of inversion ; sometimes he speaks as though it were a biological inevitability for given persons, and at others lays heavy stress on social factors. Many of his examples are drawn from youngsters who in early adolescence were exposed to situations in which pleasurable erotic sensations came to be centred on those of the same sex.

That conditions in Germany were often of the sort mentioned in the chapter entitled " In Rimmon's House " there can be little doubt ; rigid segregation during adolescence often brought with it conditions which the ordinary American would regard as peculiar, to say the least. Instance : In the academies established for the training of officers, and into which boys sometimes entered as nine-year-olds, groups for mutual masturbation were frequently organized and bore definite club names. Further, in these same academies the older boys often persuaded or forced the younger into the relation of *Leibbursch* ; literally translated, this means " body-lad ", and the gross connotations apparently were not unwarranted. Even outside of academies and like boarding-schools, conditions of this sort were by no means infrequent ; ample evidence is available.[22]

Of course, Blüher is at pains to point out that actual physical relations are not necessarily characteristic of these homosexual bonds ; there may be only romantic fixation. Following this lead, many members of the movement, while accepting Blüher's fundamental contentions, drew a contrast between *Eros* and *Sexus*, indicating thereby sublimated eroticism on the one hand and direct genital expression on the other :

Eros and sexuality are two different things ! Eros is much vaster. Eros is the god of the unity of body and soul, . . . Eros is the stream that overflows everything, and creates a paradise in a drought. But if the stream becomes stemmed, a morass ensues, and the waters stagnate—then sexuality springs forth in the midst of a barren desert land. Eros is the ever-streaming, flowing, trickling force which moves and inspires our whole soul and body—sexuality is retained need of the body, concentrated and tormenting.

Youth and Eros belong together, there is no genuine youth without the erotic. Sexuality is Eros corrupted by our present form of economic and social life, which has nothing whatever to do with real youth, and torments the not quite senile man of brains, and the not utterly exhausted man of machines.[23]

In spite of these efforts to escape from the full impact of Blüher's dogmas, no close observer of the youth movement could avoid the conclusion that Blüher's writings not only recorded some phases of youth movement history, but also helped to make that history. I have mentioned that he hinted at his general theory as early as 1912, but although there were public charges such as " The Roamers constitute a pederasty club ",[24] discussion was largely confined to youth movement circles. Here, however, debate and action had been vigorous ; as early as 1910 the Young Roamers, fifteen hundred strong, had withdrawn from other branches of the movement and had developed an ideology strongly stressing the comradeship of males. In fact, there can be little doubt that the complete barring of girls from this new group, coupled with aggressive rejection of the tendencies toward reconciliation with and supervision by friendly elders which had begun to manifest themselves among bodies such as Roamers, Incorporated, were basically determined by the homosexual proclivities of most of the Young Roamers. This fresh batch of secessionists in many instances made no bones of their overt physical relations ; anyone reading their fugitive leaflets and brochures need not be an Anthony Comstock to glean conclusive evidence.[25] When these matters came to the general knowledge of all youth movement groups through the publications of Blüher and others, roaming situations began to be more and more sharply defined in ways which rendered homosexual " crushes " difficult to avoid. The outcome was the development of a point of view utilizing the above-noted distinction between *Eros* and *Sexus*.

The ranks of those whose inclinations toward inversion were either accentuated or called into being by groups such as the Young Roamers, or by the widely diffused erotic definitions of the roaming situation, were kept relatively few in number only by the rapidly increasing recruitment of girls. From as early as 1907 onward there had been youth movement bodies which attacked the separation of the sexes [26] as one of the many youth-distorting practices " perpetrated by a corrupt older

generation " ; they charged that the Young Roamers and their
like were still in the grip of a decadent system, that they had not
yet left Rimmon's House.

Where did Karl Fischer stand in all of this ? Everyone who
knew him testifies that at the very least he showed no outward
tendencies towards inversion.[27] Indeed, the original Roamers
seemed to have been primarily romantic rebels, not self-conscious
advocates of a new " youth culture ". They fought shy of asking
girls to participate in their expeditions, true enough, but this
seems to have been primarily because of the utter absence of
facilities that would diminish the hardships of the pioneer
ventures. In the late 'nineties and early nineteen-hundreds
there were no youth hostels, no well-travelled routes, no easily
transmissible techniques of roaming. The pattern was that of
prolonged truancy or vagrancy, accompanied by more than a
little rowdyism which Fischer himself occasionally deprecated but
did not take steps to wipe out. Costume was highly individualized, and sometimes approached the rags and tatters of the quasi-
mythical " wandering scholar " of medieval times or the nondescript, dirty garb of " the raggle-taggle Gypsies, O ! " Again,
the ascetic features of almost all youth movements after about
1907 were not apparent in the early phases. Alcoholic drinks
were freely indulged in on occasion, and smoking was not barred.[28]
Still further, there may have been a good deal of Schickserei,[29]
i.e., the casual picking up of servant girls, daughters of itinerant
artisans such as coopers and tinkers, and occasionally, when
nights were spent in haystacks or peasants' dwellings in remoter
regions, the surviving remnants of old-fashioned bundling may
have proved congenial. The peasant girls who presumably
participated were not Anneles, for naturally no particular concern
for family continuity could manifest itself under such disorganized
conditions ; the only point I am making is that in all probability
male-female " relations " were not absolutely tabooed among the
" boon companions " of early vintage.

Blüher was well aware of the obstacles such evidence represented for his theory and countered, to his own satisfaction at
least, by pointing out that medical records contain many cases
of fully inverted males who are nevertheless capable of copulation
with women and are indeed " happily married "—which is to
say, sexually adjusted with their wives. At the same time,
persons of this type often claim that they feel deep romantic
attachment only as regards other males, even though overt

Heterosexual illustration from " Pluck-Fiddle Jack ".

homosexuality is never practised. This seems to be quite true, but as Blüher himself admits, cases of this sort are by no means frequent, and it is not quite easy to see just how mere chance could bring together even so relatively small a body of homosexually oriented and yet heterosexually potent youngsters as those composing the Roamers in the first five years, let us say, of their existence.[30]

The upshot of my own analysis of the evidence, fragmentarily and inconclusively presented here, is that charismatic leadership, even in the early Roamers, cannot be satisfactorily accounted for by Blüher's methods. After all, the sergeant who led his men into the drumfire at Belleau Woods with the grim challenge, " Come on, you bastards, do you want to live for ever ? " was unquestionably a charismatic leader, and the same can be said of the great warrior chieftains who have led men to victory or to destruction in last-ditch stands throughout the whole course of history. Beyond doubt a little manipulation of the ideas of " pleasure principle " and " death-drive " will satisfactorily account for such phenomena to adherents of psychoanalytic orthodoxy, but the rest of us may remain unconvinced. Add to this the *charisma* of the visionary who sees pearly gates and golden streets in a heaven where there is neither marrying nor giving in marriage, and you have another job of straining and twisting concepts to fit. Again, the *charisma* of the Buriat shaman, with his mouth-foaming ecstasies and devil-driving gongs, is a little hard to bring under one all-enveloping tent.

Whatever the erotic manifestations of the youth movement were and are, I should still be inclined to say that the " male heroism " of Karl Fischer and his early deputies was primarily heroism, however mistaken, in the garden variety sense. His smashing, emotionally surcharged assault on Rimmon's House, in utter disregard of consequences to himself, was the reason why " he spoke as one having authority ".

NOTES

1. Hans Blüher, *Wandervogel, Geschichte einer Bewegung*, 1/2 (Jena, 1912), p. 1.

2. *Ibid.*, p. 4.

3. *Ibid.*, p. 17.

4. *Ibid.*, p. 83.

5. Manthey-Zorn, *Germany in Travail*, pp. 52, 56. I have been unable to verify this reference, and Schmid, from whose dissertation I have taken it, gives no further details.

6. As a sociological concept, charismatic leadership was first dealt with under that name by Max Weber in his *Religionssoziologie*. The most convenient summary is in his *Wirtschaft und Gesellschaft* (Tübingen, 1922), pp. 140–5, 227–363, 753–78. It should be noted, however, that *charisma* had frequently been used, albeit in a more specifically religious sense, by the church historian, Sohms, several years earlier.

7. Quintus, "Grundlagen der Freischar", *Monatsbericht der Deutschen Akademischen Freischar*, 3 (1913), p. 3, quoted in Charlotte Lütkens, *Die deutsche Jugendbewegung* (Frankfurt a. M., 1925), p. 45.

8. Heinrich Roth, *Psychologie der Jugendgruppe* (Berlin, 1939), p. 37.

9. *Ibid.*, p. 45. This is a statement by Gustav Wyneken, leader of one wing of the Free German Youth, but it might well have been uttered by Fischer. The passage in square brackets replaces the somewhat esoteric "From Tao, Laotse would say".

10. Lütkens calls attention to the North German origins of the movement. See Charlotte Lütkens, *Die deutsche Jugendbewegung* (Frankfurt a. M., 1925), pp. 36–40.

11. This credo dates from the year 1924, and was the product of a young Englishman, Rolf Gardiner, whom I came to know at Hellerau-bei-Dresden in 1923. For all practical purposes, however, it could be put in the mouth of one of Fischer's followers of 1896. See *Youth ; An International Quarterly of Young Enterprise*, 2, 13 (Summer, 1924). Published at 152 Abbey House, Victoria Street, London, S.W.1.

12. *Das Lagerfeuer*, journal of the erstwhile Deutsche Jungenschaft, Plauen. Quoted by Roth, *op. cit.*, p. 27.

13. Blüher, *op. cit.*, pp. 99–100.

14. *Ibid.*, p. 134.

15. *Ibid.*, p. 135.

16. *Ibid.*, p. 138.

17. *Loc. cit.*

18. Will Vesper, *Deutsche Jugend* (Berlin, 1934), p. 13.

19. George Thomson, *The Influence of the Youth Movement on German Education* (unpublished Ph.D. dissertation, University of Glasgow), p. 31, quoted by Robert C. Schmid, *German Youth Movements ; A Typological Study* (unpublished Ph.D. dissertation, University of Wisconsin), p. 95.

20. On this knotty methodological problem, see my article, "Interpretive Sociology and Constructive Typology", with its accompanying bibliography, in Gurvitch and Moore, eds., *Twentieth-century Sociology* (New York, 1945). As every informed reader knows, this article is only one among literally hundreds of others—some of them from my pen—on the problems of type construction. I mention my own product here simply because of relative convenience and up-to-dateness.

21. Hans Blüher, *Die Rolle der Erotik in der männlichen Gesellschaft* (Jena, 1919), pp. 111–13. It will be noted that I quote from the two-volume 1919 publication.

22. Rolf Joseph Hoffmann, *Fug und Unfug in der Jugendkultur* (Griez, 1914), provides a good collection of documents, but this is only a small sample of the hundreds appearing in scores of youth movement publications.

23. Siegfried Kawerau, "Youth and Eros" in *The New Student*, 2, Special (March 3, 1923), p. 19, special supplement printed in Germany, published by the National Student Forum, 2929 Broadway, New York, N.Y.

24. Quoted by Fritz Jungmann, "Autorität und Sexualmoral in der freien bürgerlichen Jugendbewegung", in *Autorität und Familie*, Max Hork-

heimer, ed. (Paris, 1936), p. 676. The charge was openly made in the Bavarian parliament about 1914.

25. *Ibid.*, p. 670.

26. *Ibid.*

27. *Ibid.*, p. 677.

28. *Ibid.*, p. 670.

29. *Ibid.*, pp. 682–3. At least, this is my interpretation of the passage cited, although there it is *Scheckserei*. *Schickse* is slang for "light-o'-love" and I assume that *Scheckse* is merely a variant form. There is, of course, the possibility that it derives from *scheckig*, and therefore refers to tatterdemalion costume.

30. To me it seems clear that Blüher took the clearcut evidence of homosexuality to be found from at least the time of Copalle's secession onward and generalized upon it in unwarrantedly sweeping fashion. He was notably aided in this endeavour by the vagueness of the Freudian assumptions with which he was operating. For Freud the libido of which sexual conduct in the narrower sense is only one manifestation becomes virtually equivalent to "life force". The organism is dealt with almost as though it were a network of pipes, all directly interconnected and all under the same hydraulic pressure. If an opening is made at the upper levels of this system, energy spurts forth and temporarily diminishes the pressure at the lower levels— and *vice versa*. Where upper-level drainage is concerned, you have sublimation ; where lower-level, ejaculation and its counterparts. This is not the place to indulge in extended criticism of these superficially persuasive postulates, but it should be said that the notion of undifferentiated and indefinitely transferable " psychic energy " or " libido " has been unqualifiedly rejected by many contemporary investigators. (I cite, as one of many, W. S. Taylor, *A Critique of Sublimation in Males ; A Study of Forty Superior Single Men*, Genetic Psychology Monographs, Worcester, Mass., 1933.) When and if sublimation occurs, it cannot be satisfactorily explained by leafing through a plumber's handbook.

Apart from these considerations, it should also be remembered that " when something's everything, then nothing's anything ". Couched more technically : A principle which is so elastic in its application that it can be used in the supposed explanation of every aspect of life, human or otherwise, is virtually useless except for the gratification it gives to the dilettante philosopher. Instead of libido, you could just as well talk about cosmic force, Tao, or divine purpose.

Over and above this, I am inclined to suspect that a strong note of self-justification runs all through Blüher's work. He is at pains to point out that he is not himself an invert but simply a " faun "—that is, someone for whom sexual play constitutes the supreme value. He goes on to make it quite clear that he was not " exposing " the inversion of the Roamers, which is to say that he was not revealing its presence because he disapproved of it. On the contrary, he regarded the process of man-loving-man as quite as " natural " as any other—in fact, as one which in terms of creativity and intellectual and spiritual profundity far outstripped the male-female relationship. As he puts it :

It is not too hazardous to assume that the sexual tendencies of mankind have undergone periodic change. . . . The Greeks would have viewed with disdain the practice of regarding male-female " gallantry " as a worthy form of " good society " ; the fact that such gallantry is at present the only approved type certainly does not constitute anything of which our age can be proud. (Blüher, *op. cit.*, pp. 142–3.)

The ambiguities of Blüher's conception of the causes of inversion, however, lead him to plead, in the fashion of Radclyffe Hall, that homosexuality should be tolerated because of its biological inevitability :

"Healing" can affect only the neurotic character . . . [resulting from suppression of inverted tendencies] ; the sexual basis cannot be altered. (*Ibid.*, p. 135.)

As noted above this is quite in line with the popular belief that homosexuality always has its roots in some anomaly of constitutional makeup, and therefore should be dealt with as one would deal with Mongolian idiocy or a hunched back ; namely, by accepting the difficulty as essentially unalterable and devising ways and means to render the patient comfortable while life endures. Elsewhere, however—and in this instance in the succeeding sentence—Blüher makes the grudging concession that homosexuality *may* result from situational distortions in early life :

Even if it were possible to "heal" someone of his inversion by tracing it back into childhood experience, would it not also be possible to "heal" someone who focuses his affections on women and unite him with someone of his own sex? (*Ibid.*)

Part and parcel of this statement is the suppressed premise that "normality" in any period is a purely arbitrary decision of the given society. Here again there is no opportunity to deal with this widespread assumption, currently accepted in orthodox psychoanalytic circles, but in my judgment thoroughly fallacious. I can only say that it follows logically from the postulates of the orthodox Freudian system, but that if these postulates are called into question the conclusions built on them topple.

Please note that I have taken issue only with psychoanalytic *orthodoxy*. Where Horney, Fromm, and many other Neo-Freudians are concerned, I have no such sceptical remarks to make. I might differ in minor points, but that is quite another matter. To avoid misunderstanding, I should like to add that I regard Freud as a very great psychologist indeed—perhaps, to quote McDougall, as "the greatest since Aristotle". But is he infallible?

The literature on psychoanalytic orthodoxy and heterodoxy is notoriously vast, and the seemingly cavalier dismissal of moot questions in the present text and footnotes will seem presumptuous to many readers. Hence I give a minimum list of titles bearing on the relevant issues as earnest of the fact that the remarks I have made constitute my *carefully* considered judgment :

Read Bain, " Sociology and Psychoanalysis ", *American Sociological Review*, vol. 1, no. 2 (April, 1936), pp. 203–16.

Harry Elmer Barnes and Howard Becker, *Social Thought from Lore to Science*, vol. 2 (Boston : Heath, 1938), pp. 930–1.

Howard Becker, " Some Forms of Sympathy : a Phenomenological Analysis ", *Journal of Abnormal and Social Psychology*, vol. 26, no. 1 (April–June, 1931).

Howard Becker and D. K. Bruner, " Some Aspects of Taboo and Totemism ", *Journal of Social Psychology*, vol. 3, no. 3 (August, 1932), pp. 337–52.

Healy, Bronner, and Bower, *The Structure and Meaning of Psychoanalysis* (New York : Harper's, 1930).

Karen Horney, *New Ways in Psychoanalysis* (New York : Norton, 1939).

Franz Alexander, " Psychoanalysis Revised ", *Psychoanalytic Quarterly*, vol. 9 (1940), pp. 1–36.

Abram Kardiner, *The Individual and His Society* (New York : Columbia University Press, 1939).

Bronislaw Malinowski, *Sex and Repression in Savage Society* (London : 1924).

CHAPTER V

DECISION : "COME YE OUT FROM AMONG THEM AND BE YE SEPARATE"

> Name me no names for my disease,
>   With uninforming breath ;
> I tell you I am none of these,
>   But homesick unto death—
>
> Homesick for hills that I had known,
>   For brooks that I had crossed,
> Before I met this flesh and bone
>   And followed and was lost . . .
>   —BYNNER, " Hills of Home ".

Desperate diseases, desperate remedies : German youth of Karl Fischer's day loathed and hated the world of their elders, and were ready to follow any Pied Piper whose mystery and power held promise of a new realm where longings found fruition. Definite promises, clearcut goals, purposeful methods were unnecessary—indeed, no small part of the revulsion against adult life was against its very planfulness, its readiness to cast aside the joys of spontaneity in favour of crafty money-getting and the ribbon to stick in the coat. Hence it was that the boon companions and their aimless roaming exercised so tremendous a pull ; they took no thought for the morrow, and in their company the feeling—mark that, the feeling !—of being as free as the birds of the air imposed itself with compelling force on all cold-blooded schemes and calculations about " getting ahead ". Many a lad murmured, in effect, with Cyrano :

> . . . To sing, to laugh, to dream,
> To walk in my own way and be alone,
> Free, with an eye to see things as they are,
>
> . . . To travel any road
> Under the sun, under the stars, nor doubt
> If fame or fortune lie beyond the bourne . . .

Essentially, then, the *charisma* of Karl Fischer and others of his stamp acted like a spark setting off hundreds of powder trains, each one producing its own individual flareup. The Roamers came together on a basis of congeniality, no doubt of that, but the congeniality was in turn a product of the common recognition that your fellows were experiencing a sense of release

73

A knight-errant, from " Pluck-Fiddle Jack ".

and fulfilment akin to your own. The sense of belonging to a band of dissenters, to a conventicle of the elect, had a peculiar thrill for you ; nevertheless, the discovery of what you thought to be your innermost self, hitherto overlaid and almost smothered by grown-up disguises and concealments, called forth emotions to which all others took second rank.[1] " Become what you are " and " We do not want to be but to become ", sometimes spoken but more often simply felt, governed the youngsters who flocked to—what ?

To their leader and his breakaways, to the visible embodiment of rebellion against flabby school routine, insincere church attendance, flatulent concerts, boring parties designed for display and climbing, nauseous student jollifications laden with the sluggish ceremonial and spurious heartiness of the paternal *Stammtisch*, well-meant but repellent counsel about ways of getting on in the world—to escapes making you feel that adventure was still possible. . . . Then, trudging along with the beloved leader, came the new way of life : wandering at will through fields, forests, and hills, pitching camp in a ruined castle or under the lindens fringing a little cluster of peasant houses where the shams of the city were absent, returning in imagination to the cordial fellowship of roving scholars and journeymen—roaming !

> For to admire an' for to see,
> For to be'old this world so wide ;
> It never done no good to me,
> But I couldn't stop it if I tried.

Very soon—by 1900, in fact—all over eastern Brandenburg and northern Germany you could journey with Roamers like yourself : browned, travel-stained fellows in nondescript garb, here and there bedecked with fluttering red, green, and gold ribbons, on their backs a few simple belongings in knapsacks, and on the shoulders of at least a few, lutes and guitars which they merrily twanged on the *Wanderung* or around the campfire.[2] Aimless, goalless, certainly ; moved by feeling rather than thought, yes—but symbols of a great rebellion and a great awakening.

At first the heroes of the movement were likened by their followers, and occasionally by themselves, to wandering scholars of medieval times, robber knights who scattered their spoils among their henchmen and the poor, peasant Robin Hoods of *Schinderhannes* type, defiant gypsies, and savage chieftains like Uncas or Chaka. Such models, be it noted, were one and all

The faraway expeditions of the Roamers idealized.

exponents of a hard, primitive life, Ishmaels who pitched their black tents in the wilderness, every man's hand against them and their hand against every man's. Around the campfire the stories that were told were filled with the mood of romantic rebellion ; the ambivalence of Hölderlin, Kleist, Lenau, Byron, and even Cooper and the sadly juvenile Karl May found ready mouthpieces and interpreters.

Vague notions of solidarity with the folk, the intrinsically German folk, were also present, but the tinge of ambivalence remained ; the Roamers loved the peasant because he stood in direct contrast to the realm of boom and boast from which they had escaped. Now and again their expeditions took them beyond the boundaries of the Wilhelmian domain, and in the midst of Czechs, Poles, Romanians, and other lesser breeds without the law they found clusters of their compatriots who had preserved the manners of the Biedermeier time and earlier in the midst of a hostile world. Here was a living demonstration of what German virtues had once been, of The Dear Dead Days, and they felt themselves the champion of these half-forgotten Konrads and Anneles. Still and all, the Roamers did not remain among them nor take up political battle on their behalf ; the sense of kinship with the Germans of the land beyond the forest or the mountains simply intensified their own dissent and provided stimulation and example for even sharper separation from " modernity " and " progress ".

At bottom, therefore, the Roamers were initially individualists. Only with the passage of time did there arise the expectation that their cherished selves would expand and deepen in and through the surging emotions called forth by banding together with the likeminded and by undergoing the experiences of the " expedition " and the " nest ".

The expedition or *Grossfahrt* was the climax of shorter, less arduous ventures covering only a weekday evening or weekend. These more casual roamings might simply take the form of leaving the city with a few fellow rebels in the late afternoon—perhaps like this :

Arriving at a clearing in the woods at dusk or soon after dark, there the younger lads find a huge council fire leaping towards the sky—for the leader and his closer cronies have already arrived. A few bits of meat, a chunky sausage, potatoes and turnips filched from the larders of grimly disapproving but baffled parents are tumbled into the sooty kettle that has been dragged along by

The Council Fire.

some especially faithful follower, and with the simmering and bubbling *obbligato* that soon begins, someone strikes up a song. Lutes start to strum softly as the circle forms around the fire, and as the murmur of conversation subsides the music soars upward with the smoke into the trees overhead. As the last verse dies away and the hum of the plucked strings quiets, someone turns out the contents of the pot into the casually collected tins, and *Suff* and *Frasz* commences. The simple meal over, perhaps someone tells a story—in the early days frequently a tale of adventure with the Indians in America or some other romantic yarn of the remote and faraway. Other songs then come rolling out, usually in unison or with the group at least eagerly joining in the refrain and bursting into laughter or applause at appropriate points.

Before long the leader breaks into the merrymaking, outlining plans for a future meeting and telling everyone what his part in the preparations is to be. Towards eleven or thereabouts one of the more authoritative members carefully and ostentatiously consults the bulky timepiece he has " borrowed " from father or older brother, and presently the boys begin to stretch, brush off their clothes, and cover the dying embers of the fire with earth.

Then they start back to town ; if a youngster is fortunate the leader walks beside him for a while, and the spoken or unspoken assurance that the lad " belongs " gives him courage to face elders who can never " understand " what it is that draws him to and holds him within the fellowship. Whispered advice on how best to face parental wrath, hurried handshakes, exchange of " Heils ", thrilling assurance of " We'll meet again ", and then the humdrum of Rimmon's House closes down on what has become an ineradicable, cherished memory for the boy and his comrades.

If the members succeeded in standing firm, the next step in preparation for the expedition might be a weekend affair in direct opposition to the demands of homework, church, and the afternoon promenade with the family. Here is a typical Sunday excursion in the early days of the Roamers :

At the unearthly hour of six in the morning, when only servant girls and other menials are stirring about, a few bright-eyed boys clad in garments roughly adapted to outdoor needs, wearing heavy shoes and fantastic hats, begin to gather on the platform of the railroad station at Steglitz or some other centre of rebellion. For a few pennies they are admitted to a third- or fourth-class carriage, and the train takes them ten miles or more away from the town into a part of the countryside as " wild " as the sedately tilled surrounding region can provide.

Soon they are leaving the train at an isolated way-station and doing their best to lose themselves in whatever fields and woods they can find. All morning long they tramp and tussle in a realm which in fancy is far removed from " civilization ", swim naked in anything that remotely resembles an " unspoiled " stream or lake, and carry out assaults, ambushes, and last-ditch defences. Towards noon they begin to be tired and hungry, and the whole body, perhaps not much more than a half-dozen in all, ranges about a wood fire or a portable stove on which the inescapable kettle is soon stewing away. They are all keenly aware of their unconventionality, not merely in roughing it but also in cooking their own meal—for the respectable citizen goes to an inn where the despised menial work of preparing and serving food can be bought and paid for in full decency and propriety. The boys scorn napkins and the rest of the bourgeois trappings ; greasy mouths and soot-stained faces are badges of honour.

After the gorge, the ever-present " pluck-fiddle " and the pipingly boyish and uncertainly adolescent voices resound, a few pathetically romantic pictures are sketched, or there is simply the relaxation of catnapping, gazing at the sky, the clouds, the trees, and desultory chattering about the meaning of life and the stupidities of adults. As the sun falls lower, back they go to the railroad, and in the evening they tumble out on the streets of the city and clump toward the houses which they reluctantly call home.

As they pass the cafés where the good citizens sit dressed in their Sunday best, surrounded by their tame offspring and nodding and smiling at friends and acquaintances, there are ominous shakings of heads and mutterings about vagrancy, coarseness, and insubordination. Elated rather than dismayed by this evidence of rupture with the proprieties, the Roamers go back to gaol in eager anticipation of another demonstrative out-break just as soon as possible.[3]

Clear it is that this hard primitivism was highly valued, and that it took the form of a return to nature. Equally obvious : Roughing it in natural surroundings was not assigned the values which an ordinary tourist would cherish ; instead, there was

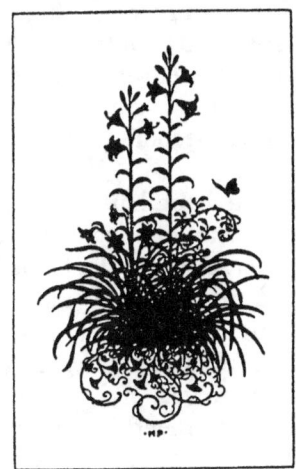

Nature treated non-naturalistically in " Pluck-Fiddle Jack ".

an effort to achieve a totally new relationship with " first things " :

> It is wholly false and superficial to suppose that we learned to revere Nature on our journeys. Our awakening eyes did not gaze on Nature but upon our own innermost selves. For what was this Nature with its meaningless disorder of sun and rain, heat and frost, fruit and hailstorm ? What did we not often endure from its sense-lessness ? What was aroused was the stubborn resolve to assert ourselves and to pierce through all of this disarray in the pursuit of the meaning of our own lives. . . . We imposed upon Nature the significance which we attributed to ourselves.[4]

Hence the Roamers did not indulge in " Ohs ! " and " Ahs ! " about blue skies and sunsets ; there was little passive observation. Instead they found a peculiar beauty and thrill in slogging through a rain-drenched countryside, laughing at torn and sodden clothing until they arrived at a shelter where they could slump and dry out before a roaring fire. Promethean defiance of nature because of success in becoming one with it was the essence of such elated experience.

Hardened and knit together by these smaller sorties and forays, bands of Roamers began to feel themselves ready for the great unifying enterprise, the expedition. All that had gone before was mere tuning up for the thundering symphony of experiences on the long trips which took the Roamers hundreds of miles afield into the mountains of Bavaria and Bohemia, the plains of Hungary, or even the forests of Finland. Such an expedition was not only an event of tremendous importance in the lives of the individual members of the group, but it also amalgamated those who triumphantly carried it out into a fusion or *Bund* that added a new dimension to their personalities :

> For the pure joy of it we clambered up and down snowy peaks and pressed onward into the beckoning distance for eight long hours. Everywhere above us lay the snow and below, by the lake, the trees were already in bloom. But we found no shelter, so we had to backtrack. At night over almost impassable, snow-covered trails ! Our leader hesitated. We, however, were in such high spirits and so eager to face the task that he was kindled by our enthusiasm. Then came the catastrophe : we went astray and could hardly flounder onward through the three-foot snow. And worst of all, a heavy winter rainstorm broke loose upon us. Our leader spoke not a single word. Slowly we worked our way forward in what we thought was the right direction, the stronger helping the weak. Every one of us would gladly have shouldered a heavier burden if only we could make things easier for the others. Then began to

come into being something that we had long felt but had never translated into living experience : we were an inseparably united fellowship. When at long last we found the right path into the valley there was aroused a feeling of intense joy which grew out of the dangers we had triumphantly endured, yes, but still more because we had stood a test proving that we were finally bound by friendly and comradely ties.[5]

The sense of fusion, the *Bunderlebnis*, was therefore the cherished outcome of the expedition, not the appreciation of nature as such. The earliest roots of the Roamers lie here ; a great month-long trip to the mountains of Bohemia in 1898 climaxed and consolidated the feeling of solidarity in revolt.[6] Thereafter one of the chief means of recruiting new members was the recounting in glowing terms of the hardships and triumphs of this or that expedition. The importance which these long treks had in the Roamers' way of life is attested by the careful avoidance of apparent synonyms such as " tour ", " journey ", " travel ", or "sightseeing ". " Expedition " came to be loaded with emotions for which nothing else offered even remote parallels.

Moreover, thorough identification with the group, as demonstrated by successful assimilation of the unique experience of the expedition, rapidly came to be the way in which the initially random conventicles of dissenters were fused into genuine sects of the likeminded and consciously elect. In a very real sense Roamers who were united by the ties of the expedition meet the requirements which the student of the religious structures of Western Christendom sets up for his sect definition :

. . . It is a relatively small plurality pattern that has abandoned the attempt to win the whole world over to its . . . [way of life] ; the phrase " Come ye out from among them and be ye separate " is followed literally. It is readily seen that the sect is a . . . body which one must *join* in order to become a member ; [it is elective]. At bottom, the sect is [exclusive in character], appeals to strictly personal trends, and . . . frequently requires some definite type of . . . experience as a prerequisite of acceptance. It therefore attaches primary importance to the religious experience [broadly interpreted] of its members prior to their [finally accomplished] fellowship . . . It frequently rejects an official clergy, preferring to trust for guidance to lay inspiration rather than to . . . [trained] expertness.

In many instances sects are persecuted, but this persecution only reinforces the separatist and semi-ascetic attitude toward the world inherent in the sect as a social structure. At times it . . . seeks to sever as much as possible the bonds which tie it to the common life of the larger . . . [society] within which it develops. In general, the sect prefers isolation to compromise.[7]

Fired by the *charisma* of overwhelmingly impressive leaders, the Roamers began with definite secession from the adult world ; they were " come-outers " from the start. Even with charismatic leadership and secession, however, the resulting social clusters were only loose-textured cults or at best conventicles.

Formless bodies such as these wax and wane with every flicker of their guiding lights, every shift in social season, primarily because almost anybody who feels tension and is attracted by the leader can push into the huddle. Very soon the situation becomes intolerable for those of more intense persuasion, and they begin to look for the outward signs of inward grace among their fellows—and these signs are not always evident.

The result is that the cult goes to pieces, sometimes to re-establish itself about a new leader whose charismatic powers include the ability to choose the utterly loyal from the mere hangers-on, or more frequently about the same leader when once he has been brought to see that he can have no consistently devoted following if he does not pick and choose on the basis of definite standards, unspoken though these often are.

For those fellowships of Roamers which survived, the standard came to be the continuing demonstration of the sense of fusion acquired in and through the supreme test of the expedition. Thus the Roamers became exclusive ; to be charismatic, secessionist, and voluntary was not enough. Not only was roaming on the expedition a new way of life ; there also arose structures which, although unstable in the long run, were sufficiently coherent for the time to mark them off sharply from the little cults with which the movement began. " The indefinable something " which set off the real from the spurious " kindred spirits " had become vaguely recognizable ; the hangers-on were excluded. Initially, the sense of fusion and its outer manifestations were in all probability but slightly tinged with the erotic (unless every feeling of solidarity can be so interpreted) ; revulsion, defiance, and self-imposed isolation as part of a presumably eternal alliance of the likeminded and congenial were at least equally important.

Another key to the sectarian character of the Roamers who had become aware of the significance of the expedition was their stress on their own peculiar hymns—or if " hymn " draws the supernatural parallel too closely, on their exclusive kind of musical expression.

At the start the music of the Roamers followed what we may

Fine Rhine Wine, from " Pluck-Fiddle Jack ".

call negative patterns ; they simply tried to avoid everything
characteristic of the Wilhelmian period.   The jingo patriotism
of the era was echoed and reinforced by truculent, bibulous, and
mawkish noise.   The banality and superficiality of the age, as
seen by the Roamers, was dramatically illustrated in what they
called the brassy, shallow, trashily sensational concert of the
popular patriotic and sentimental music of the day.

With the best will in the world, however, it is impossible for
any group, no matter how passionately sectarian, to cut itself
off entirely from surrounding methods of expressing emotion.
When the movement was just breaking out of the shell, as it were,
its cheepings and twitterings were much like the crowings and
cluckings it so earnestly condemned.   The boon companions also
chorused marching songs and ditties of Fatherland, Freedom, and
Fine Rhine Wine, differing from the beer-garden variety only in
that they harked back to earlier days.   Especially cherished were
songs of the *Burschenschaften* and the Golden Age of the dashing
knight-errant when patriotism was a hearty, parochial love of
the native land rather than a reedy hurrah for a tinsel-bedecked,
brand-new national state.

In one of the old Roamers' magazines there is a tale of noise
resounding mightily from the mouth of a mountain cave ; an
old song of 1848 was being bellowed forth for the sheer joy of
vicarious ferocity :

> Blood must flow !
> Blood must flow !
> Smear the guillotine
> With tyrants' fat !

A couple of peasants passing by the lonely spot took fright at the
gruesome outcries thundering forth from the crevice, and fled
helter-skelter down the mountain to the village with their dogs
howling and yelping in the van.   The Roamers roared with
laughter, for they felt no identity with the actual political sentiments expressed ; they were frothing for the fun of it.   Other
songs were used for more or less practical purposes : the foot-
slogging of long expeditions was enlivened by the chanting of
nonsense verses or brisk, indefinitely repeatable military jingles
putting rhythm in flagging feet and reviving jaded spirits.

Little creativity in this ! [8]   There was merely a difference in
attitude between the songs of *Turnvereine* and university fraternities
and those of Roamers who gathered at rural inns to chorus :

The rich fellow sips
Golden goblets of wine,
But more sweet to our lips
Is a rough, foaming stein.
Juvivallerallerallera !
O, the rough, foaming stein.

Sound musical talent there nevertheless was in the ranks of these boon companions and their followers, talent which a few years later led to drastic shifts in young Germany's musical folkways. First there came Max Pohl, a gifted teacher in the Steglitz school who shared the rebellious sentiments of the youngsters entrusted to his care. Close on his heels trod his student, Hans Breuer, one of the original Roamers, close friend and eventually critic of Karl Fischer. It was Breuer who was chiefly responsible for injecting the constructive and creative attitude toward music which so strongly characterized later generations of Roamers. In 1909 his efforts culminated in the first edition of *Pluck-Fiddle Jack*.[9]

" The Pluck ", as the song collection was affectionately called, was simply the visible, belated appearance of an array of songs which the Roamers had long regarded as virtually sacred to their sect. In their careless wandering through the fields and forests, and in their grubbing through tales of bygone romance and adventure, the Roamers had rediscovered a vast hoard of folk music which had not been worn to tatters in school or on platform. After the first shock of their earlier horrifying chants had worn off, and as these chants themselves fell into the discard, the Roamers began to gain the confidence and interest of the peasants and artisans whose company they so frequently sought. By singing the half-forgotten melodies of the days before the building of Rimmon's House, they broke down the suspicion that such queerly attired city youth so readily aroused among simple-minded folk. Soon the country dwellers shyly joined in with songs of Grandfather Friedl's day ; the final outcome was that many of the folksongs in The Pluck were the fruit of long evenings spent at the fireside in peasant cottages where Roamers had gently questioned aged Jockels and Bärbeles until they haltingly recalled the verses of their childhood.

To be sure, there was careful winnowing and sifting ; only those songs were finally printed which long testing " in the field " had shown to be sturdy, to stand up against endless repetition without becoming monotonous. The final arrangement shows the amazing scope of the Roamers' hymnal : Leave-taking songs ;

Title page of 1914 edition (the 22nd) of " Pluck-Fiddle Jack ".

Lieder of love and longing ; ballads of work and hardship triumphantly endured ; " spiritual " canticles ; pastorals of
morning, evening, spring, and summer ; songs for the joyous
ceremonials of life's milestones ; lays for country wayfaring,
sailors' chanties, and ditties for enlivening journeys by creaking
wagon or cart ; spinning-room melodies ; martial tunes of
Landsknecht times ; verses for country dances ; nonsense doggerel ;
rounds ; and tuneful dialect take-offs. Truly a cross-section of
the dear dead days !

In spite of such range and variety, it can still be said that the
sectarian quality of the music eventually bound into The Pluck
is unmistakable. Until the 'twenties of the present century,
when young people's organizations of all sorts and descriptions
took over the repertory of the Roamers, their songs remained
distinctive not only because of their form but also by reason of
the hotly secessionist and isolationist mood in which they were
sung. The Roamers were keenly aware of their rejection of
everything standardized and approved by the older generation ;
it was the very divergence of The Pluck from everything ordinarily
associated with German popular music that gave it the pull
towards exclusiveness, cohesiveness, and self-sufficing oddity
which it unquestionably exercised. " Your ways are not their
ways " was the insistent message of Pluck-Fiddle Jack.

The sectarian exclusiveness of the Roamers was still more
deeply underscored by the camps which were so frequently
intertwined with expeditions. After a long trip requiring at least
a fortnight of tramping, the sect would settle down in one spot
for a similar length of time. Indeed, it often happened that the
journey to the camp would be by rail direct, particularly if the
sense of fusion had already been engendered on a previous wayfaring expedition.

It was in these camps that the only specific goal of the early
movement was shadowed forth ; there was sometimes a vague
declaration that a patriotic purpose underlay the apparently self-
justifying sojourn. If patriotism is defined as deep-rooted
emotional attachment to native tongue, custom, and past, it is
fair to say that the Roamers were themselves dimly aware of
these controlling sentiments. They tried to engender or intensify
them in the various regions within Germany where they pitched
camp or, more frequently, among the Germanic minorities they
encountered when their expeditions led them to halts beyond the
confines of the Wilhelmian realm proper.[10] Bohemia, Poland,

Russia, Scandinavia, and similar outlying stretches were thus infiltrated with the Germanism of the Roamers, and the practice thus established, although innocent of deeplaid schemes for nationalistic expansion at first, was later to have fateful consequences.

In such camps, moreover, thoughtful leaders sometimes poured the energies of restless followers into outdoor labour : the clearing of a road through a patch of forest, draining marshland for cultivation, building a youth shelter in the woods—these and many other tasks were freely undertaken with no thought of monetary reward. Thus sprouted the first ideas of labour-service camps which the Nazis have so shrewdly utilized in their comprehensive compulsory programme. Add : The camps of the Roamers were often located in the borderlands, so that they functioned not only as a labour service but also as an encouraging sign of youthful preoccupation with the problems of Germanic minorities lying outside the fold of the One Blessed Country.

And yet it is hard to be positive about the extent to which these potentially Master Race objectives were consciously pursued. The streak of irresponsible romanticism evident in all of the enterprises of the early Roamers would have worked against careful plots for imperial expansion. Further, even if Wilhelmian officials had tried to capitalize on the expeditions and camps beyond the frontiers, it is highly unlikely that the sectarian temper of the Roamers would have made them trustworthy tools. Again, their rebellion against adult planfulness makes it seem plausible that the actual meaning of the expedition or the camp lay in the sense of fusion and self-expansion ; only when " alliance youth " arose in the 'twenties, with their explicit solidarity with nationalistic aspirations, their uniforms, and their programmes, did love of one's own folk become indissolubly joined with hatred of other peoples. But here we anticipate " The Tumult of the 'Twenties " . . .

Not everyone can roam freely, nor is every time or season suitable. Further, the sense of fusion thrives on the ever-repeated stirring up of memories ; paraphrasing, " He loved me for the hardships we had passed, and I loved him that he did speak of them ". The reliving of the excursions, the expeditions, the campings, and the other soul-satisfying occasions could not wait on time and place ; there had to be " sites " where the Roamers could renew their bonds whenever the spirit moved them.

Hence there came into being the " nest ", i.e., the home headquarters of each band. Its treasured features were outlined primarily by the nature of the community and the ingenuity of its frequenters. In small towns the youngsters commonly sought out an abandoned room in one of the old watchtowers above the crumbling feudal walls. There, in the romantic ruins representing the very age to which, in imagination, so many of the Roamers were returning—the era of wandering scholars, trudging journeymen, roving knights, and distressed damosels—these lads of ten to twenty would gather in deliciously furtive fashion.

Admitted with appropriate caution, through a maze of secret passwords, symbolic gestures, and fantastically exalted ritual, they revived the thrills of the great expedition on which their eternal brotherhood had been cemented and rehearsed the glorious details of the long roaming or camping projected for the holidays to come. There the initiation mumbo-jumbo for the various ranks of the sect were carried out and occasionally, if Blüher can be believed, juvenile orgies were consummated.

But regardless of the extent to which Blüher's diagnosis holds —and there is clear evidence that it holds in occasional instances —one of the major gratifications was the possession of a *place* to which the youthful rebel could flee for refuge from oldsters whom he felt to be for ever nagging and yammering at his heels. In the nest he could always find a comrade in whom to confide and a leader to idolize and take for a heroic model, and in addition it was a place where he was not only permitted to have a point of view but also where that point of view was the only one that need be considered as relevant, truthful, or important. Roth throws in this *plus* :

> The nest was the scene of much musing over past experiences, forming of new plans, discussion of youth newspapers, books, and the like. It made possible meditation on the boy's own life and his own vital manifestations. In other words, here grew the inner culture of the group. . . . The nest was not a mere utility or loafing place, but the stamping grounds for the group, a place where the members could feel at ease—which is to say that the outward setting harmonized with the inner experience.[11]

After the first bursts of demonstrative ultra-primitivism or even rowdyism had passed—and that was as early as 1903—the Roamers often decorated their nests with their own handmade furniture, carvings, paintings, and leatherwork ; aesthetic gratifications were sought and found.

Large metropolitan centres naturally did not provide the charms of ruins and hidden passageways. There the Roamers had to be content with much less romantic surroundings : an abandoned loft, a basement room, or even a corner of some paternal attic was commandeered, crudely ornamented, and fitted with a few rough tables, chairs, and couches.

By 1905 other sites for fusion-furthering occasions were devised : to the nest was added the lodge or, literally, the country home. Such a lodge or rural headquarters was generally located near enough to the city so that it could be reached in one day's resolute walk, and ordinarily consisted of nothing more than a seldom-used or abandoned peasant shelter or outbuilding, watched over during the week by the owner from whom it was rented. Very soon, however, bands of Roamers conceived the idea of using their camping time for the building of their own lodges, often pooling labour power with other sects in the vicinity in the expectation of turn and turn about.[12]

By the time the soft primitivists began to split away in significant numbers—namely, by 1907—the demand for overnight accommodations on long trips became more acute. Only the resolute boon companion continued to find joy in random haystack shelter or scraped-up pine-needle mattress ; comfort could no longer be overlooked. This was finally secured by more careful spotting of the lodges so that they could be linked up in small chains throughout certain districts. In this way a band of Roamers could begin a trip by starting from its own lodge and then passing on to a lodge sponsored by some other group, from whence it could make another day's journey to still another resting place. These tiny networks of overnight hostels, first effectively organized by Rudolf Schirrmann, were harbingers of the great national system of youth halting places emerging in the period of the Weimar Republic and since carried out to the tenth decimal place by the Nazis.

Later developments, however, must not cause us to lose sight of the essentially particularistic spirit of the early Roamers. By 1905 over seventy-eight distinguishable clusters had appeared, all similar in many respects. But in spite of similarity each little group—and some were as small as the familiar one-hand tally—clung to its own nest, its own lodge, and its own supposedly peculiar sense of fusion. The time was yet to come when the sects would be welded together, momentarily but with terrific intensity, in a climactic revival and its accompanying proclama-

"As roaming we did go."

tion of a "mission". In short, the Pentecostal day of Hohe Meissner lay in the hazy future of 1913.

Before the coming of that great event the numerous sects had already begun to fall into readily discernible larger aggregates. To be sure, each sect cherished its own presumably unique traits and kept others at a distance except when mutual aid simply had to be practised, but there were distances and distances. No matter how many leaders claimed parts of Karl Fischer's empire, for example, various groups of the hard primitivists were less antagonistic to one another than they were to Copalle's "softies". The latter in turn felt less opposition to the stern-jawed males who insisted on the exclusion of girls than they did to those tender opponents of the more obstreperous boon companions who in 1907, under the leadership of Hans Breuer, began to admit girls to their charmed circle. Still further, the homosexually oriented Young Roamers who in 1910 pulled away from the Original Roamers in a body fifteen hundred strong felt less animosity towards the soft primitivists, even though the latter let themselves in for unworthy association with the despised girls, than they did for that rough-and-tough remnant of Karl Fischer's following whose most amicable gesture in the direction of the boy-lovers was a well-placed kick.

More briefly stated : The sects survived as sects, but certain features held in common by one detachment or another make possible a rough classification. There was in 1910 a dwindling minority of aggressively rebellious Roamers of pristine stamp ; a smaller but slowly growing minority of homosexual lads subdivided into primitivists of both types, with the soft variety slightly predominating ; and a three-quarters majority as yet counting only about one girl to three boys, but with the proportions rapidly approaching a balance and with soft and hard primitivism combining into a standard, moderate form. The total membership of all these schismatic bodies was in the vicinity of fifty or sixty thousand, at the lowest estimate, shortly before World War I. The seeds sown by Karl Fischer had fallen on fertile ground.

Observing these luxuriant growths, there is some danger of exaggerating their numerical significance. High time it is that we turn our attention toward the youth *tutelage* organizations with which the youth *movement* in a strict sense stood in marked contrast. Not only must this be done for the sake of preserving a balanced presentation, but also because the opposition between youth tutelage and youth movement throws the sectarian character of the latter into bold relief.

Youth tutelage organizations were those devised by adults for the furtherance of adult interests and goals. The peculiar rebelliousness, spontaneity, and aimlessness of German youth as hitherto described were of secondary importance, if indeed they were considered at all. The youth tutelage organizations therefore became either passive recipients of adult financial support and programmes, objects of well-meaning counsel and control, or helpless tools of political or religious groups which paid little or no heed to *charisma*, sense of fusion, autonomy, and the other emotional freightage of the youth movement.

Indeed, there seemed little necessity of doing so, for shortly before World War I the various youth tutelage organizations counted over two million memberships. Even if their figures are cut almost in half to allow for duplicate enrolments, it must nevertheless be said that for every adherent of the youth movement sects there were at least twenty-five recipients of youth tutelage.[13] This is not to say that the sects were insignificant, for a single Roamer made far more stir among those with whom he came in contact than could a dozen members of a stolid physical culture society or the German equivalent of Christian Endeavour, Epworth League, and the like.

The chief effect of this overwhelming disproportion was to emphasize the sectarian character of the youth movement and to spur its devotees towards ever greater activity. Many of them felt that the creation of a youth culture for the sake of youth was all that need concern them ; if the passive surrounding lump was thereby leavened, well and good—if not, a handful of the elect could still work out its own peculiar destiny.

It would be too much to say that these conclusions were sharply formulated ; virtually every observer of the sects comments on what may be called the absence of creed, doctrine, or positively stated ideology. This is what has been hinted at in previous pages by the use of terms such as " aimlessness ", " goallessness ", " haziness of programme ". Strictly speaking, every social movement must of course have a goal of some kind, but it may proceed a long way before this goal is clearly defined in words or other symbols. " Goallessness " in the *relative* sense of inability or unwillingness to specify the objective was so marked a trait of the Roamers and the branches sprouting from them that it

Typical Roamer drawing : exalted, vaguely symbolic, romantic, goalless.

would be hard to find a " purer " type of irrational social action in any society.

This was a necessary accompaniment of their general secessionist character. Escape from Rimmon's House was so ardently desired that positive and precise commitments would have been felt as hindrances. When they were accused of vague emotionalism, nostalgia for The Linden Tree, sentimental revival of bygone days, and failure to confront the realities of their times, they were sometimes forced to reply in words, but significantly enough, such replies were negative in tone :

Our strength is precisely our lack of programme . . .[14]
Where lively people are together no one needs a programme. Our happiest hours were those in which there was nothing planned beforehand, argued out, and finally fixed. Instead, words and songs quelled out of the living present and out of the deep bonds which wove every participant into an internalized unity. There is nothing more wonderful and fruitful than communion in a small circle of confidants where no plan and no " order of the day " hems in spontaneous vitality and the spirit that, " blowing where it listeth ", unites and enthrals us. Every day is begun with eagerness and hope and every hour brings forth our wondering gratitude for rich, overflowing experience. Poor in soul are those persons who because they always have " something laid out " and always know what must be done at this moment and talked about at that never get around to the joys of simply living and being together with friends—without *any* programme.[15]

Let us analyse the implications of this anti-definiteness. Technically, every social action can be split into at least six complementary segments. These are the initiating tendency or underlying attitude, the social persons focused upon as objects of the action, the social responses expected, the social methods used in the hope of securing those responses, the social instruments with which the methods are applied, and those aspects of the selves of the persons starting the action which are internally reflected, so to speak, in the course of events.

In the case of the Roamers, the prevailing tendency seems to have been a confused compound of longing for new experience and emotionalized reciprocity with those sharing the same romantically rebellious mood.

The social objects, obviously enough, were the leaders and followers in union with whom the sense of devotion and fusion could be felt. As we have seen, these objects were at first other lads, and then, as the sects began to follow differing paths, either males exclusively or members of both sexes.

E

The social responses which were expected differed somewhat in the case of leaders and followers. The leaders did not expect adherence to a definite programme, but rather emotional attachment and manifestation of unquestioning loyalty. Followers expected leaders to respond to them by providing a sense of being in the presence of someone of extraordinary capacities and by manifesting deep comradely interest in their personalities. Followership was usually on a graded scale, but in general it can be said that as between follower and follower each one expected from the other a sense of warmth and intimacy, of solidarity and common mood, of " understanding " and sympathy —in short, a sense of fusion.

The social method was roaming, at once emotionalized symbol and expression of rebellion on the one hand and traditionally grounded way of joining forces with the likeminded on the other— even though the tradition was oftentimes of ambivalent character.

So far, then, the elements of the social actions characteristic of the youth movement were marked by formlessness in high degree—but no social action can dispense with a fixed point of some kind, even though the fixation is merely relative. The social instruments provided this fulcrum or nucleus : distinctive costume, music, preparation of food, sleeping quarters and halting places, nests, and all the rest of it. These were what we may term " positive instruments " ; they helped to give structure to the " applied Bergsonism " penetratingly noted by one French observer. Negative social instruments were at least equally definite. At the very beginning there was rejection of comfort in favour of hard primitivism and later, among the harder as well as the softer adherents, abstinence from alcohol and tobacco, refusal to participate in ballroom dancing, avoidance of motion pictures, and a host of other self-imposed inhibitions. These lent an ascetic quality to even the less rigorous contingents of the youth movement and helped to make the break with the adult world readily evident to even the most obtuse parent, school teacher, or pastor.

Still speaking technically, but shifting the frame of reference, it can be said that the ends pursued by the youth movement were extremely vague, but that the means were at least sufficiently definite to make possible the application of labels such as " traditional " and " emotional ". Otherwise put : The ends were irrational, and the means were of essentially the same character. Expediency and the values sanctioned by school, church, and home were cast aside. Nostalgic traditionalism and emotionalized fusion held sway.

Now comes the rub : People grow older. By the time the second decade of the twentieth century was well under way, many youth movement leaders and followers had passed beyond surging adolescence. Further, numerous adults in no sense identified with ordinary youth tutelage felt themselves drawn to the movement, and many of them were welcomed because of their " essentially youthful " point of view. Still further, some of the younger groups thronging about successful belittlers of ageing leaders began to threaten whatever continuity had been slowly established. Once more, the excesses of some of the jangling sects threatened to nullify several of the gains toward the establishment of a realm of youth for youth that had already been made.

The times were ripe for the formulation of a unifying credo that, it was hoped, would solidify the sects to a degree sufficient to counteract the incipient inroads of youth tutelage. Incipient inroads ? Yes, for not content with their twenty-five to one superiority, youth tutelage directors had begun to claim that their organizations gave scope for youth as youth ; they seemed well on the way towards checking or even absorbing the autonomous youth movement.

Moved by these considerations and, no doubt, by many others, youth movement leaders decided on a great meeting at which all the sects could be pulled together in a common front against outer enemies. A suitable occasion was provided in October, 1913, by the centenary of the Battle of Leipzig, symbol of the Wars of Liberation. There, on the actual battle site, official Germany, seconded by every conceivable variety of youth tutelage and every adult association ranging from the Navy League to the Westphalian Society for Home Missions, was to stage a gigantic three-day demonstration of nationalistic solidarity. In deliberately planned opposition, leaders of the youth movement sects chose another site, the hill of Hohe Meissner, and sent out a call to their followers.

Almost three thousand, representing all of the more important divisions, came thronging to the support of their cause. One contingent, more aggressively ascetic than the rest, tried to make the gathering, in its main features, nothing more than a protest against the alcohol and tobacco that so liberally saturated and swirled around the official demonstration. This seemed far too narrow in scope to most of the youth movement adherents, although they were in hearty agreement with such " life reform " proposals, and they therefore insisted on broadening their protest in such a way that practically every phase of contemporary adult respectability was assailed and the demands of youth for its own sake vigorously asserted.

Whipped up to revival fervour by the moving speeches of their leaders, many of them now in young adulthood or drawn from among elders attracted by the youthful idealism so clearly evident, the youngsters present at Hohe Meissner experienced a sense of fusion going far beyond the little sects from which it had first quelled forth.

Outcome : While retaining their individual names and unique features, nearly all the sects merged into an overarching union called Free German Youth. The merger, however, was not the result of formal parliamentary procedure. Here as elsewhere in the youth movement the leadership principle remained dominant. Liberal endowments of *charisma* were scattered throughout the assemblage, but one personality of supremely extraordinary stamp finally emerged and swept all the other leaders and followers in his train. This man—for he was then in the upper twenties—was Gustav Wyneken, founder of the " Free School Community " of Wickersdorf. Carried along by his untiring drive and kindling enthusiasm, a coterie of leaders brought out the famous " Meissner Confession "—but although the hands were the hands of Esau, the voice was the voice of Wyneken :

Free German Youth, on their own initiative, under their own responsibility, and with deep sincerity, are determined independently to shape their own lives. For the sake of this inner freedom they will under any and all circumstances take united action.[16]

This formula seems to be nothing more than an explicit statement of the attitudes held by Karl Fischer's Roamers a good fifteen years earlier, but it owed its virtually unanimous acceptance at Hohe Meissner to the fact that it could also be interpreted as an ordinary moral platitude. Hence it was agreeable to those ultra-ascetic sects already mentioned which, although making common cause with the Free German Youth, were actually much more concerned about proposals for vegetarianism, anti-alcohol, and anti-tobacco than they were with a fiery declaration of independence from all adult authority whatsoever. Further, there had begun to develop clusters of sects devoting themselves

HOHE WACHT

Frontispiece of the first Free German Youth publication, published shortly after the Hohe Meissner gathering. The artist was "Fidus", noted for his cloudy exaltation of nudity.

to the fostering of solidarity with the Germanic folk, meaning thereby those " unspoiled " elements of the population both within and without Wilhelmian boundaries which could be united, as it was hoped, in a gigantic " communion of the German spirit ". The Roamers, on the other hand, retained their strongly individualistic tendencies ; for all their attachment to The Linden Tree and The Dear Dead Days they had a good share of the ambivalence of Hölderlin and the others we have mentioned. In particular, they had come to identify themselves with certain anti-nationalistic aspects of Nietzsche's teachings, as well as with the peculiar gospel of Langbehn.

But the Meissner formula, together with the crowd elation and surplus confidence evoked by the three-day revival experience, led to the disregard or glossing over of these possibilities for new and far more profound schisms. Wyneken and his followers held the upper hand for the time, and the news of the united front presumably presented by the Free German Youth filled youth tutelage representatives with dismay. They had apparently failed in their attempts to absorb the youth movement, and it therefore seemed necessary to break it up by a direct attack.

The most obvious opportunity for such destructive effort was afforded by the youth movement magazine, *Beginnings*, which in its first issue of May, 1913, had aroused tremendous commotion because of the hitherto unheard-of sharpness of its utterances against school, home, marriage, religion, and patriotism. Wyneken was the responsible editor, but in spite of his drive and enthusiasm the radical tone of the magazine proved so great an obstacle that the subscription list never went beyond eight hundred.[17] A number of those taking the magazine, however, belonged to the Young Roamers and these, it will be recalled, represented the more specifically homosexual members of the movement. Further, Wyneken himself had let drop remarks about *Eros* which could be interpreted as evidencing homosexual proclivities.

The stage was therefore set and in January, 1914, the Catholic Centre Party brought open charges in the Bavarian parliament that Wyneken's followers and, by implication, everyone adhering to the Meissner formula constituted a " pederasty club ", i.e., an assemblage of overt male homosexuals.[18] The moderate and conservative sects incorporated in the Free German Youth were appalled by the publicity showering down upon them, and they at once took steps to dissociate themselves from those identified

with the ideology of *Beginnings* and, supposedly, of Gustav
Wyneken. They called in Paul Natorp, a well-known professor
who, although highly sympathetic with the youth movement,
had consistently fought against its extremist wing. At a gathering
of leaders in Marburg in May, 1914, Natorp and the "life
reform" groups succeeeded in pushing Wyneken aside and
replacing the Meissner confession with one capable of considerably
milder interpretation. The key passage ran thus :

> We wish to add to the store of values which our elders have
> acquired and transmitted to us by developing our own powers under
> our own responsibility and with deep sincerity.[19]

Tantamount : That part of the Free German Youth which drew
apart from *Beginnings* thereafter avoided all direct struggle with
the older generation, whereas Wyneken's cohorts rapidly became
more radical—some of them openly opposed the military preparations for World War I.

They might as well have tried to stop the turbines of Niagara
by sticking clothespegs in the whirring blades ; August, 1914,
brought the decision. Not only this : The wave of nationalistic
sentiment which swept all over Germany engulfed even the
adherents of *Beginnings*. Schisms were forgotten. The sects once
more fused in a fervent glow by contrast with which even Hohe
Meissner paled into insignificance. Members of every sect of the
youth movement flocked to the colours in what at this distance
seems like one concerted rush—frequently, because they were so
largely under military age, as volunteers. The Kaiser had
announced that Germany was being attacked, and German youth
went marching by thousands into battle, singing the very songs
which had been their campfire companions during the carefree
summertime now past. At the terrible slaughter of Langemarck,
twelve thousand young volunteers, a great number of them drawn
from youth movement ranks, stormed forth in the face of a wither-
ing fire from which seven thousand never returned.

These and other sacrifices naturally intensified the devotion
to the Fatherland which had been latent in all but a handful
of the youth movement, and those who remained at home swung
sharply toward the right. "Life reform", premarital chastity,
and inseparable alliance with the Germanic folk held the field
without serious opposition until almost 1917. Youth tutelage
and youth movement began to draw together.

Beyond this : Anti-Semitism had long been an unavowed

The soldier as romanticized in " Pluck-Fiddle Jack ".

component of youth movement attitudes, but it now blazed forth with consuming fury ; fully one-third of the youth movement became actively opposed to what was held to be Jewish rationalism, internationalism, lust for money, scheming for power, lack of the true German essence. In place of the once-hated worshippers in Rimmon's House there appeared new objects of fear, contempt, and burning rage—the Jews.[20]

Metaphorically, the great controversy between Christ and Satan was finally under way, and the children of light took up arms against the children of darkness. " Choose ye this day whom ye will serve ! " was a challenge to which young Germans returned the cry of " Our Fatherland ! " in one resounding peal. The significance of " Come ye out from among them and be ye separate " had changed almost overnight into " A righteous Germany against an evil world ".

NOTES

1. See Viktor Engelhardt, " Grundlagen der deutschen Jugendbewegung " in Richard Thurnwald, ed., *Die neue Jugend*, vol. IV, first half, *Forschungen zur Völkerpsychologie und Soziologie* (Leipzig, 1927), pp. 13–14. Consult also Theo Herrle, *Die deutsche Jugendbewegung* (Gotha-Stuttgart, 1924), p. 37 ; Heinrich Roth, *Psychologie der Jugendgruppe* (Berlin, 1939), p. 78.

2. Hans Blüher, *Wandervogel, Geschichte einer Bewegung*, 1/2 (Jena, 1912), p. 96.

3. *Ibid.*, pp. 40–3.

4. " Sendbrief des Reichsstandes ", quoted in Roth, *op. cit.*, p. 44.

5. *Ibid.*, p. 26. For an extensive discussion of the peculiar structure of the *Bund*, see Herman Schmalenbach, " Die soziologische Kategorie des Bundes " *Die Dioskuren*, vol. I (Munich, 1922), pp. 35–105. It should be noted, however, that Schmalenbach's affiliations with the Stefan George circle lead him into strained interpretations at times.

6. Blüher, *op. cit.*, p. 50.

7. Wiese-Becker, *Systematic Sociology* (New York, 1932), pp. 625–6.

8. Hilmar Höckner, *Die Musik in der deutschen Jugendbewegung* (Wolfenbüttel, 1927), pp. 24–5.

9. *Der Zupfgeigenhansl.*

10. Blüher, *op. cit.*, p. 120.

11. Roth, *op. cit.*, pp. 50–1.

12. See Karl Brossmer, *Wanderheime der Jugend* (Freiburg, 1920), *passim.*

13. Hertha Siemering, *Die deutschen Jugendpflegeverbände* (Berlin, 1918), *passim.* This definitive handbook of youth bodies, first published in 1918, but giving figures for pre-war days, contains striking evidence of the opposition mentioned on p. 131. After almost four hundred pages devoted to youth tutelage, there follows a chapter of about seventy-five pages devoted to the youth movement, and of this seventy-five over thirty are set aside for proletarian youth activities which actually took on some of the definitely

youth movement traits only after World War I. Hence less than ten per cent. of the handbook directly considered the Roamers and their offshoots. The 1931 edition of Siemering altered this proportion slightly, but even then a bare fifteen per cent. dealt with groups attempting to preserve, however imperfectly, the traditions of the days before World War I.

These figures of page allotment, even if they reflected actual membership, would of course show nothing conclusive about proportionate influence, for a very small minority, if it is sufficiently aggressive, can force its impress on a putty-like majority. That this was what really occurred few dispassionate observers can doubt, but for the time being that is neither here nor there. The present effort is simply to show that the youth movement was set apart from youth tutelage in even the handbooks designed for adult purposes.

Stepping aside for the moment, it may be as well to call the roll of the youth tutelage groups. No detailed list can be given, for there were over one hundred main bodies before 1914, and these were split into so many regional, confessional, and vocational sections that a figure of over three hundred would represent a conservative total. Now for the broad outline :

(1) Groups and directive staffs aiming at physical development primarily ; many of these derived from the old *Turnvereine*. Total membership was nearly three-quarters of a million.

(2) Army and Navy youth auxiliaries ; most of these were presided over by officers, active or retired, and total membership was small—not more than ten thousand.

(3) Preparedness and " defence " consolidations ; officers were sometimes active in these, but enthusiastic laymen also played a large part as directors and instructors. The boys drilled, manœuvred, and so on, whereas the girls engaged in efforts that would fit them for service behind the lines. Before World War I the number enrolled was insignificant—six thousand at most.

(4) Boy and Girl Scouts ; most of these organizations date from the rise of the International Boy Scouts under the headship of Baden-Powell ; after 1911 almost all of them were linked with Scout organizations in other countries. It is interesting to note that although Britishers and Americans, in particular, complained about the military character of the Scouts, Germans felt that their attitudes were much too civilian. Therefore the Scouts were in mild antagonism to the more martial bodies. Boys outnumbered girls nine to one ; all groups together had about eleven thousand members by 1914.

(5) So-called " Evangelical " youth associations, among which the Lutherans held an overwhelming majority ; the total enrolment at the outbreak of the First World War was over three hundred thousand. Pastors and devout military men headed up most of these for the boys ; the girls were directed by deaconesses in some instances, but more frequently by pastors. Some of the Evangelical organizations were of Pietist slant, and here and there pacifist bodies such as the Mennonites made themselves heard. Most frequent, however, were the Lutheran groups which combined active nationalism with stress on religiosity of " private " character. Incidentally, note that the famous Pastor Niemöller was one of the heroes of the Evangelicals after World War I, in large measure because of his service as submarine commander and his concomitant other-worldliness.

(6) Catholic young people's organizations ; here priests and laymen shared almost equally in direction, with almost no participation by officers. Women had a considerable part in heading up the girls' groups, although occasionally priests functioned in the same capacity. Catholic bodies manifested a fairly wide range of basic attitudes : all the way from mystic reconciliationists such as the *Quickborn* who tried to bridge the gap between French and German youth even before World War I, to the Catholic

Crusaders who unwaveringly espoused the cause of Germany in all things. All together, Catholic youth bodies had well over a third of a million adherents in 1914.

(7) Unions of Jewish youth, partly youth movement, partly youth tutelage. The marginal position of the Jews in Germany was reflected in their youth organizations, for they oftentimes tried to follow the pattern of the Roamers and in most instances were thrown back upon themselves. The result was that their rabbis, whether orthodox or reformed, were occasionally called in to guide youngsters who would otherwise have been glad to remain on an autonomous footing. Of course, the ardent Zionists were intrinsically bound up with the adults who aimed at the return to Palestine, so that in their case youth tutelage was definite and unavoidable. Even after World War I membership in Jewish youth groups never exceeded thirty thousand, and for the earlier period half that number would be a high figure.

(8) Socialistically inclined youth groupings; some of these had only remote connections with the politically organized Socialists. In large measure the socialism concerned lay at the ethical and ideological levels; there was Christian Socialism, "Socialism of the Spirit", Socialist Monism, and Free Socialism. For most of these youngsters the class struggle was not a vital reality, and definite membership in this or that grouping is hard to determine. A 1914 figure of about ten thousand altogether is fairly close to the reality.

(9) Political youth auxiliaries; every party of any importance tried to win recruits and assistants, but before World War I met with only a moderate degree of success; one hundred thousand all told is a generous estimate. In the 'twenties, as we shall see later, this situation was reversed; the politicization of German youth spurted ahead.

(10) Apprenticeship and vocational youth agencies—frequently cutting across political auxiliary, Evangelical, and Catholic tutelage. In fact, only bodies such as those set up for boys and girls employed in mercantile establishments, offices, and bureaus are clearly distinguishable, although a few efforts to organize peasant youngsters were made. Therefore, although some two hundred thousand *in toto* can be set down, it is difficult to tell just how many are included in the numbers enrolled in other organizations.

(11) Boundary, enclave, colonial, and intranational youth agencies, usually with "hyphenated" membership. Virtually all of these were in some way linked· with Pan-Germanism and imperial expansion, and were frequently directed, sometimes under cover, sometimes openly, by trusted officials of Wilhelm II. Over half a million members before 1914!

14. From the minority report of the Young Roamers at the Hohe Meissner conference in 1913, quoted by George Thomson, *The Influence of the Youth Movement on German Education* (unpublished Ph.D. dissertation, University of Glasgow), p. 80, quoted by Robert C. Schmid, *German Youth Movements : A Typological Study* (unpublished Ph.D. dissertation, University of Wisconsin, 1941), p. 103.

15. Wilhelm Stählin, *Fieber und Heil in der Jugendbewegung* (Hamburg, 1924), pp. 59–60.

16. Quoted by Fritz Jungmann, "Autorität und Sexualmoral in der freien bürgerlichen Jugendbewegung", in Max Horkheimer, ed., *Autorität und Familie* (Paris, 1936), p. 672.

17. *Ibid.*, p. 672.
18. *Ibid.*, p. 673.
19. *Ibid.*
20. *Ibid.*

As general guides for the topics of this and several other chapters, I can strongly recommend the youth movement writings of Paul Honigsheim, formerly of the University of Cologne and now of Michigan State College. I have not cited or quoted him directly, but all my thinking about youth movement matters has been coloured by his cogent analyses. See the following in particular :

"Die Pubertät", *Kölner Vierteljahrshefte für Soziologie*, 3, 4 (1924), pp. 264–74.

"Jugendbewegung und Erkenntnis", in Max Scheler, ed., *Versuche zu einer Soziologie des Wissens* (Munich und Leipzig, 1924), pp. 369–407.

"Jugendhilfe als gesellschaftliche Funktion", in Gerhard Danziger and Paul Oestreich, eds., *Der Jugendhelfer* (Berlin, 1927), pp. 7–33.

"Gegenwartsnot, Jugendnot, Jugendwandern", in *Der Wanderführer*, I (Hilchenbach in Westphalia, 1927), pp. 1–27.

"Die Berufswelt der männlichen Jugendlichen", in *Rheinische Jugend*, Düsseldorf, 17 (Jan. 1, 1929), pp. 1–17.

"Jugendbewegung, Politik, Friedensbewegung", in *Zehn Jahre Kampf der Jugend für den Frieden* (Berlin, 1929).

For stimulating and cogent discussion of the more general aspects of such matters, see :

Karl Mannheim, "The Problem of Youth in Modern Society", in *Diagnosis of Our Time* (London, 1943), pp. 31–53.

PART TWO

CHAPTER VI

CONFUSION : TUMULT OF THE 'TWENTIES

> Like ravelled skeins they cross and twine,
>   While this with that connects and blends ;
> And only Khizr his eye shall see
>   Where one begins, where other ends :
>
> What mortal shall consort with Khizr,
>   When Musâ turned in fear to flee ?
> What man foresees the flow'r or fruit
>   Whom Fate compelled to plant the tree ?
>   —BURTON, " The Kasidah ".

" Man lives by myth "—yes, as a statement in the generic singular this is true enough. It would also be quite possible, however, to speak in the plural. As between people and people, and even as between differing divisions of the same people, the myths men live by are manifestly of tremendous variety.

The simple lives of Konrad and Annele in a quiet corner of Suabia furnished the basis, so to speak, for a myth of Germanic peasant virtue and folk community, but as time wore on and crisis succeeded crisis, the winds of doctrine shattered The Linden Tree. Surviving shoots were piously planted or grafted to other stocks, tended with greater or lesser zeal, and trimmed into "suitable" shapes by this faction or that. Leaving the metaphor : Eventually the common element in the multifarious myths became almost unrecognizable, and when to the existing diversity were added contrasting, competing, opposing, or ambivalent patterns of " what men live by ", the name of Germany became a synonym for Babel.

This confusion of tongues was especially apparent, as might be expected, after World War I. Nowhere else on the globe could be found such a welter of irreconcilable ideas and ways of life, such a tumult of discordant voices. In the thumbnail sketches to follow, observation is limited to personalities relevant to youth movement matters—otherwise the succession of characters might be prolonged indefinitely.

I

Everywhere, everywhere ! The corridor leading to the university auditorium : Young chaps, some in academic robes, some in loose linen shirts with the Byron collar of the Roamers open at the throat, some in old-fashioned spike helmets. Hundreds. " Dead on the Field of Honour." Pathetic, awkward poses in these already-fading photographs : Rigid pride, romantic defiance, ill-concealed bashfulness, tense anxiety lest the dangling Iron Cross or the youth-organization ribbon in the tunic might not show, plain boyish clumsiness. The central post office : Alongside the ornate, oversized wall calendar with its 1924 in great red letters hangs a tablet carved in dark oak ; names in gilt curlicues—" Our Fallen Comrades ". A stroll through the city : Monuments. She-wolf suckling her young, Siegfried clutching a mighty sword, Gothic warriors hewed from granite. More names, row upon row. Everywhere, everywhere the shadow of a great and unacknowledged defeat ; everywhere the iron will to remember and avenge.

Uncomfortable recollections of Holbein's " Dance of Death " ; after awhile, death's-heads seem to grin everywhere. Especially when you see the reflected faces of Jockels and Friedls in the shiny stone of the monuments.

The lads dash away ; here come marching columns from the school around the corner. Jockel and Friedl fall into line ; scores of boyish voices ring out :

> " It may be for years but it is not for ever,
> Our Fatherland yields to its enemies never."

The marching schoolmaster : Incongruous combination of duel-scarred face, Byron collar, rune-engraved medallion of the Nordic Youth. The song changes but the marching tempo remains :

> " Each brave lad his life for the Fatherland gives ;
> What matters our death, if our Germany lives ? "

Staccato " Halt ! " On the bridge the ranks break ; route step. A few faces peer over the railing ; more reflections. Why do those mirrored smiles remind you again of Holbein ?

II

" Well," said the old Pomeranian major, " everybody knows that Bismarck was a political realist of the first order—in the direct tradition of our Frederick the Great. If he had been with us in 1914 we wouldn't see these French dandies strutting about our Rhineland towns to-day. And to think that the hypocritical

League did no more than shake a warning finger when the
Senegalese led our girls astray and murdered the fathers and
brothers who denounced them ! And the killing of our young
hero Schlageter—even if he was a little erratic, he died for
Germany ! It only goes to show that hard-headed officers of the
old school—and I am proud to be among them—are right when
they say that justice is only the law of the stronger.

"' The God who laid iron in the earth held German slavery
of no worth' said the good old Arndt, and Bismarck echoed him
with his ' Blood and iron '. He would have spoken out against
these effeminate creatures of the Weimar Republic, with their
decadent Social Democracy, who want to make student duelling
criminal ; when young men break their necks climbing mountains just for the fun of it, nobody should object to a few scars,
the marks of unflinching courage and zeal for the Fatherland.

" But Bismarck made one great mistake ; he helped Germany
start on the path of industrialism, and now comes Thyssen,
imitating your Ford, and wants to make machines of us altogether.
Perhaps, as long as the masses breed like rabbits, they must work
like machines—but the influence on our *Kultur* this mechanization
will have ! If only the war had lasted longer ; the earth is full
of the many-too-many. Thank God the French, with their low
birthrate and scabby morals, will never have the manpower to
face up to us again. If only we could be sure that their silly
friends would not come to their aid . . .

" Well, we mustn't think too long about such things, we who
have seen better days. Let me show you this porcelain bust of
our old Fritz. Isn't it fine ? And have you seen my collection
of books about Bismarck and his times ? If only these short-
sighted leaders of our patriotic youth would study him !

" Erich, my oldest son, certainly should know more about
Bismarck. He fought with the Baltic Free Corps until the
summer of 1920, and then he hid in the Mecklenburg hills until
those Social-Democratic puppies lost the scent. When he came
back he threw himself into the work of the Hindenburg Youth,
although in a way things of that kind are beneath the notice of
the nobility. As long as he was determined, however, I tried my
best to get him to join the Bismarck Alliance. It was no use ;
he's an extremist, for he wants to push the German domain all
the way up the Baltic. What do we want with those Letts and
Lithuanians ? To be sure, some of our Germanic brothers live
among them, but it would be best if we followed Bismarck's

maxim : ' Germany is a satiated state '. Of course, we won't
rest content until we restore the pre-war frontiers—that pack of
Poles in the Corridor must be wiped out—but there is no use
risking our chances to get back on top by trying to do too much at
the beginning. It's lucky that the Hindenburg Youth can't
count on more than six thousand members ; the Bismarck League
has over fifteen thousand. Maybe Erich will change his mind
when he sees that he could lead more youngsters if he followed
my advice.

" Günther, I am sad to say, has broken with family traditions
even more seriously ; he actually concerns himself with those
Pathfinders. They're just the same as the Boy Scouts, and
everybody knows that the Scouts have too many international
hookups to be trustworthy Germans. And there are so many
of them ! And they take in girls too ! All my fellow-officers
laugh at my conservatism, but I've always believed that no
daughter of a really good family would run around the countryside, sleeping God knows where and showing her legs shamelessly.
Perhaps, though, Germany needs Spartan wives and mothers—
but I can't think we will get them that way ! Moreover, what
would one or two thousand amount to ?—that's all they can count
now. Günther says that his organization has twenty-five
thousand boys ; I hope he's wrong.

" Something has to be done, I suppose, but I long for the
days when we had our conscription and the Spring and Fall
manœuvres and plenty of good noble offspring for the cadet
schools. Then we didn't have to worry about youth ; they
gladly obeyed us and had no nonsensical ideas of their own.

" Yes, yes, those were great days for Germany—yes, yes."

III

" I've been a Lutheran minister for a long time, but *I* never
preached such foolishness. Three or four years ago a few of
those crazy members of the Free German Youth were wild over
Gandhi and the Frenchified pacifism of Rolland and Marc
Sagnier, but fortunately the rest of the Free German Youth were
really German and they threw out that chattering crew. All
such stuff is Asiatic or Jewish, anyway. Turn the other cheek ?
And have it slapped by greasy Frenchmen ? See what they did
to us on the Ruhr, when we couldn't resist them !

" Of course, when you think back over the events that led
to the war and what some fools call our defeat—our armies were

never defeated in the field—you know that the British are most to blame for it all. They envied our foreign trade ; they feared our army. Well they might ; we were getting ready for them, the miserable tea-drinking scum. And to think they were once a Germanic people in the days of the Angles and the Saxons ! They're mixed up so much with those black Welsh and wild Highland Scots and flighty Irish that they're decadent.

" They've split off from us, and good riddance, but perhaps we can some day weld all the Scandinavians, the Dutch, the Flemish, the Austrians, and the Swiss into one great national group that matches the spread of our peerless language and its offshoots. It's too bad the Germans in America forget their mother tongue so readily, but it's in the blood, never fear. I think it was our great Grimm who said, ' " One people " is the idea that sweeps all before it when men speak the same language.'

" That's why I am so glad that Rolf belongs to a branch of the alliance youth ; at least that's one of the groups really concerned about our fellow-Germans scattered among Poles, Czechs, Romanians, and the rest of the sub-human lot. Rolf's followers call themselves ' Schill's Free Company ', and although only about five hundred belong to it, the faith that moves mountains is there. Who is Schill ? You mean who *was* Schill. Haven't you seen that painting of the row of young officers shot down by the French in the Wars of Liberation ? The last man on his feet, trying to hold up a mortally wounded comrade and at the same time gesturing defiance at the rifles, was the glorious Schill. What better symbol could you find ?

" They're religious, too, for they are good Lutherans. They keep themselves unspotted from the world in their inner lives, even though, as we all know, the outward life of man is a relentless struggle to kill or be killed.

" No, Rolf has chosen the right path ; my prayers for him have been answered."

IV

" Well, I wouldn't say that we're enthusiastic about the Weimar Republic, in spite of the fact that our Catholic Centre Party usually votes with the Social Democrats against the fanatical Nationalists of the Right. You see, the Church embodies the wisdom of the ages, and so long as the State leaves it free to carry on its own proper affairs, why should we get excited about the issue of monarchy *versus* republic ? A few of the Social Democrats talk loudly against religion, but they're not so vicious as the Communists, and they have left our parochial schools almost intact. Did you know that we have more than thirty thousand of them?

"Another thing that keeps us lined up with the Social Democrats and even with those Jews and sentimental liberals of the Democratic Party is the need of self-defence. Just because Erzberger was a Catholic, and signed the peace treaty, the secret societies that have been assassinating so many of the upholders of Weimar have been killing Catholics too. Between 1918 and now, in this apparently peaceful summer of 1924, there have been more than two hundred and fifty political murders; we have to walk warily.

"The amazing thing is that the bulk of the killings occurred before the Allies really began to get deadly serious about the Versailles settlement; the French moved into the Ruhr in the late winter of last year and dragged the British along with them, and that certainly makes a stupid muddle, but the Weimar leaders had been picked off in huge quantities before then. We'll just have to try to weather the storm; after all it's usually the Social Democrats who get shot or who mysteriously disappear.

"What we're really relying on in the long run is our Catholic youth. Counting all of the organizations we have almost four hundred thousand memberships. Yes, I know that a girl might simultaneously belong to the League for Catholic Apprentices and the Catholic Union for South German Girls, but even allowing for all that you can't deny us over-two hundred thousand actual members. And we're not like the youth movement tribe; we reach down into the lowest classes and up to the highest. The only youngsters who stay with them are the sons and daughters of the petty bourgeoisie—almost no peasants, and few factory workers.

"Surely, surely; some of our Catholic young people say that they are opposed to youth tutelage and really belong to the youth movement. We welcome their independent spirit, for under divine guidance it leads them to regeneration, not innovation. Even the *Quickborn*, among the most radical of all, seeks only to bring Christ into the life of every German Catholic youngster.

"Have you read about the *Quickborn* attempts to help in the rebuilding of devastated France and Belgium? Some of our brave lads, and girls too, said they were willing to offer themselves directly as workers at any task, no matter how menial, that would testify to their sincere desire to be reconciled with our former enemies. The *Quickborn* devotees didn't get very far, but that wasn't their fault. Sometimes German officials wouldn't give them passports and the French, in particular, were so suspicious of them that discouragement set in. Just the same, they did make the effort, and it redounds to the greater glory of God and His Church.

"This nest we have fixed up here alongside of the parish house is not very attractive from the outside, as you say, but I'm glad to hear you admit that the wall decorations and the carved beams are finer than any others you've seen in these parts. We did it all ourselves, and I must say that although I studied the handicraft arts while I was carrying on my theological course, I really didn't do much more than ask God to bless the work. One of our older boys is a talented artist, and with a little occasional aid from me he got fully a dozen helpers from the ranks of our group. In the long winter evenings, when we couldn't go roaming up there in the Hilly Country, we all painted and wove and chipped away as though we were those industrious dwarfs who used to help the pious artisans of Cologne.

"Oh, we sometimes go to the big youth movement gatherings, for since the war there's been less and less fuss about the differences between youth tutelage and youth movement. In general, though, we stand pretty much aloof from the alliance youth, with their talk about a folk community. What can a folk community amount to if the dear God is left out ? No, we don't have much to do with the bits and pieces of the Roamers, either. A few of them are all right, but they're so badly split up that you never know what lies behind flashing eyes and tanned faces, and they occasionally scoff at our insistence on chastity. Some of their darker sins we'd better not talk about ; they're an uncanny lot.

"Good-bye, in Jesus' name. Don't forget to send us some postcards ; if we had a dozen nice coloured ones we could make a little frieze just above the wainscoting at the entrance."

V

"Salamander for our guest ! " The steins jerked aloft with mechanical precision, tilted, came down with a resounding thud on the table. "Silentium ex ! Colloquium ! " Long double rows of students belonging to one of the minor " Corporations " they were, in their weekly *Kneipe*, where everybody drinks at least enough to get that warm, brotherly feeling. The chap opposite, head swathed in bandages (result of a fiercely-contested duel the day before), leaned across the table, almost upsetting his stein.

" Look here, you're a pretty good fellow. But th' Americans are pretty good, anyway, and you're German descent. Anyway, half German—some's better than none. Good. Say, d'y' know th' Allies would never have beaten us if the German-Americans hadn't fought against us too ? One German can trounce three of any other breed. No, I'm not drunk ! Never get drunk on less than seven, and I've had only seven. When I was with the Advance Troop (y'know that was part of the Free German Youth) I never touched a drop. Didn't smoke either, but couldn't eat those sticky mixtures of nuts and God knows what that they tried to make taste like sausage. Never was cut out for a vegetarian. Too much of a good thing.

" Anyway, couldn't stick to Advance Troop rules in the army. Officers didn't like youth movement trash—that's what they called us—anyway. Just kept a narrow black-green-gold ribbon in second tunic buttonhole so's we could recognize each other. Got together sometimes, sang songs out of The Pluck, but what's the use ? Germany doesn't need any more of that ' new world of youth ' dreaming ; we've got to stick together, old and young, and get back where we were before the whole world jumped on us. Dis'pline's what we need, dis'pline.

" Sure, three years in Telephone Corps. Same dis'pline as rest of army. Fine thing, army dis'pline, 'specially Prussian divisions. Y'had rules for everything—didn't have to worry. Y'did this, an' did that, an' when duty was done, why *you* were done, y'see.

" Telephone Corps. Got married by proxy. Telephone Corps started that business. Other fellows caught on, got too popular. Ha, no children by proxy ! 'S too much of a good thing, *nicht wahr* ? Just two ; Hans, four, Lieschen, one. Be more ; we need plenty stout Germans. Soon's they get bigger hope they go into alliance youth—any branch, I don't care. Won't push 'em though. Remember my own father—always trying to make me do something. But he left me a little money ; I'd have been able to finish my university course and get a government job if that crazy inflation hadn't wiped me out. Now I have to work and study part-time. It's slow business. Nothing like this before the war ; married man's got no business studying. Damn nuisance, but you've got to have diploma. Diplomas every-place—damn nuisance. Sometimes think war was better, if hadn't been for getting whipped.

"Not so sure we were whipped. Allies had to get th' Americans to help 'em. We had Frenchmen scared to death—mutinied in winter of '17. Even with th' Americans against us we might have held out and got a good peace; they never set foot on German soil before th' Armistice. It was all the work of those damn' Jews and Marxists. They stabbed us in the back, y'know.

" 'S I was sayin', soldier's life's a fine life. Dis'pline's good for a fellow. Didn't have to worry. Ought to have year or so of universal labour service now. When I was in th' old youth movement we built roads and log shelters and drained swamps. That's the stuff. These youngsters that run around the streets would have something to do, and they'd do it *right*. That was only trouble with youth movement camps; sometimes dance around with the girls and talk about philosophy 'stead of working. Army's fine. You have rule for ever'thing—do ever'thing right. Y'do this, and do that, and when your duty's done, why *you're* done."

VI

"Now, I always vote the way I think will do the most good. I'm a business man, I am, and my vote always goes where it will hit the Social Democrats the hardest. They stir up class hatred, you see, and you always have trouble with those cursed—pardon me—workers.

"We're keeping our eye on that fellow Hitler. He sounds like a crackpot, and he's had very little publicity yet, but we might be able to use him to fight fire with fire. All those *Gesindel* can be bought and sold, anyway; the idea is to get one that makes a lot of noise and doesn't cost too much. He's in fortress confinement now, for that Munich putsch of his didn't come off properly. Maybe he's just a fumbler, but it's my guess that he'll do things in a big way when he gets out—probably next year; we're pulling strings. All his talk about Germany's wrongs and the leadership principle and folk community and the evils of big cities make him a drawing card. These little officials and shopkeepers and small peasants might listen to him, and some of those gullible alliance youth might think he's great because he stays away from women and doesn't eat meat or drink or smoke.

What a life ! But we shouldn't get too fussy about the tools we use.

" We've got to have some good tools. There's a lot of labour unrest. Your Ford, now, he's managed to get along without much labour trouble. Is that talk about high wages in his factories just advertising ? We really do like his factory system, though ; those conveyors keep the men on the job. We're doing our best to copy him over here, but the Communists, the Social Democrats, and even the Centre fight our methods all the time. They say that we make the workers produce more and then don't give them more wages. That's true, although we don't admit it. How can you accumulate capital if you give it all back to them ? They'll only drink more beer and have more kids anyway.

" The trade unions are trying to introduce the eight-hour day. The nitwits ! The condition we're in now and the amounts we're supposed to pay for reparations, *pfui* ! They'd better make up their minds to stick to ten or eleven hours.

" But maybe the French and the British are just bluffing. Politicians have to stay in office, you know. If only we can get on a good basis with France again . . . This steel cartel that ties the German and French magnates together, and the rest of the undercover agreements, may help to ease off the tension. If only the Frenchmen hadn't gone into the Ruhr ! They won't get anything out of it, anyway, and the British certainly don't enjoy holding the tail while the French try to milk. They ought to use a little common sense. We're sick of war, but we want to live too. If we can't get our trade back and make a little money, watch out for trouble.

" I was in the States in the spring of '22 ; I was certainly discouraged when I came back here and saw what the war had done to us—the contrast would stagger you. But we'll come back if the workers don't go crazy altogether and the French and British don't give their cheap politicians too much power. I certainly would like to see a prosperous peace for a few years ; I've got to think about my family.

" Families come high if you're a man with a position to maintain. My two sons, Philip and Martin, are at the university, and that costs money. Hilde and Hertha are in high-class finishing schools, and you certainly pay through the nose for education like that. If it was only the fees and the ordinary living expenses it wouldn't be so bad, but the boys got into *Borussia*. That's a Corporation that is really tops ; before the war only those with noble connections were admitted. But money helps nowadays. When I guaranteed a monthly cheque of a thousand marks for each one—that was before the inflation —they took them in all right. They hesitated, yes, but they took them in. The girls don't cost quite so much but still it's plenty ; kid gloves above the elbows and all those Paris frocks. And then when you think of the dowries . . .

" Oh, that youth stuff ? None of my children ever paid any attention to it ; it's all right for the lower middle class, I suppose. Some of my friends have sent their boys to that expensive Free School Community at Wickersdorf just because it's expensive ; they're willing to overlook Wyneken's youth nonsense for the sake of prestige. But I won't take chances with my children ; this independence and fantastic ' youth culture ' is contagious. Besides, Wyneken does too much experimenting ; I'll not furnish him any guinea pigs. I've heard, too, that he's friendly with the Social Democrats ; that's dynamite. Moreover, there's too much talk about experimental morals at Wickersdorf. Maybe Wyneken himself isn't one of the queer ones, but you know the saying about smoke and fire. If my boys want to get a little worldly polish, I can increase the size of their cheques a little ; mistresses don't come too high nowadays. Let them do their own experimenting.

" I guess I'd better be getting along ; it's been a pleasant conversation, but you know how it is. The times are unsettled, and if you stay on top you've got to keep swimming. Business is business, as you Americans say. *Auf Wiedersehen.*"

VII

" We'll never support an imperialist war—certainly not ! But I wouldn't mind shooting some of these fat-necked bourgeois myself, if it came to that. They sold the Revolution ; Noske was their tool ; the murders of Rosa Luxemburg and Karl Liebknecht were carried out in the interest of bourgeois ' law and order '.

" It's not that they've got so much money nowadays ; the inflation put the screws on them. What makes us ready to strangle them is their feeling that they're so much better than we are. But we were good enough to stop bullets ; oh yes !

" Bourgeois society the world over is so rotten it stinks. I've got no faith in any of these bourgeois governments that belong to the League. For a while it looked as though a part of the

" Toast to Noske ! The proletariat is disarmed ! "—Georg Grosz. Left-wing
criticism of reliance on the reactionary Reichswehr by the Republic.

Officers' Corps would make common front with the Soviets against the West. Now that the Ruhr has been occupied, they're getting bolder in proposing a union of Russia and Germany. But I don't trust them ; all they want is to stay top dog. If they joined with the Soviets, they'd soon have the Red Army under their thumb.

" Our first loyalty is to Red Russia ; to hell with Germany and the Junkers. Our party is only six years old, but we're growing stronger every day. Our youth organization alone acknowledges more than ten thousand ' legal ' members, and it has lots of illegal cells scattered through the schools and factories.

" We're not like the Social Democrats. Do you know that those cretins have the oldest leaders of any party in Germany ? Some of the oldtimers from the days of Bismarck's socialist laws are still doddering along, trying to be respectable middle-class citizens and at the same time talking about revolution. When the time is ripe, we can push them to one side and take over the trade unions and the local party machines—if we want them. I'm not sure that we do. I'd just as soon wipe them out altogether and put young vigorous Communists in complete control from top to bottom.

" Our youngsters feel the same way ; they hate the silly Roamers and alliance youth, but most of all they hate the Social Democrats. Sometime when you want to see a good street fight go some place in working-class Berlin—Rummelsburg or Neukölln, say—and watch what happens when the Social-Democratic youth march down the street. Bricks, knives, kicks in the belly—that's what they get and what they need. They're cowards, anyway. You can't get ready for the Revolution without a little practice in bloodletting now and again.

" And the Revolution will come ! The aftermath of the inflation, and Fordism, and all the rest of it, will help *our* cause along. The first revolution turns out in one of those 1789 affairs ; when the next one comes it will be the real thing—the night of the long knives. Then Red Germany and Red Russia will squeeze out the Polish landowners, and with Red China . . .

" Bah, these fat-necked swine of bourgeois ! "

VIII

" Yes, during the Kapp Putsch. That was in 1920. You can see the bullet-holes in this side of our *Rathaus*. The Kapp forces were in there, and the armed workers upholding the Republic gradually drove them out. It will cost us something to fix up the stained-glass windows, I can tell you. Tears ran down my cheeks when I saw those three lovely windows at the end of the room where we performed civil marriage ceremonies. They were all my idea, too. In the middle we had a nice boat with a big square sail, and on the deck were bride and groom dressed just like those pictures you see in the history books about the Middle Ages. Then on the right we had two big yellow wedding-rings that looked like gold when the sun shone through ; they were interlocked. Then I had to have my little joke ; in the left window we put a stork. Do you know that the Kapp people inside and the republicans outside just riddled those windows ? The ones you see now are temporary ; as soon as we get funds I'll have the old designs back again.

"Oh, I'm not worried about any more putsches, no, no. Why, attempts more recent than Kapp's, that fellow Hitler's, for example—why, he was. put in fortress confinement. Yes, I know that the government has been having a lot of trouble with those secret drill clubs and officers' conspiracies, but law and order is getting the upper hand. I took my first oath to William II, and as long as he was our lawful ruler, I served him faithfully. Then I took an oath to the Republic, and I'll serve it as long as it is lawful. What matters most is peace and quiet and steady work ; although I am the *Bürgermeister*, I don't bother about politics. You see, people like myself—mayors, I think you call them in the States—go through a long course of training and are then appointed to office. As long as we do our work well and don't antagonize the party in power they let us pretty much alone. That's all I want.

"Of course, I might sometime have to take another oath. There's always the possibility that we might have a monarchy again ; many of our good people don't like this parliamentary twaddle. I certainly don't. But we'll never have the Hohenzollerns. At least not William the Woodcutter nor that slack-jawed Crown Prince.

"It's too bad that our Kaiser abandoned us in that shameful way, for he might have been the guiding star of our young people, especially the Lutherans. Now that they have no Ruler by the Grace of God to keep them steady, they get all sorts of queer ideas.

"Have you ever heard of Habertshof, in Hessia ? Two of

my own children have gone there, and I can't say that I altogether like it. It's a sort of country settlement started by the group that calls itself New Work. The members are radical Lutherans, and they're trying to live a life where all things are held in common.

" There's a farm, a truck garden, a folk high school like those they have in Denmark, a youth meeting-place, a printing shop and bindery for books, and a children's home. Everything is in one common fund, and when Leopold—that's my boy ; he does the printing—needs a new pair of shoes, they all get together and vote ! To be sure, they have to do a lot of ordinary buying and selling, but they think that's only a necessary compromise with a temporary situation ; some day, they think, capitalism will break down and we'll all live in little settlements like Habertshof. God forbid !

" Whenever there's any surplus they pour it into the children's home, where they gather orphans and waifs and strays from all parts of Germany. Grete, my daughter, takes care of the children ; they have only seven right now, but they hope to add others when they get a little more prosperous. Sometimes I think it's fine for Grete, for she's thirty now and she's unmarried. Her young man was killed at Langemarck. She washes and feeds and mothers the children and she seems quite happy. Maybe they'll get some money from the outside ; for instance, there was a vegetarian in California who heard about Habertshof —nobody eats meat there—and he sent them enough to buy two horses and some good agricultural tools.

" Oh, yes, they've had a lot of trouble from time to time. Some of the would-be members were just dreamers who had no taste for discipline and hard work. One time there was a fellow who quit in disgust because the Marxian principle of six hours a day was not being followed ; you see, twelve to fourteen hours was the rule while they were getting things started. Others had silly ideas about animals ; before they got the horses, four of the young fellows fixed themselves up a harness and pulled their light plough themselves. They said it wasn't fair to exploit dumb beasts, and quit when the others insisted on buying the horses.

" I can't see how they can all be good Lutherans and still have such queer notions ; they even hobnob with Social Democrats and Communists. But on the outside, at least, the place would do your heart good ; everything is neat and well cared for and the crops last year were wonderful. Our young people mean well, but I do wish that there was some one person to whom they could look up and who would give them good sound ideas.

"No, Habertshof isn't the only thing the New Work people are doing, but perhaps it's the most important. But that folk high school at Habertshof is just one of the forty or fifty they're running, and they do a lot for our Lutheran youth tutelage by acting as leaders. They work in the city as well as the small towns and the country ; some of the New Work nests are set right in the middle of sooty and smelly factory districts.

"I admire such good people, but I can't help being uneasy about Leopold and Grete. It doesn't seem like a natural life to me, and I still think that I could have them back home again and Germany would be quiet and peaceful if only we had somebody to look up to and give us good sound ideas. I'll always say that.

"But here, I'm telling you all about my own troubles when you want to see more of our *Rathaus*. I'll show you the council chamber. Here's where I sit, here in the middle, and over there, around the horseshoe, sit the party groups, all the way from right to left—Nazis (that's National Socialists) to Communists. Isn't it queer that those fellows away out at the ends of the horseshoe vote together so much of the time? They hate each other, no doubt about that, but they seem to hate the Social Democrats and the Centre even more. I don't know what to make of the whole business ; we need somebody to look up to.

"That blank wall space back of my seat? Oh, that's where our dear William used to bristle. We took him down after he ran away to Holland, the coward."

IX

"It's fine to have somebody to talk to. Every renter I've had in these rooms has been anti-Semitic except you. How do I know? Why, here I am near the university, and many of the students who belong to the smaller Corporations having no quarters of their own rent rooms in this district. When they're Corporation students that means anti-Semitic, almost always. They're almost as bad as those loud-mouthed Nazis. I don't look like a Jewess ; I don't believe my roomers ever find out. But I don't like to talk to them.

"Things are bad enough now, but a year or two ago it was terrible. The Nationalists said the Jews had made the revolution, and had stabbed the army in the back. They killed

Rathenau because he was a Jew, and who knows how many others !

" But they took my son, my only boy ! He was good enough to fight for them, to die for them. We Jews never expect much of the Germans, but I did think that the Free German Youth would stand by him. They let him in even though he was a Jew—he was such a good boy. But when the war came there began to be more and more anti-Semites, and he soon found that the black-green-gold ribbon he wore in his tunic didn't mean much. He wrote home from the trenches to tell me how lonely he was ; only two or three Gentiles among all his Free German friends stood by him.

" I used to lie awake so long, so long. When it was cold, that last winter, when we had no fire, I used to think so much about him, for then he was buried out there in that cold, wet clay. But I mustn't talk about it.

" And he was such a good boy. Even though he belonged to the Free German Youth he always said that he liked his father and mother. And when he was littler, I never had to whip him after he learned to keep his clothes clean . . . Such a good boy . . .

" My man died three months after we heard the news. Nothing but that killed him, nothing . . .

" And then our government betrayed us ! That terrible inflation ! Everybody who bought war bonds lost nearly everything, and the money we saved dwindled away to nothing.

" Yes, my own people betrayed me too. Last summer I sold my house in the suburbs out here to a Jewish real estate dealer, and the money he gave me for it wouldn't buy a can of sardines to-day.

" I'm afraid about what will happen to us Jews. There are so many of us in the big cities—so many lawyers, so many physicians, so many merchants, so many money-lenders. Oh, I know that for every Jew who is shady in business you'll find twenty Gentiles ; after all, our rabbi says that the Jews in Germany make up less than one in a hundred of the whole people. That doesn't make any difference ; if it was only one in a thousand it would still be bad. A few dishonest Jews make everybody think that we're all like that. They're ready to believe the worst of us. I don't know how it will all end.

" I come of a very good family, but I now rent rooms. I used to have a servant to help me, a nice little girl who belonged to the Zionist youth and wanted to go to Palestine. Maybe she's there now in one of those collective settlements ; I hope so. I couldn't afford to keep her, but I do wish she would write me a post card now and then.

" Now I do all my own work. But Americans don't think any the less of people who work, do they ? So my man used to tell me. He was in the States for a long time, in San Francisco. He used to say, ' California, the most beautiful land in the world.' But I was afraid to cross the water."

X

" My dear fellow, of course I believe in the Republic ! All the really intelligent students are republicans, and there are more of them than you might think. In Berlin the reactionary student groups are able to stay in power only by voting as a unit whenever they are threatened, and also because we, foolishly enough, have all the factional weaknesses of our parliamentary democracy. By the way, I think that our constitution, with its proportional representation making dozens of little parties possible, has some grave defects. But we can probably afford them ; I'm an optimist. Why, at Heidelberg, at Bonn, at Freiburg, the students left the German Student Federation because its policy was nationalist, Pan-German, and anti-Semitic. Don't let yourself be fooled by this swank and display you see at university ceremonies, where the Corporation students, with their duelling swords and gay uniforms, make fools of themselves with their ritual.

" They are echoes of the older generation, especially of the nobility and the officers' caste, *plus* the sons of a few plushy industrialists, who have learned nothing and forgotten nothing. They're hopeless romanticists, living in an unreal past. They're dreaming of the day when a Kaiser-Messiah will return to place his benevolent (but firm) heel on the necks of the chattering parliamentarians. Their actual power dwindles from year to year ; the gorgeous picture of the old régime grows dim in the memory of the people. The really dangerous reactionaries are those folk nationalists that you find in Bavaria and other places where demagogues like Hitler are getting a hearing. No, no, the Corporation students are not to be feared, only to be opposed as long as necessary. The old ones will die off, and the young ones will cease to be active when they can't figure in university rituals. I'm an optimist.

" Speaking of rituals, I must say that I put the great majority of Lutheran pastors in the same class as the nobility and the officers' caste. Their power, happily, has been broken along with that of the others. When the State Church was disestablished by the Republic the trick was turned. But perhaps it really means a new spiritual life for Germany—dead formalism, at any rate, no longer brings financial or honorary rewards. I can't say that I like the Catholics much better, but I must nevertheless admit that a few of their priests refused to prattle about ' our good old German God ' and the rest of the Hurrah and Hallelujah. For a time, just after the Armistice, it looked as if the Quakers would win over quite a few members of the religious youth tutelage groups, and even more from the youth movement, but that wave soon died down. There is still some mystic pacifism, but I'm afraid that not many of us are likely to be Quakers.

" Our greatest problem, I think, is economic, not political or even religious. Reparations, trade barriers, short-sighted employers, class hatred—all the heads of the Hydra. There's beginning to be some talk about a United States of Europe, but if it merely means the safeguarding of the power of the cartels, the heads will grow again.

" The League ? That's a poser. I think that the majority of the people are distrustful, if not utterly sceptical, of its sincerity and workability. The present government, supported as it is by the Social Democrats, the Democrats, the Catholic Centre, takes a more friendly attitude toward it than the feeling of our most influential people warrants. The parties of the Right of course denounce the League as ' a tool of the victors ', and in justice to the Right we have to remember that the Upper Silesia matter was not altogether savoury, to say nothing of later occurrences.

" The work of individuals, rather than the League, may bring peace nearer. Clemenceau and Poincaré will certainly never have any friends in this country ; they'd eat German babies for breakfast if they had a chance. But there are other Frenchmen whom we would like to see in power—Briand, for example. If only the French hadn't occupied the Ruhr and sent in the Senegalese ! Of course I know that they don't draw the colour line in France. A Marseilles father of the lower classes would sooner see his daughter marry a good black Dahomey sergeant, for example, than a ne'er-do-well white private. We Germans, however, can't quite take that attitude ; they shouldn't have sent black troops among us. The occasional American Negro traveller and the way German girls flock around him? Oh, he has the value of rarity, the charm of the exotic; you surely don't think that's a representative situation? Getting back to the main point: There's more hatred of the French right now than there was in 1919. On the other hand, we have come to like the British quite well since the occupation; that ' God punish England ' and other *Lissauerei* has been pretty well forgotten.

" Some of our people regret that America did not enter the League at the very first; it might have saved it from futility. Certainly you didn't do much to help realize the Fourteen Points that Wilson preached to the world! Toward individual Americans, however, we have no hostility or even suspicion. We are sometimes amused by their naïveté, but at the same time we are often won over by their frankness and lack of prejudice. To be sure, those little tradesmen and jobbers who made Unter den Linden smell to heaven during the inflation perhaps were not, shall we say, admired? I'd hate to think that they really represent the ordinary American—but we have our own share of coarse-grained Philistines.

" Unfortunately, though, our German youngsters know only what they see. It's hard to maintain an attitude of friendship toward other countries when such poor samples are sent to us. I'm one of the leaders in the organization calling itself the Socialist Working Youth of Germany, and I tell you it's not easy to keep our boys and girls internationally minded.

" Not only is it natural to blame every country except Germany, but in addition we have to reckon with the alliance youth. They're likely to be much more nationalistic than we are, even though they disguise their nationalism in terms of ' folk community '. Because they are more directly descended from the pre-war youth movement, they exercise a lot of influence. For example, we sing many of their songs and dress in much the same way, and if it weren't for the fact that we vastly outnumber them (we're over eight hundred thousand strong), they'd take us over.

" Another big pull they have is that their leadership is considerably younger than ours. They have their ' eternal adolescents ', I'll grant, but we're far worse off. You see, we're really youth tutelage, and because of this, young leaders like myself have to knuckle under to the party officials. That wouldn't be too bad if it weren't for the fact that our party officials are probably the oldest in Germany. Many of them are carryovers from the struggle against Bismarck's anti-Socialist laws ; their heroism got them jobs in the party machine. They mean well, but they really represent an oligarchy of elders ; anybody under forty is thought to be insignificant. Unless we get some young blood at the top, our numbers won't save us.

" Oh, well, something will turn up ; I'm an optimist. When you go back to America, tell your comrades that they must have faith in us. The German Republic will survive, and with it the Social Democratic Party ; don't overrate these old-fashioned Monarchists and new-fashioned Nationalists. The day will come when our Social Democratic song will be realized : ' The international party will be the human race '."

XI

" How can you spot fellow-Americans so easily ? My German is pretty good, and I've got a youth movement rig on. Oh, the shell-rimmed glasses ! I suppose they do make me look like Harold Lloyd. And then you saw me with my coloured friend Harvey over there ; unless you mistook me for a French lieutenant in disguise, with his Senegalese orderly trailing along, you'd have to conclude that I was an American. Yes, those three girls belong to our outfit too. There are seven of us all told, and we're here to study the youth movement—National Student Forum, you know.

" I've been here for more than a year, but the others just came this summer. We've been roaming all over Germany, from the Baltic to Lake Constance, and with every youth group you could imagine—atheistic anarchists to pious Catholics. Why do I carry this heavy rucksack ? That's easy. Every blessed thing I've got is in it—clothes, food, books, diary, and all. It weighs about sixty pounds, but what else can you do ?

" What are you doing now ? Well, as long as you're just killing time until the next train, let's go on over to the café there and have a beer and a sandwich or two—I've got the bread and cheese in this big pocket on the outside of the rucksack.

" This beer is what they call ' upper fermentation ' ; it's a little bitter, but you'll like it. Say, would you be willing to listen to some fragments from this diary here ? I'd like to see how it strikes an American who hasn't been in touch with some of these things that are going on in Germany ; if I can hit the right note, I might be able to publish parts of it. Here is something I wrote

F

last winter when I was visiting a family in Solingen ; the mother of one of my friends is talking :

" Hans told me you would have to spend Christmas alone, so I said, ' Write to him, Hans, and ask him to come to us. We can share our Christmas with a stranger, surely.'

" So this is the first Christmas you've ever spent away from home ? How lonely your poor mother must feel, and you the only child ! I told Hans I could be mother to three boys this Christmas.

" Do they have Christmas like this in America ? Trees and andles and everything ？ So ？ Even in Chicago ？ With all those gangsters ?

" Take some of the cookies. That kind there, that's Speculatius. Yes, all those funny little fat men and dogs and kittens are made of Speculatius dough. I always make them for the children at Christmas. They're grown up now, but they like them just the same.

" Hans told me that you gave him a book about American students for Christmas. Do Americans like us any better than they did ? We must obey the government, after all. Hans tells me that the Frenchmen and the rest called us very bad names. I'm afraid some of our people called the others bad names, too.

" I don't know, I can't understand, why the dear God sends war. But if we only trust in Him, and do His will, and honour the Christ Child, everything will someday come right. When war comes, we must obey the government, even if we don't like it, mustn't we ? Saint Paul said that ' The powers that be are ordained of God ', and ' Whoso resisteth the power receiveth unto himself damnation '. Luther liked Saint Paul, too. And I've heard our Catholic neighbours say that the Pope talks much the same way. They're good simple Germans, but I can't see why they think so much of that Italian Pope. He says lots of other things that you can't find in the Holy Scriptures.

" So when you go back, you'll tell your friends that we're not wicked people, won't you ? It was very hard to know that everybody thought we were wicked and that we had to write it down in that nasty treaty. Our Kaiser was foolish, like a little boy with a tin sword, but he didn't want war—he only wanted to make a big noise. I know that none of our good people wanted war. I was so glad that Hans was too young to go ; when Paul came back he looked really dreadful. So thin ! And then all that winter, after we'd been misled by the Jews and Catholics into signing that nasty armistice, they kept food away from us. That's why our daughter's little girl waggles her head that way.

" Don't look so hard at Paul ; he's moody and thinks sometimes that people are spying on him. He used to belong to the Good Templars—that's a society for young people that keeps them away from alcohol—but now he drinks a little too much. Beer and wine are all right, but brandy burns your stomach.

" Hans, as you know, escaped all that ; and he belongs to the Kronacher Alliance. They're abstinent too, thank God, and although people say that they're just a branch of the Roamers, that isn't true any more. The Roamers may have been all right, but after the war they didn't try to forget about themselves and help the German folk.

"The Kronachers are really alliance youth; they are trying to build up a great folk community where all Germans will be brothers and sisters. And they don't run around in those queer costumes that the Roamers used to have, every one different. The Kronachers have nice uniforms. Maybe they're not exactly uniforms, but they're pretty much the same. Hans didn't want me to make his, but we couldn't afford to buy one in the store. I turned one of Father's old suits and dyed it, and with a little cutting and sewing I made a nice one.

"I'm glad, too, that the Kronachers are beginning to stop their mixed roaming. Boys and girls used to make long expeditions together, but now they stay separate except when they have singing evenings or something like that in the nest over there on Vorgebirg Street.

"Hans says that they're growing, too, but I can't believe that they have as many as two thousand. But that's what he says. If they keep on getting more members, and outsiders like you get a chance to see what good German youngsters they really are, it may help to make the world think more kindly of us. Germany's only hope is in her good young people. Old folks like Father and me make so many mistakes, and we're so easily confused . . .

"But when you go back you'll be sure to tell them that we're not wicked, won't you? That we just try to obey the government and trust in God?'"

"What do you think of that? Well, I know it's a little sentimental, but that's the way it struck me at the time. Maybe you'd like to hear something that just describes what happened instead of putting words in other people's mouths. Listen to this :

July 6. A group of students headed by Günther Keiser, a tall fair-haired chap with an eccentric leather vest, met us at the train. He is the leader of the Young Nordic Alliance, a group that is just starting but already has more than five hundred members. He had about a dozen other Germans with him. We were taken to a vegetarian restaurant, where we ate the most weird compounds imaginable, and met some very odd people. Immediately after the lunch we were rushed to a lecture on the political situation of Germany, given by a young professor from a folk high school somewhere near Hamburg. Then we were taken by subway to a wine or beer garden where we had coffee, marmalade, and bread and butter, and where discussion really broke loose. I discovered that what even the most liberal German youth think about the war and our part in it doesn't agree with anything I've read.

July 8. This morning we headed for Lüneberg, and after a

short ride got off the train about ten o'clock. We wandered through town looking for bread for the rest of the crowd, I with my big new rucksack on my back. We bought the bread, and then we and our German guides roamed—I see I'm beginning to talk that way too—out in the country to find the others ; they had gone ahead to find a suitable picnic place.

We had heard rumours that the Germans were going to pull their youth movement stunt of mixed nude bathing, and we were afraid the girls in our party would be drawn into it. I am not opposed to such bathing in principle, but in practice, in a strange country among strange people, it is a little apt to be disconcerting. We got there in time to find the group all ready for lunch, so we added our bread to their marmalade and fruit juice. The German youngsters were nude with the exception of a Turkish towel around the waist, and the girls, with the exception of our three, were in their underclothing. Our party seemed to be meeting the unusual situation with considerable calm and composure—in fact, more than I had expected from the girls. It turned out that they had already been swimming, nude, but with the sexes separated by some fifty yards. After lunch the Germans played ball with nothing but their birthday clothes on.

I can see and agree with the fundamental idea of all this, which is that morbid sex curiosity, smutty stories, obscene imaginings, and all the other train of sexual evils would be ended if people only saw each other as they really are, but I doubt if it could be put into general practice, at least in our own country. I went in swimming by myself, as I was a late comer.

Then there was a lecture about expressionistic art and afterwards more bathing and ball-playing in the nude. I made a remark that got a laugh out of Bob and Nancy, but which I feel was perhaps a trifle unkind : " These people seem to have an exposure complex." In spite of my so-called witticism what really struck me most was the very evident simplicity and naturalness of the whole affair.

On the way back I talked with Irma Hinnenthal about the matter ; I could understand her German and she my English. She said that for her part she thought that such practices were all right, but that she had to be very sure of the group she was in. I still think that it isn't very practicable, although it may be quite all right otherwise.

July 9. I bought a green sportshirt that I like very much ; I look like a youth mover in it. Slush ! This afternoon we tramped for about five miles to the youth hostel where we were to stay. A hurried dinner, some singing out of The Pluck by the Germans, and then to bed on some dingy straw ticks thrown on the floor.

July 10. An early start to the beach. One of our girls made a crude pair of swimming trunks for me out of the skirt of her bathing suit—that is, the outside skirt. I was in the water almost all morning, and after lunch I took a nap with a kettle over my head to shade my eyes. I woke up about an hour later with the nastiest case of sunburn a man ever had.

July 11. Started early in the morning for Hamburg. All of us felt weak and ill from the sunburn yesterday, and the insufficient food. I fainted for the first time in my life when we changed stations at Lübeck. As soon as I got to Hamburg I had a glass of beer and a couple of cheese sandwiches. How these Germans stand the undernourishment I don't know.

July 14. Here we are in Marburg. Harvey and I got up early to hear a theological lecture by the famous Rudolf Otto. He spoke so rapidly that I didn't get much out of it. In the afternoon we went to tea at his home, and in the course of the conversation I was amazed to discover how strong his anti-Semitic tendencies were. There was one German Jew in our party, and things got very uncomfortable. I'm sorry to see racial prejudice popping out in a man who is attempting to form a World League of Religions. This is to include Jews, Hindus, Buddhists, Mohammedans, and every other faith under the sun. Huh! Perhaps we misjudge him, however.

August 1. We went to a meeting at which the internal political situation of Germany was discussed, and were thoroughly nonplussed. The learned professor who led off read a paper of an hour-and-a-half's length, full of talk about the German Spirit and the leadership of Stefan George, but not a word of politics. After a little comment on the speech by the Scandinavians, Harry voiced the feeling of all the Americans when he said that he could not get the point of view at all. He said he wanted something concrete and practical, something that an American could bring home and put before his hearers in such a way that they could understand him.

At this point Babel broke loose. Poor Heinrich, who was chairman, could not control the meeting at all because of the lack of parliamentary rules—characteristic of the youth movement, I am told. Any donkey who thinks he has something important to bray about can grab the floor and hee-haw as long as he likes. Out of the whole mess one man emerged, a chap named Landsberger, who attempted to give us what we asked in the way of facts, but even he got so tangled up that he was finally forced to quit by his shouting opponents.

Such discourtesy and continual interruption I have never seen in my life before. The German impotence in politics is now explained, as far as I am concerned. They cannot hold their tempers or their tongues, and so accomplish nothing.

August 11. We arrived in Nürnberg yesterday, and there was nothing much doing this morning, so we slept late. In the afternoon there was great excitement, for a counter-demonstration against the nationalists was being planned by the Social Democratic youth, and it was thought that bloodshed might result. Max and Heinrich, who are back with us again, decided to go, and I went with them—the only American. The rest looked too foreign; they would be too easily spotted. The demonstration was a huge affair; about fifty thousand working youths from all parts of Germany, Austria, and the Tyrol were in line. Heinrich and I marched near the head of the column, but after a mile or two we dropped out to watch the rest go by and, incidentally, to keep an eye on some emergency police who were extreme National Socialists and who promised no good to the marchers. From time to time, a straggler from the column would fall foul of these chaps, who would then beat him up until the regular police slowly plodded up and stopped the amusement.

August 16. We got to Rothenburg in time for dinner, and got good clean rooms in one of the inns. Our party is having a lot of trouble, for the Germans have split into two factions. One is apparently composed of those who want to shove the girls off to one side, and the other continually mocks at what they call the " male harem ". I was a witness at the controversy between Ludwig, who headed up the exclusively male clique, and Heinrich, who stood for letting the girls take part in all our activities. Ludwig was positively disgusting ; his language outmatched anything I have ever heard in both violence and volume. Heinrich was quiet, but every reply he made was deadly—like a skilled swordsman against a club-wielder. I like Heinrich, but they all make me sick.

" Well ? So you think I'd have to revise this a lot before showing it to a publisher ? Maybe you're right, but so far as I know nothing of this kind has yet appeared in English. Oh, really ? Ye-es, I suppose it is a little naive, but I didn't think it was provincial or self-righteous. Perhaps I'd better give up the idea, and just write something based on the diary.

" Of course I can boil down what I've observed ! For example, it's pretty clear that the war has almost totally changed the character of the youth movement. The Free German Youth and all the others who suffered through trench life and the collapse of morale in 1918 have gone over almost entirely to an anti-individualistic position. To be sure, I suppose they never were completely individualistic, for the sense of fusion was strong even among the early Roamers, and after Hohe Meissner solidarity within the youth movement was pretty heavily stressed. Just the same, I think that until the World War the fusion and solidarity were valued chiefly because they helped to expand and deepen single personalities. I shouldn't say that everyone was gazing at his own navel, like a Hindu mystic, but there was a lot of self-worshipping. Nowadays that's beginning to be *passé* ; there's more and more of this alliance youth business. Sure, they talk about the sense of fusion, but now it means pretty close identification with the Germanic folk community as a whole ; they're trying to regenerate Germany instead of themselves.

" And it's pretty clear, too, that youth tutelage and youth movement are getting all mixed up. If you'll go among Lutheran or Catholic or Socialist or even Communist youth, you'll find that they all wear clothing which, although of increasingly

uniform-like character, still copies a good deal of the youth movement pattern.   And now with these hostels scattered every place,
everybody seems to be on the roam.   Why, in 1920, from everything that I've heard, I'll bet that there were more than three
million footloose youngsters, and right now, in 1924, there must
be two million or more buzzing and swarming around the country
like so many bees.   Over two-thirds of them probably belong to
church-sponsored groups or to one or another kind of political
auxiliary, but you'd never know it just to look at them.

"I've noticed, too, that the old practices of boys sticking
together on the one hand, and flocks of boys and girls roaming
far and wide in close-packed little clusters on the other, are both
getting less popular.   These alliance youth are beginning to join
up into exclusively boys' and exclusively girls' groups, with their
own separate leaders of their own sex.   When they do get
together, it is usually only at the nests or the hostels or these
infernal conventions they're always having ; when they're out
on the road they rarely see much of each other.

"Another funny thing : Have you noticed what a big bunch
of youth movers you'll find who are getting long in the tooth ?
I've seen men of thirty and more trying to cut folk-dance didoes
as though they were sixteen.   And the old maids !   They're the
people called ' eternal adolescents ' ; I don't know how on earth
they're ever going to find their way back into ordinary life.
Maybe papa and mamma will get tired of supporting them after
awhile, or maybe the police will force them to go to work.
I don't know much about this mind stuff, but I can't help feeling
that some of them are just teetering on the edge of nervous
breakdown.   After all, these people have got to get married
sometime, but they certainly do go in for indefinite postponement.

"It is true, though, that some of the younger fellows, like
Flueth of the Young Nordic Alliance, have lots of girl friends ;
somebody told me that Flueth was hooked up with about four
and that there had been several children.   Most of that, though,
you'll find among the ' youth culture ' crowd who come from the
biggest cities.   The small-towners are pretty much devoted to the
customary moral standards.

"What really bothers me is the way politics is dominating
both youth tutelage and youth movement.   Even when the
Social Democrats or the German Nationalists haven't actually
lined them up as members of their parties, the youngsters split
up along party lines.   And when they get to arguing they can't

seem to stick to the main points ; first thing you know they get all mixed up and ready to fight. True enough : you don't expect the Communists or the Hitler Youth (that's a little bunch that goes under other names now because their idol is in prison) to do anything but break each other's heads. Most of the others, however, are showing the same signs. Those who don't, go and hide out in country settlements or get shot full of religious mysticism. Yes, I know that you'll find quite a few pacifists here and there, but when the Communists, for example, are yelling ' No more war ' all they mean is no more international war. A good rousing fight between classes would suit their taste exactly if their leaders would let them turn loose.

" I must say, though, that the youth movement music and art is sort of attractive. It's a little feverish, but just the same it has its good points. What I like most about it is that almost everybody uses whatever talent he has, no matter how little. There's what you'd call a general creativeness, I suppose ; when you contrast that with the flat, cheap, commercialized stuff that we soak up in the United States, the youth movement looks pretty good.

" After all, though, I don't think that anybody should try to transplant the German youth movement to the American scene. It probably wouldn't take root anyway ; what could you do if you translated The Pluck and imported a batch of lutes ? You'd just be a laughing-stock. And suppose the music or something else did catch on ? I'd hate to think that along with it there might come a flock of these other features of the youth movement that couldn't help but be damaging to us. We certainly have our faults, but I don't know that I would trade a happy-go-lucky American youngster, with all his bad taste and unwillingness to think, for one of these high-geared youth movers. Perhaps I set too much value on just getting along in life, but I know mighty well that this German youth movement is headed for the rocks somehow. If the members don't go crazy singly, they'll go crazy as a mob.

" So that's what I ought to write about ? All right, maybe I will—if I can't find a kinder critic of this other stuff than you seem to be. You know I'm only kidding ; let's pay the waiter and get started. Your train is due in ten minutes."

XII

" German university professors have always had attentive audiences outside the classroom, I suppose. Yes, there were

Treitschke, Wagner, the Weber brothers, and many more. In spite of that, I do think that since the collapse of our old political leadership we have received much more attention. The middle classes, at least, don't have much confidence in the politicians of the Weimar Republic, and they turn to us instead.

" Even the alliance youth, all the way from groups that are almost indistinguishable from the Roamers to those *Artamanen* who want to make Germany over into a folk community of completely peasant character, call in professors to talk to them. It may not be very good for the professors to be cast in the roles of youth advisers and leaders, I sometimes think ; they get into the habit of preaching in almost revivalistic fashion. At the same time, there is a lot of discussion or even the preaching of contradictory gospels by the youngsters ; the professors don't perpetually have things their own way.

" Occasionally their influence on the more romantic alliance youth and the more restive protégés of youth tutelage is healthy. Why ? Oh, most of the professors are sceptical about the possibility of creating a new world in which all the ideals of youth will find fruition. Thus they counteract the tendency to withdraw and set up little settlements pervaded by religious communism, as well as the notion that a German folk community, mentally and socially isolated from the rest of the world, can have any hopeful prospects.

" I once heard a colleague of mine, Paul Honigsheim, tell a tumultuous crowd of boys and girls that what they really ought to try to do was to carry the spirit of the youth movement into all walks of life, to be ' the little leaven that leaveneth the whole lump '. What ? Certainly his interpretation of the spirit of the youth movement is open to question. Honigsheim seems to think that the sense of fusion, the Hohe Meissner conception of youth's mission, and longing for a Germanic folk community come to the same thing as the mutual aid that Kropotkin talked about. It's possible, of course ; but for my own part I think that not more than two or three out of every hundred of our youngsters extend the idea of mutual aid beyond their own class, or at the most, any farther than their German nationalism will carry them. The few who do try to leaven the social lump and practise all-inclusive mutual aid have a hard time ; their fellows, for the most part, don't understand them, and the adult world is hard and unyielding almost everywhere.

" Did you ever hear about Otto Zirker ? There's an instance

of the kind I'm talking about. He was a brilliant young Jew, so thoroughly identified with the idealistic elements in German culture that he was more essentially German than most of his ' Aryan ' associates. I imagine that is why Honigsheim, who is not a Jew, admired him so much. Moreover, Zirker didn't fit the ordinary German ideas of what a Jew is like ; he was slim and rather tall, and his dark hair and eyes weren't particularly different from what you'll find all through the Rhineland and southwest Germany. I suppose, though, his extreme sensitivity and his consuming ambition reflected his Jewish social heritage ; he was keenly aware of the discrimination which virtually all Jews suffered in Germany—and in the United States too, I'm told ! —and he knew that any Jew has to be about three times as good as his ordinary Gentile competitor if he is to achieve distinction.

" He came under the influence of the League for Basic School Reform in which Paul Oestreich and Honigsheim were active. They wanted to get more freedom into our system of public instruction without getting mixed up with that rot of Wyneken's. Zirker, among others, got the idea that these educational reforms could be carried over into the rehabilitation of juvenile delinquents, and he decided to prepare himself to be a pioneer in the field.

" You see, his mutual aid enthusiasms derived only in part from the alliance youth—how could it be otherwise ? The decisive influence, I think, was his devotion to Dostoievsky. Don't raise your eyebrows ; in this post-war turmoil ' The House of the Dead ', ' Crime and Punishment ', and ' The Possessed ' have been avidly read and accepted as revealed truth by many persons, young and old, who are troubled by our harsh treatment of social outcasts. Zirker thought that he could combine the Dostoievskian gospel with mutual aid ideas ; if all men are brothers, exalted and lowly alike, they ought to help each other in prison or out.

" Otto worked like a Trojan, graduated from the university with high honours, and then went to that Home of Adult Education at Dreiszigacker bei Meiningen. There, as you may perhaps know, factory workers go for vacation courses ; most of them are six weeks or three months long, but many week-end arrangements also are made. Zirker learned to talk the workers' language, as you Americans say, and he got excellent results as teacher—after he had gone through one of the three-month courses they promptly assigned him teaching duties.

" The future looked bright, and when he got a call to take charge of the educational programme in the Eisenach Reformatory—Eisenach is in Thuringia, and was the birthplace of Luther and Bach—everyone thought that the ideology of mutual aid would win a great victory. But Zirker, as I have said, was highly sensitive and impressionable, and he soon became profoundly depressed by the difficulties confronting him.

" Not only were the older reformatory officials highly sceptical and even antagonistic, but the boys and young men in his charge perpetually disappointed his hopes. His notions of what delinquents and criminals were really like were far from ' realistic ' ; his absorption of Dostoievsky had led to so much idealization that the contrast became harder and harder to endure. And yet everyone, except for some of his more critical superiors, felt that he was doing remarkably effective · work, considering the handicaps under which he necessarily operated ; his self-torture and steadily deepening pessimism weren't at all warranted.

" Then came the final act of the tragedy ! A suspicious official discovered that Zirker, moved no doubt by his reforming zeal as well as by his compensatory ambition, had falsified his age in order to be eligible for the Eisenach post. He was called in and told that there was no major fault to find with his efforts as educator, but that under the circumstances his resignation would have to be tendered. Some people who were incensed about the affair have harshly criticized the officials, but given the mentality of the ordinary German bureaucrat it is my opinion that it was all one could expect. In fact, much harsher measures were possible, and Zirker was even told that no obstacle would be placed in his path if he tried to find a position for which his age made him eligible.

" The combination of disillusionment and detected deception, alas, was overpowering ; just six months ago, at the age of twenty-five, Otto Zirker committed suicide.

" Maybe I shouldn't have told you all this, for it is my firm conviction that Zirker's fate in no way reflects on his teachers or on the ideals of mutual aid. I fervently hope that more and more of our romantic youth movers will go into adult education, psychiatry, the training of the mentally deficient, and social pedagogy. If they do—and some have already done so—something worthwhile may come out of this frenzied chaos in which we now live.

" If the youth movement remains apart from ordinary

German life, or if it succumbs to the demagogues who conjure up visions of a new world in which all Germans will fall on each others' necks in brotherly love and at the same time hate everybody outside their sacred fraternity, I haven't much hope for us.

" We need thousands of young men like Zirker, but they'll have to be made of sterner stuff."

XIII

School is out. Here they come, with their book-satchels on their backs, knapsack fashion, marching and singing. Some a little ragged, some a little pale, some with fanatical devotion in their eyes, all clean and neat. Six-year-olds, eight-year-olds.

Everywhere, everywhere, these little Hänsels and Gretels.

The World War ended in 1918—six years ago. How many centuries from the Biedermeier time ? How much " progress " ?

Struggle ; bitter, grinding struggle. Poverty. Twisted, contorted offshoots of The Linden Tree. Shouts of " Germany, awake ". Pied Pipers with promises of a world where all dreams come true. Myths of regeneration ; myths of hatred ; myths of self-sacrifice ; myths of revenge.

The good will in man. Is it real ? Will it flicker out ?

What lies ahead of these children ? Of the children they have been taught to love, of the children they have learned to despise?

More of those shiny granite monuments ? Everywhere ?

NOTES

As in the case of Chapter I, detailed notes for this chapter would be absurd. It is only fair to the reader, however, to give some indication of the sources from which these impressions and personality sketches have been derived.

In the Preface, I mentioned the fact that I participated, in a sense, in several branches of the youth movement during part of 1923, the inflation year, and also that I thereafter returned to Germany on several occasions enabling renewed observation. In 1923 I kept a diary which probably runs to well over fifty thousand words, and on my return became editor of what was fondly thought to be an American youth movement periodical, *The Student Challenge*. This publication experienced a not altogether untimely death in the summer of 1925, but not before a considerable amount of material bearing on the German youth movement had appeared. Naturally, I was also in close touch with *The New Student*, organ of the National Student Forum—which was the organization financing the 1923 expedition.

My German sojourn in 1926-7 was not primarily for the study of the youth movement, but I renewed a few of the earlier associations, talked with many youth tutelage officials (a group previously overlooked), and gathered a few of the rarer items from the flood of youth movement literature. In 1934-5, from various points in France and Belgium where I was carrying on research, I made five separate trips into Germany and again saw a good deal of the youth movement, this time in the period of transition from the voluntary to the compulsory stage.

Consequently, the sources of this chapter are first-hand. For the personalities sketched, with but two exceptions, specific individuals whom I knew directly provide the basis. I do not wish to deny that there has been some alteration of dates (1924 instead of 1923 and 1926-7, in particular) and sequence of events, the telescoping of many episodes into one, and other "fictionizing"—nevertheless, there is no "pure fiction" anywhere in the chapter. Everything said in the long note at the end of Chapter I is relevant here. In the case of the exceptions to the "specific individuals" basis mentioned above, namely, the priest in charge of a group of Catholic youngsters and the Dostoievskian reformatory worker, my information is in a sense secondary. I had close contact only with lay Catholic youth leaders and with a friend and teacher of the unfortunate Zirker.

It might also be noted that my diary and several other documents were read, within a short time after being written, by youth movement members, and inaccuracies corrected. Further, the chapter as it now stands has been thoroughly analysed by a refugee scholar, here nameless, who was himself active as a leader of youth activities and who has written extensively on these and related topics.

The reader can therefore be reasonably certain that in spite of the form of presentation no liberties have been taken with essential truth—at least, truth as I then saw it and, with minor qualifications, as I still see it.

CHAPTER VII

CUNNING : THE ACCOMPLISHMENT OF PERVERSION

> Tongue, you are a tongue of fire,
> Shrivelling like a white-hot wire,
> Blackening like a dragon's breath
> Flower-fluttering fields with death.
>
> Tongue, you are a tongue of brass
> In the jawbone of an ass,
> Slaying what was most divine—
> Not the reeking Philistine.
>
> —BENET, " Brazen Tongue ".

" Nothing Sacred " was a first-rate motion-picture title in the sense that it appealed to the American sophisticates of the late 'thirties. The picture itself, however, was not altogether palatable to the devotees of the brave new world, for it discreetly pointed out one very important truth : namely, that it is impossible to maintain stable personalities or a coherent society unless there is *something* sacred.

This sounds like hard doctrine, and perhaps it is, but it need not carry all the customary implications with which the word " sacred " is freighted. Most Western Europeans and Americans identify the sacred with the supernatural ; they think that always and everywhere awe, reverence, and sacrificial devotion are inseparably linked with divine blessing.[1]

Witness : When the Puritans relaxed a little in their task of wiping out the practitioners of " ye beastlie customes of ye heathene ", a few missionaries tried to save Indian souls from the grasp of Satan. Some of the kindlier preachers of the Gospel made inquiry about what their prospective converts already believed. This proved hard to discover, for " belief " presupposes a kind of religion bearing strong resemblance to something like the Christian faith, and in particular to Protestantism. What is done rather than what is said, ritual rather than creed, is frequently far more important.

Hot on the trail of belief, these missionaries found words in the various Indian vocabularies that seemed to point to a God who, although not the Jehovah of the Scriptures, nevertheless had the attributes of personality. Among these words *manitou* was rapidly singled out and embellished with a capital M. The rest was easy ; Manitou became the Great Spirit. With supposedly natural theism of this sort already in existence, it was thought that the missionary need only cast out the old god and replace him with the Three in One, the One in Three. But conversion did not come as rapidly as was hoped, and the missionaries decided, with reluctance or with grim determination, that Manitou was that old Satan who goeth about seeking whom he may devour.

The Indians were puzzled and astonished by all of this, for to them *manitou* was not a person, benevolent, fiendish, or otherwise. When a medicine man proclaimed " Me got plenty *manitou* ", he oftentimes made his assertion graphic by clutching his belly. Why ? Because *manitou* was nothing more than extraordinary power, force, stuff. It could be concentrated or diffused, transmitted to others or retained for private use, localized in rocks or embodied in persons. The medicine man's world was not split in two parts, one natural and the other supernatural ; *manitou* was simply concentrated nature, so to speak, or nature in its more unusual manifestations. In short, although the awe evoked by demonstrated capacity to manipulate *manitou* was definitely tinged with what may be provisionally termed sacred emotion, nothing remotely akin to our notions of the supernatural was involved.[2]

It is entirely possible, therefore, to have a value-system of sacred character without theism, without a reference to a personal God. The parallel with *charisma* is not far to seek ; the leadership principle is definitely coloured by the sacred, but it is not necessarily supernaturalistic. Instead, naturalism and this-worldliness may rule.

Moreover, the emotions roughly designated as sacred in their bearing are not called forth by charismatic manifestations alone. Indeed, if this were a place for certain finer distinctions essential in some contexts, " holy " might be substituted for " sacred " in what has been said thus far with little basic change in the analysis. Disregarding this, however, it is fair to say that another part of the sacred is contributed by the emotional halo surrounding the old, the familiar, the intimate. Said Schiller :

> For of the wholly common is man made,
>   And custom is his nurse ! Woe then to them
> That lay irreverent hands upon his old
>   House furniture, the dear inheritance
> From his forefathers ! For time consecrates ;
>   And what is grey with age becomes the sacred.

Illustrations in "Pluck-Fiddle Jack" for sacred songs of originally theistic character, radically changed in significance because of inclusion in a non-theistic value-system.

Still more : All peoples with limited horizons believe that they live in the One Blessed Country and represent the Chosen People ; the aura of naïve conceit fringes the native land, tongue, and race. Exhibits : " Among flowers the cherry-blossom ; among men the Samurai " ; " The difference between Arabs and Persians is the same as that between a date and its stone " ; " The Italian is wise when he undertakes a thing, the German while he is doing it, and the Frenchman when it is over " ; " The Englishman bawls, the Irishman sleeps, but the Scotsman goes till he gets it ". When the impious stranger—impious because strange—challenges these attitudes by word or deed, feelings of uneasiness, distrust, and outrage are stirred up which represent the other side of the sacred shield.[3]

Enough : German youth activities of the sort I have been describing, with few exceptions, were at bottom random, " goalless ", but persistent attempts to replace the crumbled valuesystem of Rimmon's House with another which would in some way focus the longing for sacred experience. At first, it will be recalled, self-expansion and the sense of fusion with the likeminded seemed sufficient ; after the shattering impact of the First World War the folk community came more and more to represent the one thing needful.

Alliance youth groups afford the clearest example of this search for a new value-system, although many of the youth tutelage organizations, likewise remoulded in the crucible of the World War and its aftermath, took similar form. Leadership principle, yes ; self-realization, yes ; sense of fusion, yes ; ardent desire for a new way of life, yes—but all inseparably bonded and fundamentally transmuted in the service of the folk community, in the creed and practice of a new this-worldly religion.

Religion ? Of course. Any value-system for the sake of which its devotees sacrificially live and gladly die is a religion, regardless of whether or not it has a god in the traditional sense. Granting that Hitler is the earthly god of the Nazis, it is nevertheless true that he achieved his quasi-divine position only because he visibly and tangibly embodied values which German youth had long been learning to hold dear. I am not saying that any other fanatical leader emerging in the Tumult of the 'Twenties would have achieved the same results ; there were probably several alternative possibilities of development. Nevertheless, I should regard it as highly likely that any of these alternatives would have had to sluice most of the longings of the new religion into channels leading to an outlet. Permanent damming up of the faith that had found such manifold and clamorous expression would have been impossible.

The religion sought the prophet, and he then became its god. Once godhead had been accomplished, the alternatives that once existed were wiped out. From that time on the line between heresy and saving belief could be sharply drawn. The only problem for the priests of the new religion was the defining of the creed and the standardizing of its ritual so that the greatest possible number of adherents could be gained and the dissenters cast into outer darkness.

Now, repellent though many of the features of the alliance youth and their " tag-along " associates unquestionably were, it is barely possible that developments might have taken place which the rest of the Western World would have been willing to call good had it not been for the perversion accomplished by the Hitlerian priests. Perversion is a word of many meanings ; it is used here in a sense familiar to most social scientists :

> The [planful] substitution of goals other than those proper to particular . . . [social groupings] and their derivative institutions and functionaries is denoted. This should not be confused with the changes brought about by unforeseen consequences of apparently trivial actions ; such consequences may entirely divert the . . . [social grouping] from its original goal, but genuine perversion does not take place, inasmuch as only the *intentional* substitution of other goals falls under the latter head.[4]

The ideologists and propagandists in the tow of Hitler skilfully perverted the new religion of German youth in ways which eventually led them to rush, like the Gadarene swine, down a steep place into the sea. Thorough regimentation, militarization, and enthusiastic support of and participation in the Second World War represent that rush.

To see clearly how these things came about, it is now necessary to trace the growth of the Hitler Youth in some detail.

Even as early as 1923, the available wisps of information make it seem altogether probable that little bands of Hitler enthusiasts as yet out of close touch with the then inchoate Party had begun to take shape. Further, it can be definitely shown that a Nazi youth group, disguised as a harmless roaming alliance, did extensive organizing and propaganda work for the Party in the region known as the Vogtland (Saxony near Silesia) during 1923. In a short time the disguise was dropped, and the Nazis proclaimed the establishment, pretentiously enough, of the Greater German Youth Movement.   No sooner was this done, early in 1924, than the ranks were swelled by the entry of various other youth groups who found the Hitlerian programme attractive.[5]   At a party convention in Jocketa in the summer of 1924, funds were appropriated for an intensive propaganda campaign, and by the end of that year Nazi youth groups were shooting up throughout the region centring around Upper Saxony.[6]

The most effective leader in this area seems to have been Kurt Gruber, a seasoned Nazi veteran.   He gathered about him so many fiery-eyed youngsters who zealously fought for the Party that in 1926 Gruber, following a hint from Julius Streicher, was able to persuade Hitler that the time was ripe for the official recognition of the Hitler Youth, long active under that and other names.   With impressive fanfare, Hitler announced the creation of this Party auxiliary at the 1926 Weimar convention, and proclaimed Gruber as his youth deputy.

Thus blessed and headed, the organization spread like wildfire. The brown-shirted, swastika-waving patrols burned consumingly among the youth of both the alliances and tutelage organizations. Soon the movement was banned in several regions, but the threat of persecution and martyrdom only added fuel to the flames.   In 1929 Gruber marched at the head of more than two thousand Hitler Youth at the Nazi convention, and these represented less than a tenth of those actually enrolled.[7]   Moreover, only boys and girls from ten to eighteen were counted, whereas many youth tutelage organizations ran the age of their " youth " up to twenty-five and the alliance youth took in numerous eternal adolescents.

What accounts for this amazing upswing in the face of the most intense competition ?

First, alliance youth, to say nothing of youth tutelage, had begun to sink into the ruts of routine as early as 1920.   The social methods and instruments, i.e. roaming and all that went with it, had lost the charm of novelty ; everybody knew what to expect from the expedition, the camp, and the nest.   Further, the ways in which social objects, expected responses, and reflected selves were defined had become relatively standard.   They were still strongly tinged with irrationalism, but it is a little hard to feel elation at its fullest intensity when thousands of others have undergone the same experience and have told all about it to everyone willing to lend an ear.   In other words, the esoteric, highly intimate aspects of youth movement life were flooded by the light of common day ; revelations supposedly undreamed of were described in advance with guidebook thoroughness ; and the mood of " Is that all ? " became harder and harder to down.[8]

Second, charismatic leadership itself, at first highly spontaneous and unpredictable, grew increasingly matter-of-fact and even traditional. Youngsters learned to distinguish between types of charismatic leaders ; the youth magazines were full of descriptions of this or that kind of extraordinary personality which, by being thus ticketed, began to recede toward ordinariness.[9] Boys and girls supposedly possessing one or another of the combinations of classifiable traits were expected to become leaders whether they themselves were initially convinced of their " call " or not. Once stamped with the mark of " potential leader ", the ineluctable result ensued : " calls " were felt with ever-increasing frequency. Leaders, good, bad, and indifferent, appeared on every hand, and the followers of the mediocre or positively incompetent began to long for some overwhelmingly impressive Führer.

Third, the extent to which youth tutelage had taken on the external traits of the youth movement had damaging effects on both. Youngsters who, if they had been born ten years earlier, would have been active participants in the Free German Youth, expected far more of the youth tutelage into which they drifted than the imitation of surface similarities could possibly vouchsafe. Those who joined the post-war successors or survivals of the earlier sects, on the other hand, could not avoid disappointment ; the glorious days of pioneering were over, and flatly conventional youth tutelage was a nextdoor neighbour instead of a foe. Rimmon's House seemed well on the way towards being rebuilt.

In a sense that is more than analogical, then, the erstwhile sects were taking on the traits of denominations :

Denominations are simply sects in an advanced stage of development and adjustment to each other and the secular world. The early fervour of the self-conscious sect has disappeared, as a general thing, by the second or third generation, and the problem of training the children of the believers almost inevitably causes some compromise to be made in the rigid requirements for membership characteristic of the early phases of sectarian development. Thus, for example, the Presbyterians inaugurated the Half-Way Covenant in order that children whose " calling and election " was not yet sure could be held within the fold, with the consequence that in time the greater proportion of professing Presbyterians were those who had gone no further than the Half-Way Covenant. Similarly, the Baptists have gradually lowered the age of " adult baptism " so that at the present time, in some branches of the denomination, it is possible for children only twelve years old to be baptized.[10] . . . [In the same way,] with the aid of the prosperity prevailing in the days of good Queen Anne, middle-class tendencies [, replacing the aggressively espoused poverty of George Fox,] were introduced [among the Quakers], and eventually the earlier origins of . . . [the sect] were almost lost from view. It continued formally to hold the tenets of its social programme, but they were pruned and pared to fit a . . . [conformist] denomination rather than a radical sect aiming at complete social reconstruction. This was especially evident in America.[11] . . . Similar instances can be gleaned from the history of almost any sect one cares to name ; age inevitably brings [the denominational] compromise.[12]

Fourth, many of the fragments deriving from the Roamers, and the alliance youth in addition, began to pay considerable heed to expediency, to calculation, to planning. Confronted by the competition of youth tutelage (particularly various political auxiliaries), membership in the " youth for youth's sake " bodies failed to increase as rapidly as was hoped. In the struggle to maintain themselves, they therefore began to set up bureaucracies of their own.

These centralized and routinized office staffs usually drew their personnel (1) from among well-disposed elders who while youngsters had never been actively functioning members of genuine youth groups, or, more frequently, (2) from the ranks of youth movers who had begun to pass out of active participation because of age.

In all too many cases these ageing " youths " were of that personality type several times referred to as the eternal adolescent. Unstable of purpose, diffusely emotional, dogmatically idealistic, intellectually fuzzy, and erotically fixated on leaders or followers, they found the gates of the adult world too high to scale or too forbidding to enter. Compelled to eke out a livelihood in one way or another—for even when the inflation of 1923 had not wiped out the surplus funds of middle-class families to which they so predominantly belonged, parents sometimes tried to force their errant children to cease being " youthful " by withholding the monthly remittance—they came to form a sizable proportion of the officials upon whom the presumably " spontaneous " youth groupings eventually became utterly dependent.

For a time, to be sure, things went fairly well. New organizations with the prestige of old names behind them kept halting pace with the rapidly expanding political branches of youth tutelage. Moreover, they were instrumental in getting favourable legislation passed, in establishing new hostels and linking up hostel chains, and in regulating and administering youth affairs in efficient bureaucratic fashion.[13]

As might be expected, however, the needs of the central organization soon came to seem more important than the preservation of those youth movement practices which had become traditional. *Ergo*, measures were often adopted which ran directly counter to the best interests of " youth for youth's sake " or even of " youth for the sake of the folk community " ; " youth for the officials' sake " became the unadmitted but nonetheless effective maxim.

Fifth, the very efficiency with which the " youth for the officials' sake " organizations secured governmental support for hostel chains, to take only one striking example, helped their opponents greatly. These opponents, notably the Hitler Youth, hated the youth denominations and youth tutelage, to say nothing of the Weimar Republic from which aid had been secured, but they nevertheless made use of the hostels for their own ends. And well they might ; the hostels were ideal centres from which systematic propaganda could be conducted among the youngsters who were becoming increasingly dissatisfied with the standardization that had been introduced.

Sixth, standardization hurt the denominations greatly because many forceful and thoughtful boys and girls who might well have become Roamers of original vintage, had they been born in the 'eighties, remained aloof from movements which had begun to show signs of middle age. Even if such youngsters did find their way into the denominations they oftentimes quietly withdrew, forming little clusters of their own. Such withdrawal and reconsolidation was especially evident after 1927, and might have resulted in a revival of the earlier cults, conventicles, and sects. As it was, however, events were moving too rapidly ; the expansion of the Hitler Youth began to overshadow all other developments. The little secessionist bodies remained too small to find their way into the official handbooks and directories— one of which, incidentally, had swollen to nearly five hundred pages by 1931—before they were swallowed up in the maw of the Nazi Behemoth.

Seventh, and finally, routinization, type-casting of charismatic roles, imitation by and of youth tutelage with ensuing denominational adjustment, official expediency for officialdom's benefit, capture of propaganda centres, and quiet withdrawal of the élite acted concertedly to generate the " *charisma* of office ". That is to say, " pure " *charisma* arising from overwhelmingly impressive, extraordinary personalities became increasingly rare ; instead, *charisma* presumably transmitted in appropriate official ways was the general rule.[14]

Parallel : Jesus, Paul, and the other founders of Christianity were altogether extraordinary men ; their disciples and converts followed persons rather than rules and doctrines. Eventually, as the Christian sects stabilized, and particularly when the great State Church or ecclesia was established under Constantine, *charisma* came to be more and more a matter of faithful service to the communion of the saints, the passing of standardized doctrinal tests, the laying on of hands, and the donning of ecclesiastical vestments.

The ultimate outcome was the appearance of the Papacy. The Pope, however an extraordinary personality he may be in certain historical instances, does not owe his position, as the topmost pinnacle in the pyramid from which divine grace flows downward, to his own extraordinary attributes. Instead, he is elected by the College of Cardinals through a carefully devised system of balloting. There are always several candidates for the exalted office, and as the voting goes on the results are known to the assembled cardinals only ; an elaborate ceremonial of ballot-burning is part of the routine. When, after the various "favourite sons " have been successively eliminated, only one candidate remains, the result is necessarily unanimous, and a new Pope is announced to the world. Thereafter he possesses, to the fullest extent, the *charisma* of office ; during his lifetime all other ecclesiastical *charisma* flows through him as the sole earthly source of the divinely imparted " power to bind and to loose ".

The various sects of the old youth movement, it must be granted, had not yet become mere parts of a great ecclesia. They were simply denominations throughout the 'twenties. At the same time, it seems clear that denominational *charisma* of office did frequently manifest itself, and in many instances the result was a slackening of aggressiveness, compelling fervour, and follower-holding magnetism. The glorious days of the early Roamers and the youth of Hohe Meissner called forth the " longing for things past " in the precise degree to which they receded into the haze of romantic tradition. Hundreds of

Horst Wessel as the ideal young Nazi.

thousands of followers were hungering for the opportunity to chant with the passionate intensity once called forth by Karl Fischer, "Leader, we follow thee and shout 'Yea!'" But among the denominations there was no Karl Fischer, nor any place for his like.

Yet . . . yet was there not an altogether extraordinary man named Adolf Hitler whose followers, for all their brutality, vulgarity, and downright ignorance, were challenging a presumably " effete " social order?

Questions like this ran through the minds of many young Germans, and although by far the greater number were unable to overcome the revulsion which the first shock of contact with the Hitler Youth produced, they were nevertheless rendered hesitant, or even became disquieted and fascinated. Failing to act vigorously in opposition, they thereby made it possible for the Leader to be heard more widely than ever.

The *Führerprinzip*, the leadership principle! Was this anything more than the homage which genuine *charisma* should receive? Doubt, confusion, passive waiting for ever newer, more startling manifestations of " the wave of the future " . . .

What a chance for the skilled perverter! Hitler, Goebbels, Rosenberg, *et al.* seized time by the forelock, and exploited the existing attitudes of youth movement and youth tutelage so cleverly that by 1933 determined, fight-it-out opposition was to be found only among the Communist youth and scattered handfuls of Lutherans and Catholics. The objects and methods of perversion were simple but potent; as they pass in review they fall in divisions which must now be inspected in detail.

It is already apparent that the perversion of the leadership principle was fairly easy. German youth had become more and more accustomed to the *charisma* of office, a capacity which Hitler, as head of the Nazi Party, automatically acquired. Joined to this, of course, was the undeniable extraordinariness or even uncanniness of the man himself: apparent readiness to be a martyr for the sake of his cause, oratorical skill astounding and fascinating to a politically untrained people, obvious power to evoke unquestioning loyalty from his intimates, and so on. Confronted by mediocre *charisma* of office devoid of personal *charisma*, on the one hand, and *charisma* of office infused with personal *charisma* on the other, it was a simple matter for the propagandist to exalt Hitler and abase his feeble competitors.

Closely linked with this was the example of asceticism. Scores of alliance youth groups, to say nothing of youth tutelage, had adopted a "life reform" programme of vegetarianism, anti-alcohol, and anti-tobacco.[15] Hitler himself was a total abstainer in these regards, and his propagandists saw to it that everyone was duly impressed.

Similarly, Hitler's apparent immunity to the compulsions of sex provided an example which helped thousands of youth movement neurotics and eternal adolescents to rationalize their impotence or continuing masturbation. Even the rumours of Hitler's homosexuality—rumours probably unverifiable in his own case but well attested where Roehm and many other intimates are concerned—were not necessarily harmful. Beyond doubt thousands of lads, many of them grown to maturity by the late 'twenties, had passed through homosexual episodes or had continued in their abnormality. What better self-justification than the Supreme Leader could be found?

A closely related vein : "The beautiful Adolf" was a watchword among German girls and women. This may seem incredible, but the evidence is there. The decimation of German men in World War I, plus the class and caste stratification of German society, had led to a situation in which daughters of German professional men, let us say, had the choice either of marrying men far older or much lower in status, or of resigning themselves to spinsterhood. Analysis of the vote polled by the Party plainly shows that middle-class girls and women flocked to Hitler's banner in droves. And youth alliance groups, in particular, were prevailingly middle-class ! The *jugendbewegt* old maids and girls who saw their chances of happy marriage steadily diminishing found a dream hero in a man differing considerably from ordinary, pudgy, closecropped, beer-dulled German males : he had a full head of hair, a reasonably slim figure, flashing eyes, and an enthralling moustache !

Anti-Semitism likewise was capable of ready perversion. Among the Free German Youth and their successors it did not become explicit until well along in the World War, but once it had been brought into the open it harmonized excellently with youth movement ideals. The Jews had never been Linden Tree peasants, roving journeymen, wandering scholars, knights-errant, or effervescent *Burschenschaft* patriots in numbers at all significant. They were identified with mechanistic science, economic rationalism, detached internationalism, and metropolitan culture—all of them anathema to the youth movement. All of these anathema-

" Life Reform " Appeals.

tized traits and many more were present among and utilized by the Nazis, but they were cleverly concealed by Goebbels and his like. To cap it all, even the ascetic features of youth life were dexterously linked with anti-Semitism. Exhibit :

The Jew knows very well how he can harm the German people. In open battle he is beaten by the German, because the latter is by nature warlike and soldierly, and is a really stout fellow, a *man*. . . . Exactly this factor is cleverly taken advantage of by the Jew, who persistently, through propaganda and influence on the customs of society, emphasizes the idea that " To be a man and a good fellow means to be able to drink a lot and smoke a lot " . . . the German people fall for this Jewish swindle with open eyes, . . . and the Jew laughs uproariously as he for the first time brings to the ground the race which through its strength and health is so dangerous to the Jews. . . . It is no accident that the entire cigarette industry is controlled by Jewish capital.[16]

Anything " anti " is almost necessarily tied up with something " pro ". The zeal for those of one's own kind, justifiable enough in any people as long as it does not lend itself to arrogance and the use of violence, was a well-marked characteristic of the Roamers from the earliest times on, and among the alliance youth had taken shape in systematic striving towards folk community. Notions of the superiority of German blood were widely diffused in the youth movement, and had even found a rationale in the writings of the much-quoted Gobineau and Chamberlain. Nevertheless, it remained for Rosenberg, Günther and lesser lights to take this reverence for the Nordic, with whom the sadly mixed German races were skilfully identified, and mould it into catechism and creed. The relatively mild preferences and sympathies for those thought to share in one's own superior lineage were shrewdly played upon ; the upshot was utterly fanatical belief in the necessity of keeping Germanic blood free not only of Jewish taint but also of debasing admixture with virtually every people west, south, and east of the Master Race. From this to the contemptuous segregation and expulsion of " first- and second-class hybrids " was but a step, and the greater part of the youth movement kept pace. Another step readily taken was in mate selection : Nordics and other authorized inhabitants of the Nazi Valhalla were encouraged to marry and multiply—in any case, to multiply.[17]

Nationalism is sometimes regarded, in whatever form it appears, as either already wicked or well on the way to become so. If the analysis of youth movement nationalism is approached on the basis of such assumptions, however, it is almost impossible to see precisely how Hitlerian perversion took place, and it therefore seems wise to define my own contrasting position in advance. I do *not* regard nationalism as necessarily evil :

> . . . let me state . . . my own arbitrary choice among contending values. I stand for an ethic of responsibility towards those I know most intimately, whose way of life I can directly understand. I am an internationalist, yes, but on a basis of nationalism. The sentiments that cluster about the native land, the familiar language, and the accustomed way of life certainly represent nothing that is absolute, but the absolute can be attained only in and through the relative. Men who do not respect themselves cannot respect others, and in the larger life of the nation the analogy seems to hold good : only through devotion to the values closest to us can we be genuinely loyal to the values that take in all mankind. There is a real place for patriotism, albeit a chastened and reticent patriotism. The poorest way to be an internationalist is to begin by apologizing for your nationality.[18]

With this benchmark established, it can now be said that although there were many aspects of alliance youth nationalism, in particular, with which there can be little quarrel, there were many others which readily lent themselves to the uses of the perverter. Sample :

> The source from which the ranks of alliance youth and of the young nationalist movement derive is the conservative middle class, which contains the highest percentage of Germans of pure race. The middle class cast down by the war and the revolution, the proletarized officials, teachers, scholars, and engineers, together with the skilled workers of the factories—these form its broad membership.
> Outwardly regarded the great youth alliances represent an educational enterprise with a definite purpose . . . and it is the beloved practice of the jejune foreigner and " good European " to range the German movement alongside the movement for international regeneration. . . .
> [Instead] . . . the youth alliances constitute a faith. . . . The alliance youth stands with his God and his nation in direct connection. . . .
> We have not been defeated with arms, but as the result of hunger-blockade, internecine treachery, and moral calamity we have fallen to pieces. . . . The business of alliance youth is not that of pacifistic confirmation of Christian brotherly love, not the rebuilding of the devastated areas of France, but the recovery of the intellectual, political, and financial sovereignty of Central Europe.
> The reconquest of the unredeemed territories in the south, north, east, and west of to-day's little German Republic is inseparably linked with national unity, with a true German democracy. . . . The whole passion of our older comrades and young leaders is devoted

to the task of standing side by side with the alliance youth in the lost provinces and preserving their heart for Germany. . . .

We love our race, our people, our blood, and our fair upright youth, but never the intellectual who is at home everywhere, who knows neither friendship nor fatherland. We are all young nationalists. . . . We . . . are a proud people ; our young manhood was undefeated in war, unbroken in revolution. Pacifists can seal no compact, they lie when they say they are a nation. . . .[19]

This turgid Chauvinism, widely spread among German youth of every description long before 1924 (the date of the sample), needed only systematic expression and propagandizing to bring it hand in glove with Nazi doctrines. Note : The hatred of internationalism ; the reiteration of the " stab in the back " legend ; the demand for the reconquest of the Polish Corridor, Alsace, northern Schleswig, and all the other territories reassigned by the Treaty of Versailles ; and the identification of efforts to develop a peaceful Germany with spineless pacifism. Hitler rang the changes on these themes with unwearied vigour and startling success, and study of the votes cast for the Party shows conclusively that it was the younger men and women who did much to swell the tide of National Socialism.

Chauvinism of such intensity is itself a religion, but traditional Lutheranism and Catholicism, as held by both young and old, have features of which the perverter can avail himself.

Orthodox Lutherans draw a sharp line between the realms of private devotion and public action ; the combination of personal piety and ruthless use of force is often characteristic. The objection which Lutherans had to National Socialism was neither to the nationalism nor, in many instances, to the socialism ; rather, exception was taken to the claim that the State as such can properly interfere with the internal affairs of the Church.

Referring to Pastor Niemöller : not only was he a submarine commander in World War I, but also, at the outbreak of World War II, he earnestly asked Hitler to be allowed once more to fight for Germany. He was refused, not because his nationalism was suspect, but because he insisted that the Nazis would have no right to appoint his successor or in any other way to interfere with strictly religious matters.

This same attitude manifested itself among the Lutheran members of youth alliance and youth tutelage organizations.[20] After the seizure of power, for example, they suggested that religiously-minded youth be included in the Hitler Youth as a special division, to be called Hitler Youth Devouts or *Feld-*

geistliche.[21] The plea was rejected, but what is significant for our analysis is the fact that it was ever made. The maxim of "Render unto Caesar the things that are Caesar's, and unto God the things that are God's" lay at the root of the proposed compromise—but the compromise would have left everything but the inner life of the Hitler Youth Devout to Caesar !

In justice to the Lutherans, however, it must be noted that when their plea was rejected they were consistent enough, where the more courageous leaders and youngsters were concerned, to attempt to go underground. They took full part in the activities of the Hitler Youth, and then tried to meet in secret for the preservation and furthering of their own faith. Even now news occasionally filters out to the effect that one more " subversive " Lutheran group has been discovered and broken up. Yet, in the very nature of the activities involved, there is no serious threat to the supremacy of the Nazi régime ; ultranationalism goes unchallenged.

The Catholics were somewhat harder to handle, and the struggle went on until 1937, at which time all hitherto un-affiliated Catholic groups were incorporated in the Hitler Youth.[22] In many cases reservations similar to, although certainly not identical with, those of Lutheran youth were made, and underground meetings have likewise been going on.

Still and all, it must be remembered that Hitler, by birth a Catholic, has never been excommunicated, and that at Rome, in 1933, he signed the famous Concordat with the Pope by which non-interference with " proper " Catholic activities was guaranteed. *In return for this the Pope gave his official recognition to the new German government.* Hitler did not observe the guarantee, and a campaign of defamation was launched against nuns and priests which eventually swung public opinion far enough towards Hitler's side to make possible the totalitarian incorporation of Catholic youth already noted.[23] The Pope bent before the storm. When Austria was invaded, Cardinal Innitzer of Vienna officially greeted the Hitlerian hordes. Vigorous protest against pagan tendencies, however, still continues, for even though nothing fundamental in Nazism can be altered under war conditions, the record is thereby kept straight. Observe, in conclusion, that the Vatican is still outspokenly neutral.

Utilizing these ambiguities, doubts, and confusions, Hitler's propagandists went to work. There was zealous denial of pagan tendencies in the Hitler Youth :

I want to say this morning that the Hitler Youth is devoted to God as no other nation's youth is, that it will have no one doubting its religious character, and that we all are determined that no one shall question us in our loyalty to God, to our leader, and to Germany. . . . Youth stands here to-day and it bows its head.[24]

The Hitler Youth is not a church, and the church is not the Hitler Youth.[25]

From this there readily followed the major perversionary slogan : The State shall not interfere in matters of religion, *and the Church shall not interfere in matters of politics*. By ceaselessly dinning this into the ears of both Lutheran and Catholic youngsters, religious belief has been pushed over so far into the private sphere that few priests or pastors dare say anything that has the remotest bearing on political life—and in Hitler Germany, with its complete *Gleichschaltung* or co-ordination, virtually everything that is said or done has political implications ! Perversion can no further go.

What is the result of all this ? Simply that a new value-system of sacred character has been constructed by the adroit utilization of every fragment of other value-systems to which German youth has been loyal. The transformation seems almost magical, but " It's done with mirrors ". Everything from " Heil ! " and the ramrod arm salute which the Roamers re-introduced into German life to the definition of religion as other-worldly and strictly personal has been picked up, twisted, trimmed and fitted into the Hitlerian system.

Perversion, to be such, must always be intentional, and it is difficult if not impossible to escape the conclusion that Hitler and his lieutenants know exactly what they are doing. They are fanatics, beyond question, but fanaticism can be coldly calculating even when it reaches the stage of paranoia. Witness the way in which the " martyrdom " of sixteen-year-old Herbert Norkus was exploited ; German youngsters were given a Horst Wessel of their own age and generation. The fatal mistake made by the outside world was the effort to judge the Nazis (1) in terms of ordinary rationality and (2) without detailed knowledge of the society in which they were operating. The upshot was underestimation of the skill and foresight which Hitler and his higher deputies possessed ; the consequences we know.

The new sacred system, moreover, is a very stable structure ; there is nothing ramshackle or jerrybuilt about it. Admittedly, it lacks a supernaturalistic capstone; in spite of tactical concessions to traditional religion, Nazism is essentially godless. Before we take too much comfort in this fact and assume that the National Socialist edifice will crumble as soon as victory has been won, it is well to remember that the sacred and the supernatural are not identical. Many societies enduring over long periods have lacked belief in a God of the kind we know—indeed, some of them can be said to have lacked any god whatsoever in the theistic sense. Perversion can take effect only when there is something to pervert; the Nazis have built into their edifice many phases of German life about which sacred emotions cluster. There seems little reason to think that those German youth who were devoted to National Socialism in its days of glory will ever lose the feeling that it represented everything essentially German, so cleverly has the perversion been accomplished.

Stop! Perversion is an utterly colourless term; in itself it is neither good nor bad. The ends towards which perversion is directed determine the moral value ultimately laid upon it. Is it too much to submit, with due humility, that the results of Nazi perversion can be undone only by *another kind of perversion* conforming to the moral judgments of mankind as a whole and skilfully reshaping the sacred components of German life to its own peaceful purposes?

NOTES

1. See my chapter in Becker and Hill, eds., *Marriage and the Family* (Boston, 1942), especially the bibliography on pp. 22–3; and Howard Becker and Robert C. Myers, " Sacred and Secular Aspects of Human Sociation ", *Sociometry*, 6, 3 (Aug., 1942), pp. 207–29, and *ibid.*, 6, 4 (Nov., 1942), pp. 355–70.

2. Harry Elmer Barnes and Howard Becker, *Social Thought from Lore to Science* (Boston, 1938), 1, pp. 23–6, 32–9 and xii–xiii (notes).

3. *Ibid.*, pp. 17–18.

4. Wiese-Becker, *Systematic Sociology* (New York, 1932), p. 393.

5. Anonymous, in Hertha Siemering, *Die deutschen Jugendverbände* (Berlin, 1931), pp. 251–2.

6. Details of the early years of the Hitler Youth will be found in Hermann Bolm, *Hitlerjugend in einem Jahrzehnt* (Braunschweig, 1938).

7. Siemering, *op. cit.*, p. 252.

8. In 1923 and 1926–7 I talked with many youngsters who spoke in this vein.

9. See the material collected in Ludwig Hemm, " Die unteren Führer

in der HJ : Versuch ihrer psychologischen Typengliederung ", *Zeitschrift für angewandte Psychologie und Charakterkunde* (Leipzig, 1940), Beiheft 87.

10. Wiese-Becker, *op. cit.*, p. 626.

11. *Ibid.*, p. 638.

12. *Ibid.*, p. 626.

13. See the self-eulogies in Siemering, *op. cit.*, *passim*.

14. The classical discussion of "*charisma* of office" is found in Max Weber, *Wirtschaft und Gesellschaft* (Tübingen, 1922), chapter 3, sections 11, 12, 12a, pp. 143–8 ; and chapter 10, pp. 758–78.

15. The Advance Troop programme spread to virtually every part of youth movement and youth tutelage.

16. Quoted in Robert C. Schmid, *German Youth Movements : A Typological Study* (unpublished Ph.D. dissertation, University of Wisconsin, 1941), pp. 215–16, from *Die Kameradschaft*, special number for summer camps (Berlin, May, 1939).

17. It should be noted, however, that publicized official encouragement of illegitimacy was discontinued about 1941 ; Goebbels remarked that illegitimacy, even when both parents were Nordic, had certain " population liabilities ". Apparently the difficulties of caring for illegitimate offspring had become too great. Without publicized official encouragement, however, the Élite Guard still propagates freely.

18. Howard Becker, " Irrational Factors in International Relations ", in Brown, Hodges, and Roucek, *Contemporary World Politics* (New York, 1940), pp. 582–3.

19. Heinz Rocholl, " What Does Young German Nationalism Want ? " in *Youth : An International Quarterly of Young Enterprise*, 2, 13 (Summer, 1924) —Published at 152 Abbey House, Victoria Street, London, S.W.1. Pp. 170–2, 199.

20. This was startlingly apparent even at the outbreak of World War I. See *Freideutsche Jugend : Eine Monatschrift*, 1, 1915, pp. 3, 32, 35, 79, 148.

21. Baldur von Schirach, *Hitler Jugend, Idee und Gestalt*, p. 46, cited in Schmid, *op. cit.*, p. 206.

22. Schmid, *op. cit.*, p. 204.

23. *Der Angriff*, June 6, 1936, quoted in M. B. Schnapper, *Youth Betrayed* (New York, 1938), pp. 55, 58, *et passim*.

24. Baldur von Schirach, " Über uns ein Gott ", in *Revolution der Erziehung* (Munich, 1938), p. 150.

25. Quoted in Santoro, *Hitler Germany*, 3rd ed. (Berlin, 1939), p. 317, as quoted by Schmid, *op. cit.*, p. 208.

CHAPTER VIII

POSSESSION : " DOWN A STEEP PLACE "

> Out of the depths a cry
>   Rings, rings and is still !
> Out of the night a voice :
>   " Ye that were taught to kill
> Youth blinded, cow'd and bled—
>   Who planned your agony ?
> Ye brave unnumber'd dead,
>   Have ye not seen the Lie ? "
>   —ALLINSON, " Challenge ! "

Like the Gadarene swine, German youth rushed to their own destruction, and like those same swine the boys and girls perverted by the Führer's grace were possessed by evil spirits leading them astray.

On the surface, the truth of such an assertion seems in doubt. German youngsters were told and unhesitatingly believed that they were leading themselves, and their own emotions, surging as they did about things sacred to them, powerfully reinforced their convictions. And had not the Führer himself issued the proclamation : " Youth shall be led by youth "—and that in the very days of his struggle for power ? And was not that proclamation followed to the letter ?

The regional leaders, responsible for from one to two hundred thousand youngsters, are usually not less than twenty-one but rarely more than thirty years of age, while the battalion leaders range from twenty to twenty-five. The leader of a platoon of from eighty to one hundred and fifty boys will usually be a little under twenty, while the squad leaders in charge of about a dozen lads are most frequently in the vicinity of sixteen or seventeen.[1]

The top rung of the ladder is the exalted office of Youth Leader of the German Reich. The first occupant of this post was Baldur von Schirach, who at the age of twenty-seven was appointed by Hitler in June, 1933. He was succeeded in 1941 by the similarly youthful Arthur Axmann.[2] Note, now, that each person in the hierarchy takes his orders from someone whose age differs so slightly from his own that adult-youth conflict as such does not arise. Apparently, then, youth is really led by youth.

The " apparently " is just that and no more. Viewed from

"Youth shall be led by Youth."

a standpoint regarding the Hitler Youth and its counterpart, the League of German Girls—together, with their junior contingents, making up the Youth Service—as units functioning within the National Socialist state, it is at once obvious that the slogan is false. Youth is not led by youth but by the same group which controls the nation as a whole ; namely, the supreme command of the National Socialist Party. In this command the Youth Leader of the Reich is an important figure, but he has no more power than, if as much as, the other high party officials—and certainly much less than the chief of the secret state police, the ill-famed *Gestapo*.

At bottom, then, the activities of youth are as much dominated to-day by the will of the adult rulers of the nation as they were in the days when the Roamers assaulted Rimmon's House. Indeed, considering the fact that such an open revolt would be impossible to-day, it is clear that the domination is far more complete. " Possession by evil spirits " goes beyond a mere figure of speech ; it might be said to be literally true.

The possibility of this peculiarly contradictory situation, viz., that youth should think it leads itself when actually adult power is still supreme, is vouchsafed by the pattern of leadership effective throughout Nazi Germany.

This is of course the famous *Führerprinzip* as perverted for Nazi purposes and characteristic of all branches of public service in the Third Reich. Before perversion had been accomplished, the youth movement leader announced himself and then selected those whom he wanted for his followers. The bond between leader and led was therefore a personal one, responsibility resided in the leader rather than in the membership, and rule was by charismatic pronouncement rather than official decree. In the Hitler Youth the principle is applied quite differently. First, following systematized adult standards, there was until 1941 a rough process of selection whereby the organization was divided into two unequal parts. One was composed of ordinary or general Hitler Youth : dull, physically weak or sluggish, un-imaginative, unenthusiastic, doubtfully loyal, or " just average ". The other was a much smaller group called the Select Cadre, to which were admitted only the brightest, most fanatic, aggres-sively authoritative, and strongest of German youngsters. *Only from this group could leaders be selected.*[3] Since 1941 the division has not been openly made, but it nevertheless persists in practice.

At the top of the leadership pyramid, responsible directly to

Adolf Hitler, stands the Youth Leader of the Reich. He represents the followers of Hitler the Supreme Leader, and has been selected from among them by Hitler, in accordance with the Nazi version of the leadership principle, as worthy of inclusion in the highest circles of authority. The Youth Leader of the Reich in turn personally selects the leaders in charge of the four great regions of the State Youth organization. He is directly responsible for their conduct in that he must answer for any of his subordinates' actions, carried out by his command, to Hitler himself. Each of these subordinates selects the leaders who are to command the districts in his area, and is likewise responsible for what they do. This process continues down to the platoon leader, who is responsible for the selection and conduct of four or five squad teachers, and finally, these young squad leaders are immediately responsible for the ten or fifteen boys in their charge.

The shibboleth of " Youth led by youth " therefore means that in every case the followers are given marching orders by other young people, but where do the ultimate marching orders come from ? Clearly from the adult Party leaders, the men who make the master plans ; the initiative and responsibility of the genuinely youthful leaders can never go any farther than these master plans permit. The whippet greyhound chasing the mechanical rabbit around the track undeniably has energy and enterprise, but who designed the track and installed the rabbit ?

Further, the Nazis make much of the charismatic aspects of the leadership principle ; they recognize the fact that the ability to lead others is a kind of " natural " trait in some persons, a trait which can be cultivated and perfected but never created *de novo*. Von Schirach, for example, speaks of " natural authority " which cannot be achieved by " passing examinations " : " The ability to lead others cannot be learned ".[4]

Well and good. Does it follow that such natural leaders can assert themselves, *à la* Karl Fischer, without the benediction bestowed by the Party hierarchy ? Obviously not. There is only one final source of pure *charisma* anywhere in Nazidom ; namely, Hitler himself. (Even here, of course, strictly personal *charisma* has been steadily changing into the *charisma* of office— but let that pass.) All other leaders derive their power from him, and there can be no belittlers to challenge his authority— at least not while the Elite Guard and the *Gestapo* continue to function.

The situation could hardly be otherwise in a compulsory,

totalitarian machine. Where the State Youth organizations are concerned every youngster, with the sole exception of the complete racial outcast, is forced into the ranks or, if " forced " is too strong a term, let us say that he and his parents know what will happen if he does not enter " voluntarily ". This is not to deny, of course, that the great majority of German youth enter the totalitarian organizations freely and gladly. It most distinctly is to say, however, that opportunities for withdrawal and the rise of schismatic sects clustering around self-appointed leaders were until quite recently very rare indeed.

In fact, it is quite safe to put forth the generalization that no group in which membership is ultimately compulsory can sustain pure charismatic leadership, for this demands that the followers implicitly reserve the right to refuse recognition, at any time, of the leader's prerogative to issue decrees and otherwise exert control.

Present-day German youngsters are locked within a vast youth tutelage organization from which only the most reckless can escape. Pushing our religious line of analysis further, it can be asserted that they are members of an all-encompassing State Church or ecclesia devoted to the perpetuation of the value-system sacred to Nazi Germany. To define :

The social structure known as the ecclesia is a predominantly conservative body, not in open conflict with the secular aspects of social life, and professedly universal in its aims. The phrase " Come ye out from among them and be ye separate " has no place in the ideology of the genuine ecclesiastic ; " Force them to come in " is likely to characterize his thinking. The fully developed ecclesia attempts to amalgamate itself with the state and the dominant classes, and strives to exercise control over every person in the population. Members are *born into* the ecclesia ; they do not have to *join* it. It is therefore a social structure . . . [which] is in no sense elective. Membership in an ecclesia is a necessary consequence of birth into a family, folk, or similar structure, and no special requirements condition its privileges.

The ecclesia naturally attaches a high importance to the means of grace which it administers, to the system of doctrine which it has formulated, and to the official administration of sacraments and teaching by . . . [authorized agents]. It is in a very real sense an educational system which, when functioning properly, trains its youthful members to conformity in thought and practice, and thus fits them for the exercise of the religious " rights " they have automatically inherited.[5]

Originally the Nazi Party was a cult which rapidly became a

sect. This sect, however, was peculiar, for instead of isolating itself from the elements in German life antagonistic to it, there was from the beginning the iron resolve to convert all doubters to the One True Faith. Sect was envisaged as potential ecclesia from the start. To be sure, there was a strong trace of isolationist endeavour even in this ; the totalitarian ecclesia represented by Germany as a whole was to set itself apart from the decadent and racially inferior peoples to whom the promise of salvation had not been given. The grand finale was to be the domination of lesser breeds by the Master Race :

> To-day we hold the Fatherland,
> To-morrow the world is ours.

Further light on the ecclesiastical structure of the Nazi Party and its State Youth—or Youth Service, a synonymous term—can be gained by tracing the process by which the early cult clustering around its charismatic leader developed into a standardized, routinized State Church.

A cult, or even a sect, refuses to make any compromise with the world even in the realm of economics ; it is specifically aloof from economic considerations. " Be not anxious for your life, what ye shall eat, or what ye shall drink ; nor yet for your body, what ye shall put on." Provisions for the ordinary needs of life are extremely loose and tenuous ; there are, for example, no such things as regular dues for the membership or salaries for the leaders. All necessary outlays are made with a fine disdain for niggardly reckoning ; each member of the group contributes what he can to the common fund, and leaders and followers alike draw from it as much as the needs of the hour demand.[6] It will be remembered that among the Roamers one of the first cleavages appeared because wealthier members insisted on providing luxuries for themselves which could not be shared by the others. Even if they could pay in money, the Roamers usually preferred to " work out " their obligations for shelter and food—when furnished by peasants, in particular—by performing some direct service such as draining a meadow or digging a ditch. Ordinary economic considerations were despised.

There is ample evidence to show that the National Socialists started out with a large measure of this primitive communism. Salaries, dues, regular meals, and ordinary sleeping arrangements were quite secondary to the campaign. Subsidization by calculating industrialists there was, beyond doubt, but at first the funds

flowed directly into the struggle. Once in power, however, the
National Socialist Party became an almost perfect case of the
collapse of sectarian communism ; salaries and perquisites were
rapidly seized.

Rank-and-file followers of course could not be permitted to
become too keenly aware of the shift towards ecclesiastical
arrangements. Dependence on booty snatched from heretical or
devilish opponents and upon free-will offerings provided by the
faithful was and still is part of the creed. This helps to produce
the illusion that for the really important things compulsory
measures are not necessary, i.e., that the German nation is really
a great folk community which unhesitatingly recognizes its duty
to contribute to the mission of its charismatic leader. Street-
corner hat-passing in the interests of various poor relief and
public welfare projects, for which prominent Nazis personally
solicit to the clicking of camera shutters, is a neat way of sug-
gesting that the informal mutual aid practices of the original sect
are still supreme. Among the State Youth this takes the form of
endless canvassing from door to door to collect funds for youth
hostels, nests, and lodges. During the present war, furs, warm
clothing, valuable metal, and the like have been gathered in the
same way. Begging is sanctioned and glorified when it can be
said that it is in the interest of the folk community or any part
thereof.

Yet no better proof of the shift from personal *charisma* to the
charisma of office, from sect to ecclesia, can be found than the
fact that leadership in the Youth Service—to say nothing of the
rest of the Nazi system—has become a paying profession. When
youth leaders begin to draw salaries for their work, cult and sect
have been left far behind.

A youth leader is of course supposed to have unusual qualities
lending him personal fitness for his task, just as a school-teacher
ultimately derives whatever authority he possesses from his
students' recognition that persons in his position have ordinarily
demonstrated their professional adequacy to someone. But this
is a far cry from personal *charisma* ; neither the Youth Service
leader nor the school-teacher derives his authority from the daily
demonstration to *youth* of his peculiar capacities for his office.

This is especially evident in the vicissitudes undergone by
Hitler Youth or Youth Service leaders. Kurt Gruber, who
persuaded the Führer in 1926 that the time was ripe for inte-
grating the Hitler Youth with the Party, held *de facto* control

until about 1929, but then began to give ground to one of Hitler's favourites, the well-known von Schirach.[7]   Organization head-quarters were moved to Munich, and the future of the State Youth began to be conceived in dimensions far more sweeping than Gruber's.   The whole of Germany was divided into ten regions for organizational purposes, and a beginning was made in the development of special literature.

It seems evident that Gruber, although a charismatic type, either clashed with Hitler or was unable to change his own ideas rapidly enough to meet the needs of a sect shifting with tremendous speed towards ecclesiastical structure, for by 1930 he exerted relatively little influence and was clearly being eased out.   In 1931 Gruber resigned, and a few months later, in June, 1932, von Schirach was appointed National Leader of the Hitler Youth.

Baldur von Schirach is not a charismatic type ; rather, his rise to power seems to have been largely the result of Hitler's liking for him.   Born the son of an officer in 1907, he encountered the small group of National Socialist fanatics active in Munich, where he was studying art history and Germanic lore, in 1924. By 1925 Hitler was referring to him as " a true follower and a dependable lad ", and a close friendship seems to have been formed, partly on the basis of their common interest in art.   The " fair-haired boy " also possessed some poetic gifts, and Hitler encouraged him to intensify his efforts at verse-writing.   His poems met with Hitler's approval, and before long von Schirach was the poet laureate, so to speak, of the Nazi movement.

His first major political responsibility does not seem to have resulted from any extraordinary powers of leadership ; in 1929 he was *appointed* by Hitler as Leader of the National Socialist University Student Movement.   Nazi eulogists claim that " he brought the whole German student body under Nazi control and put the German universities in the very front rank of the National Socialist revolution ".   Less partisan observers maintain, how-ever, that as late as 1943 German university students were still resisting the efforts of the Nazis, with the underground remnants of the famous Corporations among the most determined recalci-trants.   Be this as it may, von Schirach probably made some headway into hostile territory at a time when the Nazis were not taken seriously by the educated classes, and his Party comrades seem to have been pleased with his work.

At any rate, he soon began to overshadow the other leaders in the Hitler Youth organization, and in 1931 he was appointed

National Youth Director of the Nazi Party in preparation for his 1932 elevation to Gruber's position. This achieved, and with the power of the Party organization behind him, he further boosted his prestige by organizing a huge youth demonstration at Potsdam, just outside Berlin, in 1932. Over one hundred thousand brown-shirted Hitler Youth marched grimly past the reviewing stand where Hitler himself stood at attention, perpetually saluting, for seven hours.

Other honours followed thick and fast, and in 1933 von Schirach was appointed Youth Leader of the German Reich, without whose permission no youth group could exist or be organized. In 1936 a decree was published providing for the inclusion of all German youth in the State Youth organization, and in 1939 detailed plans were revealed by which Hitler's favourite was to project National Socialism, through German youth, " into eternity ".

When he reached this pinnacle of glory, von Schirach was a moderately tall, plump, placid young man of thirty-three, charged by his enemies with homosexual proclivities. His picture then graced as many walls as those decorated by Goering or Hess—indeed, he probably took up more space than any other Nazi leader except Hitler himself. The publications of the period represented him as a kind of demi-god who embodied, somehow, all that was fine and noble in German youth.

Having always enjoyed Hitler's protection, von Schirach never had to modify his views in answer to criticism ; sheltered under the cloak of the Supreme Leader, he was beyond criticism in spite of the frequent impracticality of his projects. In short, he was Youth Leader by the Führer's grace ; he had been given a share of Hitler's *charisma*.

But in spite of the frantic adulation which this brought him, he retained power only as long as Hitler and the Party saw fit. His *charisma* was only the *charisma* of office, after all, and in July, 1941, he was " kicked upstairs " to the governorship of Vienna, a much less significant post. Arthur Axmann, formerly an assistant in the Hitler Youth headquarters, became heir to von Schirach's title and office. Ironically enough, the new Youth Leader now receives the same fervid respect and homage from the youth who have rushed down a steep place as was formerly accorded von Schirach the Blessed. The Nazi machine works so efficiently that demi-gods, at least, can be made and unmade to order.

Examples like this demonstrate how complete the possession of German youth can be. They still talk as though their Youth Leader has personal *charisma* when actually he has nothing more than the support of a tremendous, highly institutionalized ecclesia.

The German Youth Service, sharing in this institutionalization, has swallowed many of the functions of other institutions such as school, family, and traditional supernaturalistic church. Formally organized and tightly integrated within Nazi society, the Youth Service is a respectable, recognized authority for the dispensation of the sacred value-system and its buttressing means of grace. In short, conformist education for every phase of life in Nazidom is its major responsibility. Like any other ecclesia, the Youth Service organization takes full account of the varying abilities of its charges :

> The [ecclesia] . . . is the great educator of the nations, and like all educators, she knows how to allow for various degrees of capacity and maturity and how to attain her end . . . by a process of adaptation. . . .[8]

Let us now follow through in detail the differing methods used by the State Youth system for the inculcation of the Nazi faith. The later phases of the war have brought many minor changes, but the main features persist.

By March 15 of the year in which he will celebrate his tenth birthday, every German youngster must be registered with the local State Youth headquarters. After thorough investigation of the child's and the family's record, with special attention to " racial purity ", he is admitted, if free of " taint ", to the year's group of initiates. In a magnificent ceremony on April 20, Hitler's birthday, the Führer or some highly placed deputy personally inducts the ten-year-olds into the organization which will have virtually unquestioned authority over them for from eight to eleven years—indeed, which exerts the first grip of the Party and makes it almost certain that control will never be relaxed as long as the Nazi régime exists.

The two major divisions in the system are those for boys and girls. Each of these is then further subdivided into two age groups.

For the boys there are the Junior Boys, ages ten to fourteen, and the Hitler Youth, fourteen to eighteen. Significantly enough, the State Youth system feeds directly into the Party, for at the age of eighteen the young man must enter either the Storm Troops or the Élite Guard. Under peacetime conditions, he would then pass to the Labour Service, and then back to the Storm Troops. Thus the Party never relinquishes its grasp from the age of ten onward.

The girls are organized into Junior Girls, ten to fourteen, and the League of German Girls, fourteen to twenty-one. It will be noticed that the German girl is held three years longer in the Youth Service than is the boy ; this differential was inaugurated in 1939 to compensate for the fact that the girls do not have to spend two years in the army and because the one-year Labour Service for girls was not yet completely organized at that time. (What has happened during the war years is somewhat obscure.) The three years from eighteen to twenty-one, however, are spent in the organization called Faith and Beauty, where the girls undergo training in domestic science and preparation for marriage.

Reference has already been made to the squads, platoons, and larger units ; the latter are necessary in order to handle the hundreds of thousands of youths who are sometimes called out for the great mass demonstrations and festivals. There are separate leaders for the younger boys' and girls' groups until the higher organizational levels are reached ; above these control is centralized in the offices of the organizations for older youth. (By this time, however, it may be that there are special leaders for all levels in the four age-sex divisions ; plans in this direction were being laid in 1939.)

As might be imagined, the administrative staffs are very large ; the task of housing them has become a real problem even for the Nazis, free as they are to confiscate any property they need. Bureaucracies are notorious for their tendency to expand indefinitely, and the Youth Service is no exception. Locally, at the various regional headquarters, and in the national capital the buildings occupied by the State Youth functionaries and the youngsters they dominate are conspicuous even in a country long accustomed to elaborate provision for officialdom.

The full title of the State Youth organization is the Youth Leadership of the German Nation and of the National Socialist German Workers' Party. The accompanying diagram and explanatory figures give the main outlines, and I here quote, slightly modified, a passage from Schmid which makes the complicated structure reasonably clear :

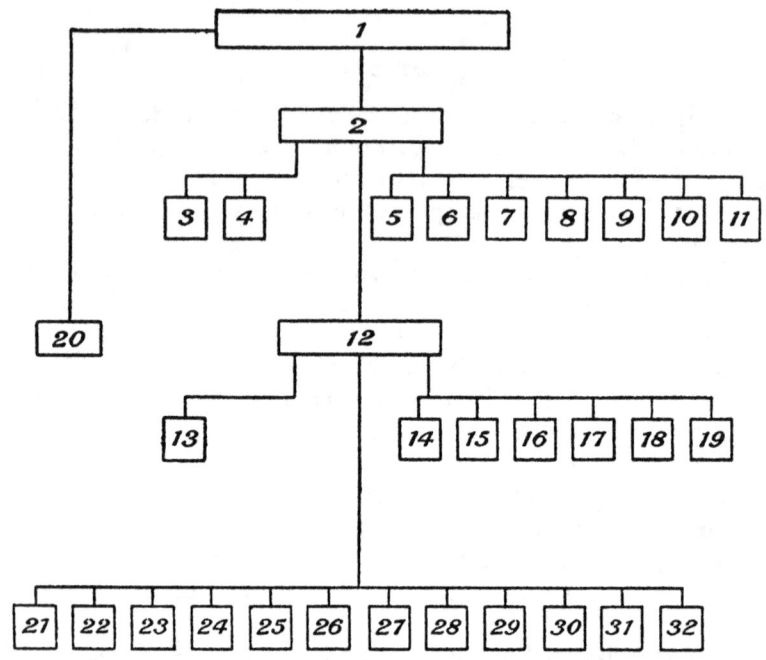

Organization Plan of the Youth Leadership
of the German Nation and of the National
Socialist German Workers' Party
(NSDAP) (1)

Youth Leader of the German Nation
and of the NSDAP (2)

Legal Adviser (3)
Adjutant (4)
Director of Physical Education
   for All German Youth (20)
Youth Hostels (5)
Brunswick Academy for Leaders (6)

Girls' Sports School (7)
Adolf Hitler Schools (8)
Langemarck Committee (9)
Memorial Committee (10)
Youth Library (11)

Chief of Staff (12)

Office of Chief of Staff (13)
Leadership Schools (14)
Inspection (15)
Construction of Youth Homes (16)

Munich Liaison Office (17)
Cabinet Liaison Office (18)
Legal Adviser (19)

Administrative Departments :

Physical Training (21)
Physical Fitness (22)
Female Youth (23)
Personnel (24)
Social Work (25)
Ideological Training (26)

Health Leadership (27)
Radio (28)
Press and Propaganda (29)
Foreign Affairs (30)
Trips and Roaming (31)
Executive (32)

Dominating the entire organization is the office of the youth leader of the nation . . . [no. 1 on the diagram]. It will be noticed that directly appended to the youth leader's office are seven organization divisions (nos. 5–11). Number 5, the National Association of German Youth Hostels, is the Nazi version of the association which began two decades ago under the leadership of Richard Schirrman. This office provides not so much for the construction of hostels as for their maintenance and co-ordination with the total youth programme. The hostel custodians are selected here. [Naturally, the youth leadership academy at Brunswick (no. 6)], and the office of the national girls' sports school is a further responsibility. . . . The Adolf Hitler Leadership Schools (no. 8) . . . [were] von Schirach's special hobby . . . ; his early experiences in the Nazi Party brought him into intimate contact with the whole student movement. The Langemarck division (no. 9) concerns the Nazi version of the commemorative ceremonies which, since 1920, have been held to honour the thousands of youth movement boys who lost their lives in the famous battle of Langemarck. The office in charge of Hitler Youth killed in action (no. 10) will no doubt be expanded during the present war. Previously its authority was limited to the commemoration of the fifteen Hitler Youths who were killed during the street fighting and political brawls which characterized the party's march to power. The chief of staff also has a series of special responsibilities. The first of these (no. 14) is the leadership schools [these are outside of the Adolf Hitler Schools initially fostered by von Schirach ; the present status of the latter is not well known, but they probably continue to hold high prestige]. . . . The committee for the construction of youth homes is a very important office. It is here that architects and landscape artists efficiently designed . . ., according to Nazi principles, an artistically genuine network of youth homes. This includes not only hostels but all the other kinds of Hitler Youth shelters. [The directorship of physical education for German youth (no. 20) requires no special comment, and] . . . main departments in the Hitler Youth (nos. 21–32) do not all require explanation. The personnel department (no. 24) is the focal point for a great deal of psychological testing (aptitudes, personality characteristics, etc.). The social work department (no. 25) has taken over many of the old youth . . . [tutelage] activities, against which " free " German youth used to protest so violently. Social hygiene, juvenile law, rural service, and vocational education and guidance, including the national vocational competitions, constitute subdivisions of this department. Also all technical questions of reduction of railroad fares and the remission of fees in connection with organizations and establishments for youth welfare are handled in this department.

The department of . . . [ideological] training is, from the point of view of indoctrination and propaganda, the centre of the effort to mould the minds of German youth. Most of the youth publications are sent out from here in a continuous stream of literature, educational pamphlets, and the like. The radio department (no. 28) has been of increasing importance. From this office is directed the widespread network of youth broadcasts ; most important of these is the weekly home evening broadcast at 8.00 P.M. each Wednesday, when for a whole hour the entire German youth assemble about the radio to hear a specially prepared educational programme. Subsidiary broadcasts are made and directed by the Hitler Youth during the week. The department for press and propaganda takes care not only of Hitler Youth publications but also keeps the daily and weekly newspapers informed of Hitler Youth activities. This work is, so far as possible, left to the initiative of the youth themselves. The foreign affairs department (no. 30) was formerly the borderland and foreign affairs department (apparently border problems are considered to be liquidated and no longer need special attention in the Hitler Youth leadership).[9]

Running all the way through this elaborate structure, as a major preoccupation, is training for youth leadership. " Training " is, of course, in direct contrast with the old youth movement conception of the inspired, self-appointed leader, but that makes no difference. The ecclesia has learned a lesson from the disastrous experience of the early sects, and is determined to see to it that an authorized, skilled priesthood attaches due " importance to the means of grace which it administers, to the system of doctrine which it has formulated, and to the official administration of sacraments and teaching." [10]

Many Nazi writers state over and over again their belief that the basic reason for the failure and eventual disappearance of many powerful social movements of the past has been in every case the lack of a leadership training scheme which would ensure the perpetuation of the original successes by their speedy institutionalization. They mean to make their characterization of the Nazi state as the Eternal Reich something more than an idle boast through the leadership programme of the Youth Service. This falls into three main divisions : Regional Leadership Courses ; National Leadership Schools ; and the Hitler Youth Leader Schooling Work.

Regional Leadership Courses are set up both for weekends and for longer periods, but from the standpoint of the numbers of young men and women exposed to their influence, the weekend courses are perhaps the most important. They are given in about sixty centres scattered throughout Germany, with the boys' and girls' schools roughly equal in number. All leaders in the Youth Service are given at least preliminary training here, sometimes over a series of weekends and sometimes by means of intensive three-week sessions. Training in the National Socialist outlook on life, group leadership and response, and the utilization of sports, camping, and military equipment prevails, but everything serves the common end of perpetuating National Socialism :

Actually, the most important part . . . is the philosophical-political [ideological] ; that is, our main effort must be expended in so channelling the natural play-adventure activities [of our youth] . . . that their behaviour will have the *meaning* to them that we National Socialists consider to be all-important . . . the significance of all this activity is not the satisfaction of individual recreational interests, but *the preparation of youth for responsible positions in* . . . [our folk community].[11]

The National Leadership Schools represent a higher level of training. At present they are probably six in number, three for each sex. The minimum period is one year, and may be longer ; training is very thorough and facilities lavishly supplied. The régime, especially for the boys, is one of monastic rigour with constant stress on bodily perfection and fierce, unquestioning, fanatic faith in Adolf Hitler's mission in the establishment of the " True and Eternal Germany ". The qualities of leadership necessary to persuade less enthusiastic youths to dedicate themselves to their task with the same selflessness are carefully cultivated, for a religion of the sword must have stout followers as well as determined leaders.

At the very apex of the training programme stands the Academy for Youth Leaders at Braunschweig, completed in 1939. This is for young men only : an imposing edifice topped by a colossal statue of two muscular striding youths—a proper finishing school for those who choose leadership in the Hitler Youth as a profession. The period of training is one year, and no one is accepted who has not actively served in the movement for a considerable time ; novices are barred. After the year's training, which follows the lines of the National Leadership Schools, but much more intensively, the candidate must spend at least six months in the foreign service of the Hitler Youth— Norway, Slovakia, Italy, and so on.

The Adolf Hitler Schools are not, strictly speaking, a part of the Hitler Youth Leadership training programme, but close connections demonstrably exist. At present there may be as many as thirty throughout the Reich, each one planned to accommodate some four thousand students. They got under way in 1934, and were at first named after various " old fighters " in the Nazi Party.   This proved embarrassing, however, for one bore the name of the notorious Ernst Roehm, purged in 1934 under disgraceful circumstances.   Since 1937, therefore, they have all been rendered sacrosanct by being named for the Immaculate Adolf.   These schools, too, remorselessly select according to merit—at least, so the Nazis claim, and if merit be construed as ability to lead other young Nazis, the claim is probably justified.

The tie-up of the Adolf Hitler Schools with the regular Youth Service comes from the fact that the lads chosen for super-training are selected from the ranks of the Junior Boys.   They are withdrawn from their ordinary fellows at the age of twelve, and although the basis of selection is not known, it must certainly include demonstration of potential capacity for higher leadership.

For six years these lads pursue a course of physical, mental, and so-called " philosophical " training, akin to that of the National Leadership Schools but not aimed at preparation for specialized service.   At eighteen the Adolf Hitler students enter the Labour Service and the army, and in peacetime were then to spend seven years in practical experience ; namely, learning a trade or profession or working in a governmental bureau.

This period elapsed, the plan calls for the choice of a quarter of each graduating group ; these ultra-elect are to be sent on to the highest training centres of the ecclesia, viz., the Castles of the Order.   Of these there were three in 1939, located in Pomerania, the Rhineland, and Bavaria.   The lower divisions of the Adolf Hitler Schools have been munificently fitted out, but they are far surpassed by the Castles of the Order.   Luxury of equipment, beauty of surroundings, and effectiveness of design are noteworthy.   Such super-schools are literally intended to develop a " new aristocracy of leadership " in Germany.   Geared to a long-time programme, however, and getting under way only in 1934, they will have turned out relatively few finished products before the collapse of the Nazis brings on the Twilight of the Gods.

The Nazis, however, have also had an effective short-time programme complementing the Regional and National Leadership Work as well as that of the Adolf Hitler Schools.   This is the system, launched in 1937, called the Leader Schooling Work of the Hitler Youth.   Participation is voluntary, and is carried on through the Work Fellowships of Hitler Youth leaders who meet on their own initiative once a week throughout the year to expand and deepen their knowledge and skill in leading German youngsters. The chief guides of these Work Fellowships are not always Hitler Youth leaders ; they may be Party officials, scholars, scientists, or others whose interest and local availability make them convenient rallying points. On the average, the Fellowships enlist about twenty participants, consisting of Hitler Youth leaders from all levels of the hierarchy, with the lower of course predominating. Schnabel comments :

As in the general schooling in the Hitler Youth, this leadership training is not concerned primarily with transmitting facts and knowledge to the leaders. Much more is the leader to be directed towards thinking for himself and independent action. He must be politically activated, and must learn to fit every individual happening of the day into a total picture of the world. . . . It is therefore obvious that we shall not work with endless theories . . . but upon the basis of objective and exact scientific research results.[12]

How " objective " and " exact " are the scientific research results on which the discussions are based can be indicated by saying that many of the programme outlines read like the table of contents of *Mein Kampf*. Externally, however, there is no lack of pedagogical aids ; printed materials, special broadcasts, phonograph records, sound motion pictures, projection slides, models and maps are abundantly available, and first-hand contacts with the various fields studied are fostered by subsidized trips and out-of-town accommodations.

Considered as a whole, the Leader Schooling Work follows a pattern much like the Home Evening of the State Youth. This is the regular Wednesday evening meeting where each squad of ten to fifteen boys or girls meets at its nest for several hours of carefully prepared indoctrination.

Of course, there are striking differences between the Home Evening and the Work Fellowship, primarily because of the age levels involved and the fact that the Fellowship workers are already leaders trying to better their skills and, no doubt, to rise in rank. Constantly dangling before them is the prize of a year's training at one of the Adolf Hitler Schools ; ardent demonstration of attention and initiative is thereby ensured.

The voluntary attendance at these meetings is consistent with Nazi notions of leadership. The high priests of the Party recognize that leaders who have to be forced into training are not likely to carry responsibility successfully later on. As always, however, " voluntary " has a string to it.   Those who do not take advantage of the Work Fellowships languish, like Boanerges Blitzen, " in a district desolate and dry, while they see promotion yearly pass them by ".   Before 1941, they could even be openly transferred from the Select Cadre to the " ordinary " general body, with no chance of holding public office, with its preferments and emoluments, in the great ecclesia of the National Socialist State.

The transmission of the sacred value-system thus far outlined has gone on outside the educational system in the narrower sense ; " extra-curricular activities " have absorbed our attention. What of the ordinary schools ?   Have the Nazis left them untouched while concentrating on the State Youth system ?   Far from it ;   pressure towards " co-operation " has been steadily increasing, primarily because the Nazis have insisted on redefining the role and function of the school-teacher.   They claim that under the conventional teacher training system the great majority of pedagogues are uninspired, mediocre pension-seekers in spite rather than because of whom German boys and girls gain insight into the world.

These attacks soon brought about a situation in which aggressive, thoroughly Nazified youngsters showed so much impatience with everything that they could not immediately apply in the interest of the Eternal Reich that systematic class instruction in some subjects became almost impossible.   Instructors in the higher schools, and even the universities, began to complain that their more ardently Nazi charges lacked knowledge essential to sound work in medicine, engineering, industrial chemistry, and other utilitarian subjects, to say nothing of advanced science and scholarship.   A running battle between the conventional school system and the educational aspirations of the State Youth has gone on year after year, but the Nazis seem to feel it necessary to deny that it is the intention of the State Youth organization to dominate the educational scene completely :

We are not reaching out towards other fields of work, but at the same time it is not a matter of indifference to us whether the youth who have been entrusted to us, and whose hearts belong to us, are happy in the schools. . . .   We do not consider the teacher to be our enemy.   Whoever says that should take into account that more than ten thousand teachers have co-operated voluntarily and with high enthusiasm in the Hitler Youth principle of training and education. . . .   With us it is a matter of education, not of legal authority and offices. . . .   But because of the responsibility which we bear

Pictures of Hitler appearing in official youth handbooks frequently had the Black Eagle of Prussia in the background ; Hitler Youth flags also bore it.

for the future of our people, we must and will apply ourselves to the solution of the total problem of National Socialist training.[13]

It must be remembered, of course, that the State Youth versus School System controversy does *not* revolve about the question of whether the schools should be Nazified, co-ordinated, regimented. After the seizure of power in 1933, one of the first moves of the Nazis was toward the complete control of education.

Each school day is begun and ended with a ceremony exalting the National Socialist State ; this includes the two national hymns : namely, the old, once innocuous *Deutschland über Alles*, now given world-dominating meaning, and the new Nazi theme song, the *Horst Wessel Lied*. Moreover, all teachers are sworn to support the Nazi movement and to give the " German greeting " to their students, i.e., the stiff-arm Nazi salute borrowed from the old Roamers. A special manual distributed by the Nazis to all teachers early in the co-ordinating process contained this admonition :

The primacy of politics, especially in the teaching of history, must replace the detachment of traditional education. . . . The teacher must lead his pupils to adopt a decisive position which clearly distinguishes friend and foe in politics at home and abroad. The Ministry of Education expects the teachers of history to espouse National Socialism positively.[14]

Thus *how* to Nazify rather than *whether* to Nazify was envisaged as the problem. Should the State Youth restrict itself to extra-curricular activities, or should it completely take over all educational functions ? Everything that can be learned about developments since the outbreak of World War II makes it seem probable that complete regimentation would have been achieved had it not been for the draining off of younger teachers by the war effort.

Earlier, von Schirach expressed his view of the situation about as follows :

Leadership in the State Youth is to come no more from the teaching profession than from any other occupation. Carpenters, lawyers, dentists, and mail carriers have as much to contribute to the training of youth as have teachers. The natural ability to command respect is not a monopoly enjoyed by the educational craft alone.[15]

If this were to be taken as a definitive standpoint, the role of the teacher in the Reich becomes clearer. His responsibility, apparently, is simply that of presenting for absorption the masses of " facts " which Nazified " science " has produced. His effort is not to inspire youth except, possibly, as his conduct provides an example ; rather, he is simply to transmit the information which the authorities of the ecclesia regard as essential. All other educational processes lie in the hands of the State Youth leaders.

Such limiting of the teacher's duties seems to conflict with the Nazi demand that the teacher must possess " a leader personality ". In all probability, however, the apparent contradiction can be resolved by viewing the limitation as purely temporary ; it is simply a means of making use of existing personnel until such time as the Nazi teacher training programme can turn out—if it can—the all-round guides, companions, friends, and teachers who constitute the ideal of National Socialist pedagogy. Until this can be achieved, the Nazis do not want to run the risk of bungling the inculcation of sacred values by entrusting the task to holdovers from earlier days ; extra-curricular functionaries must carry on until the new priesthood can take over entirely.

Passing over the Nazification of theological training and supernaturalistic instruction which is just one aspect of the religious perversion previously analysed, and which in any case is rapidly diminishing in importance in the Third Reich, we now turn to a phase of education possessing many novel features. This is in the vocational field, long neglected and disdained by the Roamers and even by the alliance youth, in large measure because of their middle-class affiliations. Youth tutelage, with its organizations for apprentices and factory workers, had given somewhat more heed to the matter, but usually had little to say about vocations as such ; instead, " culture " designed to remedy the deficiencies of lower-class training was offered, all too often in forms hard to digest. By contrast, the State Youth system has made much of vocational education ; it is now one of the pillars of the ecclesia.

In discussing differences between the Roamers and the State Youth, von Schirach made this significant statement :

The symbol of the old youth movement was the expedition, but the symbol of the Hitler Youth is the National Vocational Competitions ! [16]

Profiting by the unsettled conditions prevailing when they first seized power, the Nazis redistributed the boys and girls just

Vocational Competition glorified.

beginning work in the trades and crafts with an eye to preparation for war. On every kiosk there appeared placards : " The Selection of Your Life Work Can No Longer Be Left to Chance ! " The newspapers, radio, motion pictures, and all other devices of communication were utilized to hammer home the same message. Vocational guidance stations were rapidly established, and youngsters were shunted back and forth so that shortages of skilled labour, both industrial and agricultural, would not cripple future nationalistic efforts, and so that awkward surpluses of unskilled and unemployed workers would not accumulate revolutionary impetus in the large cities.

In 1934 the first National Vocational Competition was held ; approximately a million German youth, one-third of whom were girls, took part. As the plan developed further, it embodied careful preparation of competitive " practical " examinations by the German Labour Front in co-operation with the office of the Youth Leader of the Reich. These examinations are offered to all comers between the ages of fourteen and eighteen, and a wide range of occupations is covered.

Usually the " examination " consists of a specified task to be completed to the best of the applicant's ability in a given time. Apprentice bricklayers, for example, are given the necessary materials and are then required to put up a section of wall. The local winners are then sent on to regional competitions, from whence those not eliminated go on to the finals in Berlin. The ultimately victorious are honoured at a luncheon at which Hitler or someone touched with his grace appears in person, and where scholarships and prizes are handed out.

Noteworthy is the fact that although the preliminary contests are based on vocational skill alone, the winners of the finals must have skill *plus* : personality, family background, physical appearance, and other attributes are considered to an extent relevant to the tasks at hand.

Over and above reliance on ordinary Nazi motives, the scheme is designed to bring the spirit of competitive sport into vocational training. Constant propaganda appeals persuade German youth to " train " as eagerly for the vocational com-petitions as they would for football, running, or swimming. The pattern of preliminaries, semi-finals, and finals is a direct carry-over of traditional sports methods.

If Nazi leaders are to be believed—and here there is little reason to doubt them—a double purpose is fulfilled by this vocational competition. Not only is the interest of the trainees in their occupation heightened, but in addition the national authorities easily get an annual census of potential labour supply in various fields, as well as the opportunity to estimate general advances or setbacks in skill. With this information and increasing totalitarian control, youngsters can be switched from one field to another as national needs dictate. Totalitarian planning therefore has one more known quantity with which to reckon.

Beyond all this is the substantial gain registered even by those who fail to get beyond the local competitions, for they are coached by older fellow-workers, and there is always the hope of getting farther up the list next time. One of the reasons why German war *matériel* has remained so relatively good in spite of scarce raw materials and frequent bombing undoubtedly lies in this aspect of the totalitarian economy.

Further, the vocational competitions provide one more opportunity to inculcate the sacred value-system. " By your work you win not only for yourself, but also for the German folk community ! " Here as elsewhere the ecclesia runs smoothly.

The vocational competitions of course differentiate between girls and boys. Housework and the tobacco industry list no male competitors, and the girls are not offered vocational examinations in lumbering, mining, and similar tasks where heavy physical strain is certain. Sex differentiation, however, appears most clearly in other phases of the State Youth programme ; these should now be inspected.

The National Socialist conception of the importance of woman's reproductive role dominates the training of girls from the very outset :

We know what we are doing when we give the small girl a doll. We are making sure that this child is exposed to the symbol of her future motherhood, and we are unanimous in the desire that this playing child will, if possible, become that which she is constructed to be : a mother . . . the substance of womanhood is motherhood.[17]

The training of the future mothers of the National Socialist population is fundamental in Nazi plans. Girls are segregated from boys and handled as vital cogs in the operation of a totalitarian society. It is not assumed that woman's biological structure will automatically dispose her towards efficient motherhood ;

a carefully controlled process of training moulds the biological
" raw material ".

The three main divisions of the Youth Service for girls have
already been noted. Differential sex treatment most clearly
appears in the fourteen to eighteen and the eighteen to twenty-
one brackets. The former, characteristic of LGG, the League
of German Girls, has physical health as the cornerstone of its
programme.

Flowing directly from the idea that woman's destiny is motherhood, there is a conscious effort to remould aesthetic, sexual, and
economic attitudes as they bear on the female figure. Artists are
encouraged to glorify the peasant type ; in the 1939 Exhibition
of German Art at Munich the sturdy, robust, buxom girl was
exalted. Careful discrimination was shown : not only was the
hipless and bosomless boyish figure avoided, but so likewise were
the flabby, soft models of Rubens-like mould, as well as the
chunky, hard-muscled " lady wrestler ".

This is not to say that the Nazis discourage athletics for girls
—on the contrary, they merely insist that men and women should
not try to achieve the same results in athletic competition. The
ideal female athlete must be a *female* athlete, which means that
eventual motherhood is the chief criterion of fitness. As early
as 1935 nearly half a million girls participated in over three
hundred sports festivals designed to further the process of " buxom-
ization ". A sports achievement badge is now liberally bestowed :

> The requirements for this decoration are determined by the
> basic principles of LGG sports : namely, no supreme efforts by
> virtuosos in particular specialties, but a fairly good record by every-
> one in all fields. Supplemental to this a sound grasp of open-country
> and hiking practices is required, as well as a knowledge of first aid.
> All gifted girls are given the chance to develop themselves further
> by work in the Calisthenics and Sports Clubs.[18]

Some girls and young women are prevented from joining in
LGG physical training because of age, type of occupation, and
the like, and for these there are free summer camps making
possible excursions lasting from a week to a month or more.
Thereby such girls " can gather fresh resources for the strain of
their work days throughout the year ". Since 1939, of course,
camps of this kind probably have been greatly curtailed or
eliminated altogether.

Leadership in the LGG is provided for by thirty-six regional
and three national leadership schools, with a yearly output of

nearly twenty thousand. These schools have programmes similar to those offered to boys and young men, with the modifications necessary to fit the Nazi conception of woman's role.

Extensive planning for the vocational schooling of girls has been undertaken ; it is designed to place them for a year either as farmworkers in the country or as household helps in the city. In either case the vocational competitions are strongly stressed in the hope that otherwise monotonous toil will be rendered vital and interesting.

It must be said that Nazi youth publications are surprisingly realistic about the hardships encountered by those who choose to spend their year of service in the country. Hoeing, for example, is thus described : " Four consecutive days down endless rows you have to dig along on hands and knees ".[19] Back of this almost brutal frankness undoubtedly lies one of the sacred values of the Nazi ecclesia ; the hard primitivism of the early Roamers has been glorified in order that the German people may be prepared to live in a country either at war or ceaselessly getting ready for it.

In the city the training of domestic help is carried out with the assistance of relatively elaborate facilities, not overlooking the devices of ideological indoctrination. The girl is established in a home to help the housewife with the care of children, preparation of meals, and general domestic tasks. True to the objectives of the totalitarian state, the women to whom these girls are apprenticed are encouraged to bear another child, inasmuch as the " home economic year " assistant can help with the training of other children and in keeping the household running smoothly.

Thus far this hasty sketch of the girls' programme has focused on the fourteen to eighteen age group. The Junior Girls' activities are essentially in preparation for the adolescent period, but the eighteen to twenty-one brackets require more extended comment.

After passing through the LGG, Faith and Beauty training begins. Much attention is given to personal attractiveness achieved in a " natural " way through " health and spirituality " and general cultural refinement. The physical training programme is maintained with unabated zeal, but in other matters a considerable range of choice is possible. Those who like music, painting, sports, and similar avocations or accomplishments are given a chance to become proficient. Moreover, there is a strong effort to develop general aesthetic appreciation, particularly in the

" everyday " things of life, in the hope that all Germany, sooner or later, will learn to value " what we National Socialists believe to be in good taste ".

When twenty-one is reached, the young women leave the ranks of the State Youth, but are still members of the Party. If they marry before this time, they withdraw from Faith and Beauty in order to enter the National Socialist Married Women's Organization.   The ecclesia never relaxes its grip !

The general Nazi ideology in these matters has been thus set forth by Adolf the Bachelor :

Along with the training of boys, the Folk State can direct the education of girls from the same points of view. Here, too, the main emphasis must be put on physical training ; after that comes the cultivation of spiritual values, and finally, attention to . . . [the intellect].   The goal of female education must always be the future mother.[20]

Vital in the whole scheme of conformist education, whether extra-curricular or regular, are the external symbols.   The methods and instruments of the Roamers have been directly copied by the Nazis in many important respects ; the differences lie primarily in the vastly greater scope and systematization.

Anyone observing a squad of Hitler Youth on an expedition (at least before 1939) would see lutes, fluttering ribbons, knapsacks, and cooking pots, and would hear roaming songs which, although not drawn from The Pluck (which the Nazis have prohibited), would sound much like the old repertory.   Even the uniforms would not strike an utterly false note, for the alliance youth of the 'twenties had abandoned the individualistic raggle-taggle of Karl Fischer's boisterous crew.   The same observer could overhear talk about the extraordinary qualities of the squad leader, the sense of fusion, folk community, and Germany's mission which would sound surprisingly like the stock-in-trade of the Free German Youth.   The actual meanings attached to these externally similar symbols would have little resemblance to even those of the two or three years after Hohe Meissner, but the accomplishment of perversion has been so skilful that our observer, if he were a mere outsider, would see little if any change.

Moreover, the nests and lodges of the old Roamers have been copied on a grandiose scale, in the Small Home system of the State Youth.   Usually located in open spaces, but often quite accessible by means of ordinary city transportation, they serve

all the traditional purposes of both nest and lodge, and gear into
the propaganda system by providing meeting places for the
Wednesday Home Evening at which indoctrination is carried on.

Some of the best architects of Germany have lavished their
talents on the designing of the Small Homes.[21] Apparently
unlimited funds flowing from taxes, gifts, and the incessant
cup-jingling of State Youth youngsters are at the disposal of the
architects and builders. Hundreds of plans fitting varying needs,
groups, and surroundings have been turned out, and construction
was going on rapidly. even in the early years of World War II.
Oftentimes the plans provided for extensive terrain (the military
term is used advisedly) around the home : sports fields utilizable
as drill grounds ; hills, ditches, and hedges for skirmishing ; and
water barriers which also serve as swimming pools, along with
less obviously military facilities, were meticulously plotted and
built.[22]

The Small Homes are not designed as hostels ; they serve
supplementary or complementary purposes. The hostel system
itself was well under way before the First World War, and with
the coming of the Weimar Republic it underwent rapid growth.
During 1920, there were nearly a million overnight hostel stays,
and by 1933 these had increased to five million.[23]

To be sure, some of the hostels were crude and poorly kept,
but in the face of Nazi clamour to the effect that the Party started
everything worthwhile in Germany, it is well to remember that
the largest German hostel, the House of Youth in Frankfurt am
Main, was built by Social Democratic and Socialist youth groups
with the aid of subsidies from the Weimar Republic. It has
more than one thousand beds, a lecture hall and motion picture
auditorium, a large restaurant, hot and cold running water, and
showers. A well-organized programme of social activities ran
throughout the year under the Republic. The large new Nazi
hostels at Leipzig and Dresden virtually duplicate the Frankfurt
model. Moreover, abandoned or unused castles were adapted
to youth hostel purposes long before the seizure of power ; the
Nazis have simply taken a good idea and pushed it to its logical
conclusion.

Nevertheless, it cannot be denied that there has been much
improvement and expansion under the Nazis. In 1938 almost
eight million overnight stays were registered,[24] and cleanliness
and efficiency, sometimes lacking in a few of the more amateurish
centres of pre-Hitler days, were everywhere fostered. The only

difference between a good hostel and a first-class hotel is the
necessity for self-service, simplicity of accommodation, lack of
privacy, and the tremendous hubbub which swarms of adolescent
boys and girls naturally perpetrate. Ideal as propaganda centres
for any cause, good or bad, the hostels served the Nazi perverters
well.

But after all, roaming is unsettling unless very closely controlled ; the Nazis really prefer substitutes "just as good as the
original ". Such substitutes have been found in the Rural
Service Homes, for these help to foster, far more effectively than
can the hostel system, the sacred ideology of Blood and Soil.
The idealizations of The Linden Tree are revived in altered guise ;
the peasant becomes the source of solidly German racial worth,
steadiness, unquestioning devotion to the task at hand, and conformity to the demands of the powers that be. The soil on which
he labours is ennobled and sanctified by his efforts ; Germany the
Blessed is presented as a tangible cluster of peasant holdings
rather than an abstract entity called a nation. The folk community, in its ideal outlines, becomes a large peasant family
living on diversified but essentially united and sacred plots of
soil. An absurd ideology for a highly industrialized nation ?
Yes, but "if men define situations as real, they are real in their
consequences ".

Over and above the gains registered by the ecclesia through
such use of the Rural Service Homes, there was also a definite
economic purpose. In the effort to establish autarky, i.e.,
complete economic self-sufficiency, the Nazis tried to start a Back
to the Land movement. They realized that the approaching war
would bring blockade with it, and that food supplies were crucial.
In conjunction with the Rural Service Homes, therefore, they
launched the programme of Land Service.

The Land Service section of the State Youth springs directly
from the work of the *Artamanen*, conservative alliance youth with
agrarian reform as their goal.[25] They were drawn into the Hitler
Youth Service in the fall of 1934. With this impetus, the Land
Service began with forty-five groups and about five hundred
participants, mostly unemployed from sixteen to twenty. Of
these about one hundred and fifty remained in the country during
the winter of 1934, representing what the Nazis hoped would be
a permanent precipitate. In succeeding years the Land Service
rapidly expanded, and by 1938 the number of Land Service
workers in the Hitler Youth rose to eighteen thousand, and of

these the percentage who chose agriculture as their life work—
or said they did—was slightly over twenty. Quoth von Schirach :

I see in the Land Service of the Hitler Youth a claim which the
land of our nation makes upon all those who live in the cities of
the Fatherland. The time which one spends in his lifetime working
on the land is never lost, and if nothing else were to be achieved than
that a great portion of to-day's youth in their later life would have
a clearcut and intelligent attitude toward agricultural work as such,
then a great deal would have been accomplished.[26]

Voluntary measures, however, were not trusted ; 1934 saw
the enactment of a law for a compulsory Country Year. All
youngsters completing eight years of elementary schooling were
required to spend nine months of the following year in the country.
Officially, this is a kind of introduction to the regular Labour
Service which comes at the age of eighteen. It is described as
the initiation of the child into " the reality of the duties involved
in the privilege of participation in the German folk community ".
Here is a day in the Land Service Home :

6.00	A.M.	Rising bell, followed by setting-up exercises and a cross-country run.
6.30–7.00		Cleaning up.
7.00		Flag raising in full uniform, followed by breakfast and orders for the day.
8.00–12.00		Work, followed by luncheon.
1.00–2.00	P.M.	Free time (compulsory rest in bed for the girls).
2.00–3.15		Sport, followed by tea.
4.15–6.00		National political schooling and group work.
7.00		Flag lowering in full uniform, followed by evening meal.
7.30–8.30		Campfire circle.
9.00		Lights out.

In general the morning period of work consisted of agricultural
work and gardening in the fields, usually with the neighbouring
peasants. This type of work also included cooking and house-
keeping for the girls in the peasant families and work of a similar
nature in the homes of the city people recently settled on the land
by the National Socialist administration. The girls had an opportunity to run a harvest kindergarten [really a day nursery for children
under six whose mothers are at work at harvesting] for the families
of the region.

. . . The two-hour period of group discussion and national
political schooling was largely made up of discussion of current
problems which arose from the daily contacts of the children with
the agricultural population : race questions, agricultural questions,
discussion of the peasants' attachment to the soil, the question of

settlement of excess city populations on the land, geography and
geo-political discussion, the World War and the Treaty of Versailles.
Especially in connection with these discussions is the National
Socialist point of view ever again brought up and interwoven. In
addition great importance is laid upon the stressing of the local
peasant holidays and celebrations.

The evening fireside hour is very important, particularly to
acquaint the city children with the local peasant folk dances and
songs. Many times the natives are brought into the evening life
of the home and quite often groups of the children are invited to
the peasants' homes. The local priest or pastor is invited to interpret
the religious sentiments of the local population. Local officers of the
National Socialist Party are at all times drawn into these evening
discussions, prominent among whom is the local peasant leader
(*Ortsbauernführer*).[27]

The connection of the Land Service Homes with the Land
Year Programme should now be fairly clear, but it should also
be noted that the homes are an important adjunct of the voluntary
summer harvest work started by the State Youth in June, 1939.
Under this scheme it is possible to choose between going to a
regular summer camp for a month or helping peasants to get
in the crops. In that very year thousands of university students,
as well as younger Hitler Youth and even Junior Boys, spent
their summer vacations in the harvesting effort, thereby releasing
many older persons for military service. This has gone on ever
since. The enterprise was probably thought of as temporary,
but the officials concerned would no doubt be glad if a goodly
portion of the volunteers decided to remain among the peasants ;
autarky is a crying need during the war. Moreover, the sacred
value-system of the ecclesia, with its focus on what are believed
to be peasant values, is thereby reinforced.

The mass of detail presented here has perhaps been wearisome,
but the whole notion of an elaborately devised and shrewdly
marshalled set of schemes for the perpetuation of a great ecclesia
is so foreign to most of us that reasonably full presentation of the
evidence has seemed unavoidable. It would otherwise have
been hard to see how the Tumult of the 'Twenties could ever have
issued in the totalitarianism of the 'thirties and thereafter, no
matter how adroit the perversion.

Manifestly, the Nazis never deluded themselves into thinking
that their early twistings and trimmings of youth ideas and
activities would carry the movement beyond the stage of revival
fervour. Once their converts had " hit the sawdust trail ", so
to speak, the perverters immediately began to institutionalize

Hitler Youth idealizations.

everything that would in any way contribute to the perpetuation of the new sacred system.

They had to guard against possible backsliding and fresh sectarianism, but not only that : they had to stir the emotions and provide for the instruction of the oncoming generation. The youngsters who had experienced the thrills of the struggle for power pulsed with vivid memories of bloody fights, hardwon victories, doctrines imparted in the glow of unprecedented happenings. The new recruits felt the *élan* of excitement, true enough, but still they had never been " old fighters ". Nothing dared be left undone that would ensure fresh possession and its accompanying willingness to die for the Führer and his Eternal Reich.

Moreover, the great mass of the German people had been whipped up to a frenzied demand for territory, population, and power which could not be won by peaceful means. Morale-sapping penetration, tactical compromise, diplomatic jockeying, divide-and-conquer strategy were all used to gain time ; the Nazis well knew that they had aroused expectations which in the end only war could gratify. And they needed time : time to amass raw materials, shift production of weapons into high gear, extend and intensify agriculture, and exploit every source of fuel and oil.

These things, however, are merely dead matter and its agents ; they are inert unless filled with fierce life by an all-powerful ideology. Time was also needed for the perfecting of the work of the great ecclesia, for the callousing, subordinating, and regimenting of mind as well as body. Six strenuous years passed by, each one witnessing greater stiffening and hardening of the sacred value-system and its ecclesiastical framework. At last doom's thunder-peal sounded, and millions of German youth, demoniacally possessed in heart and soul, rushed exulting down a steep place.

NOTES

In this chapter I have drawn heavily from the dissertation of Robert C. Schmid mentioned in the Preface and in the Notes of several previous chapters. Although I have paraphrased a few passages from Schmid here and there in earlier pages, I have done so much more frequently in this chapter, and have also quoted some of his translations without checking the originals (inasmuch as they are inaccessible).

1. Albrecht Möller, *Wesen und Forderung der Hitler Jugend* (Breslau, 1935), p 71.

2. The first name is sometimes given as Gerhard, but this is an error.

3. Many difficulties arose because of the split between the Select Cadre (*Stamm*-HJ) and ordinary State Youth. Therefore, in March, 1941, it was decreed that *all* youngsters received into the organization from March 31st on would be classified as belonging to the Select Cadre! The real purpose, of course, was to conceal the compulsory features thereby introduced.

4. Baldur von Schirach, *Revolution der Erziehung* (Munich, 1939), p. 101.

5. Wiese-Becker, *Systematic Sociology* (New York, 1932), pp. 624–5.

6. Max Weber, *Wirtschaft und Gesellschaft* (Tübingen, 1922), pp. 144–8, 758–78.

7. Schmid's dissertation has an illuminating section called "The Story of Baldur von Schirach".

8. Ernst Troeltsch, *The Social Teachings of the Christian Churches* (Wyon translation, New York, 1931), I, p. 339.

9. Schmid, *op. cit.*, pp. 170–3.

10. A repetition of the passage on p. 229.

11. A statement made by a young Hitler Youth leader in Cologne in 1939, stenographically recorded by Schmid.

12. Reimund Schnabel, *Das Führerschulungswerk der Hitler Jugend* (Berlin, 1938), p. 10.

13. Von Schirach, *op. cit.*, p. 121.

14. J. W. Taylor, *Youth Welfare in Germany*, p. 167, quoted in *Pädagogisches Zentralblatt*, 1933, pp. 537 ff.

15. Baldur von Schirach, reference not available, quoted in Schmid, *op. cit.*, p. 200.

16. Baldur von Schirach, *Hitler Jugend : Idee und Gestalt*, p. 49, quoted in Schmid, *op. cit.*, p. 209.

17. Albrecht E. Günther, *Geist der Jungmannschaft* (Hamburg, 1934) p. 20.

18. Hilde Münske, *Mädel in aller Welt* (Berlin, 1936), p. 13.

19. "Mädel vor der Berufswahl", *Die Mädelschaft* (Berlin, August, 1938), p. 17.

20. Adolf Hitler, quoted in von Schirach, *op. cit.*, p. 95.

21. *Das Klein-Heim der Hitler Jugend* (Berlin, 1939), *passim*.

22. Helmut Höckel, ed., *Das Jugendgelände* (Berlin, 1939), *passim*.

23. Schmid, *op. cit.*, p. 230.

24. *Ibid.*

25. *Das Landdienstheim der Hitler-Jugend* (Berlin, 1939), p. 9.

26. Von Schirach, introduction to *ibid.*

27. Taylor, *op. cit.*, pp. 173–4.

CHAPTER IX

PREMONITIONS : "WHAT OF THE NIGHT?"

Ye know who use the Crystal Ball
(To peer by stealth on Doom),
The Shade that, shaping first of all,
Prepares an empty room.
Then doth It pass
Like breath from glass,
But, on the extorted vision bowed intent,
No man considers why It came or went.
—KIPLING, "Before a Midnight".

The temptation to say " Thus endeth this lesson " is strong, but responsibility to the reader who has followed the toilsome path up to this point cannot be so lightly dismissed. A backward glance along the trail seems to be called for, and more or less well-grounded speculation as to where it may eventually lead is likewise in order.

Toward the beginning of the Wilhelmian era German youngsters, particularly those of the middle class, found themselves caught up in a dizzy whirl of social change while they were at the same time expected to yield reverence to a moral world still defined for them in terms of Grandfather Friedl's childhood. Irreconcilable contradictions soon made themselves agonizingly felt, and the idealistic revolt began.

It was aimless and almost formless ; escape from an intolerable present by almost any loophole was the one thing ardently desired. The past of the Biedermeier time provided an enthralling myth of not wholly imaginary character, for it had indeed been a span of years during which humble and unassuming albeit stolid contentment had prevailed in sheltered nooks and corners. Even when the youthful escapists found the bucolic society of 1825 too placid and inert to inspire fantasy, there was still the remoter past of the pirate, the Indian fighter, the soldier of fortune, and the peasant rebel to furnish ecstatic release.

Roaming arose, and its youthful practitioners rejoiced at what they held to be the discovery of their essential selves in and through the hardships they encountered. Rejecting the despised wisdom of their elders, they rendered homage to their own leaders, following them with a devotion that only the conception of a naturalized *charisma* or " grace " can explain. Belittlers and challengers made their divisive appearance ; little cults and sects mushroomed everywhere.

The unhappy effects of boy-from-girl isolation became manifest here and there among the divided ranks ; lads found their surging emotions rushing towards their particular hero and others who followed in his train. Even the bristling thickets of German convention, however, could not long separate Pyramus and Thisbe ; by far the greater number of youth movement adherents broke through the barriers. Girls and boys roamed afield together ; only a hopelessly warped minority held to the ideal of Damon and Pythias. True, that handful continued to make its distorting presence felt through the whole course of subsequent events, but it could not stop the natural mingling of the sexes.

Eventually the cults and conventicles drew together, shortly before the First World War, in an unstable union that heightened feelings of self-realization, sense of fusion, and " grace-endowed " leadership to a pitch engendering vague ideas of a great mission. Nothing less than the regeneration—how, no one knew—of a depraved Germany was the hazily outlined vision. Character-istically enough, the formula embodying these adolescent aspira-tions was interpreted in scores of ways ; at one pole clustered chastity, vegetarianism, espousal of the folk community ; at the other, full response to any deep affection, " living dangerously ", utter contempt for adult standards. Back and forth and in between were scattered anti-Semitism, pacifism, cloudy exalta-tion of nakedness, self-abnegation, fervent mutual aid, nationalism, socialism, theosophy and anthroposophy, romantic Catholicism, Lutheran communism, and almost anything else one cares to name.

As the crises of the war grew more searching and severe, and as the trials of the early 'twenties bore down with full weight, groups embodying attitudes congenial to Germanic solidarity gained the upper hand. Until late in the 'twenties, however, almost every creed that had begun to clamour for attention decades earlier could still count on little flocks of the faithful, waning in significance though they were.

The dwindling influence of diversity was clear to every informed observer, but to the superficial eye the youth movement had always presented a semblance of unity. The distinction between youth movement and youth tutelage, to take only one instance, had never greatly impressed the foreign admirers of lute-strumming, folk-dancing, and romantic expeditions ; any German youngster with linen jacket, shorts, and sandals was thought to be much the same as any other. By 1925, however, the superficial visitor could no longer be taken so strictly to task ; the youth movement had succeeded so well, where its externals were concerned, that the old distinction between youthful spontaneity and adult manipulation began to lose its meaning. Organizations that had once avoided the youth movement like the plague began to play the sedulous ape, and sects that had formerly drawn aloof from ageing leaders fell increasingly under the sway of eternal adolescents.

Brutal struggle as glorified by the Nazi :
" Science teaches us that the weaker peoples must perish."

But soon the cooling cauldrons were heated afresh ; fires kindled by the Nazis brought simmering at the edges, bubbling in the centre. Boys and girls who had tired of the flat, lukewarm sedatives of accustomed routine found the hot concoctions of the Hitler Youth strangely appealing. Most of them could do no more than taste and spew out the near-scalding mixtures, but the fumes held them entranced ; they did little or nothing to extinguish the fire, and some of them piled on fuel. Here and there, to be sure, there were shouts of " Poison ! " and frantic attempts to overturn the reeking vessels were made, but the thronging bystanders, in their fascinated passivity, formed an outer ring so dense that the scattered assailants who pierced their way to the centre were easily defeated and trampled underfoot by aggressively defiant Hitler Youth.

Dropping the figure : The weakening sects were transformed

into denominations which could not withstand the combined effects of dulled indifference and fervent attack. The Hitler Youth, at first only a handful of brutally fanatic devotees led by maniacally cunning perverters, successfully transformed their new faith into the dogmas of what is in all essentials a great State Church, and triumphantly applied the injunction : "Go out into the highways and hedges, and compel them to come in, that my house may be filled ". After the seizure of power, heretics and dissenters were silenced or crushed ; finally, perversion by the Führer's grace was accomplished.

What of the future ? Has conformity to Hitler's gospel been so thoroughly enforced in word and deed that even the imminent collapse of Nazidom will not undo the work of perversion ? Questions such as this are easily asked ; answering them is another matter. Indeed, the conscientious investigator is often prey to a mood which makes him feel that silence is the better part of honesty. Guesses about the future of Germany, usually decked out with the tawdry finery of "estimate", "forecast", and "secret sources" have recently been tumbled forth in such rank profusion that they are now worth the well-known dime a dozen. Anthropologists ordinarily would venture no generalizations about a tribe of one or two hundred without a prolonged field work sojourn and intimate knowledge of the language and social structure *plus* multifarious other details. Yet some of them twitter persuasively about what is going to happen in a nation of at least sixty millions having more than a dozen differing regional mentalities—and this without any direct experience in the country itself or even reasonable familiarity with the tongue spoken. Psychiatrists who have hardly poked their noses outside the four walls of the clinic pompously belch forth their jargon : Germany is paranoid, or schizophrenic, or maniacally elated, and everything from mass shock therapy to individualized functional treatment is soberly proposed. Political scientists ponderously and prophetically intone the clauses of a new German constitution which will ensure the effective working of that oh-so-loosely-defined "democracy", or blithely outline the structure of a World State that is to bring healing to Germany and to all mankind. So one might go on throughout the range of scientific and scholarly specialists, to say nothing of the journalists and hack writers—but why be nasty without cease ?

Even when prophecies far less grandiose are projected, Everests of difficulty loom up. No one knows with any accuracy what the constellation of forces within the Germany of to-day actually is, nor does anyone, with the possible exception of a tiny coterie of experts, know what the announced policies of the Big Three *vis-à-vis* Germany will mean in detailed application. Moreover, there is no way of telling what modifications and adjustments may have to be made to meet changing circumstances, shifts in Big Three or United Nations' alignment, or the whims of parliamentary bodies and electorates. Prophesying later phases in a necessarily unique series of equally unique events can never be entirely scientific in any case, but when there are half a dozen unknown variables for every one that can be even approximately located and characterized, a crystal ball is an indispensable item of equipment.

What I shall have to say, therefore, must not be dignified with the adjective deriving from my professional specialty ; I am not indulging in " sociological " discourse. Granted, it is highly probable that anyone possessing a few elementary notions gleaned from the social sciences and having been a reasonably close student and observer of the matter in hand is a less capricious and prejudiced prophet than is the ordinary newspaper reader. In some realms of life, it may be true that Patrick Houlihan is right when he shouts that " Ivery man is as good as ivery other ", but even friend Patrick makes room for exceptions in the next breath—" an' some are a damn' soight betther ". In an equalitarian democracy, where one man represents one vote, it is of course literally true that one man's opinion is as good as another's, but I should be the last to admit that questions of scientific import can be adequately settled by counting noses or totalling arbitrary guesses : " Six here, six there, take your choice ".

With all due humility, qualification, and recognition of inescapable bias, I therefore think that I am not about to engage in guesswork pure and simple. In any given context of unique phenomena, some developments are possible and some are not. Only the megalomaniac would claim that he can unerringly lay his finger on that one of the alternate possibilities which will be realized, but even a relatively modest investigator may be able to cancel out the utterly fantastic forecasts.

What has been said amounts to this : There is no remotest assumption that the ensuing discussion of what may happen to German youth after the Nazi collapse is other than speculative.

Yet, speculation has limits, and these limits may be set carelessly or
with caution.   It is my fond belief that I shall err on the side of
caution.   This announcement made, I rush in where angels fear
to tread.

Until well into the third year of the present war, and perhaps
even the fourth, it is altogether likely that the external grip of
the Nazi party grew stronger and that the ideology of the folk
community as embodied in the Nazi system was hammered home
with ever greater energy.   In other words, the physical and
mental straitjackets within which the German people were confined were laced up more and more tightly.   Many Germans
tolerated or even welcomed the increasing rigour of control, but
here and there, particularly among youngsters not yet used to
such complete confinement, a good deal of restive wriggling unquestionably occurred.

Again, there is little reason to doubt that within the State
Youth system itself there was a further consolidation of routine and
a wider and wider reliance on the " grace of office ".   A nation
at war cannot undertake new enterprises designed primarily for
peacetime ends, nor can it avoid the draining off of young leaders
whose capacities lend them some touch of " personal grace ".
The established grooves must be followed and relatively mediocre
leaders must function on the home front.   Granted, the Party
did its best to exempt as many youth officials as possible ; there
was liberal use of the classification " u.k."—" indispensable ".
These officials strutted about in their uniforms as usual, but even
when they possessed the necessary personal qualities they could
not hope to compete with the *charisma* of the fighting forces.   In
the best of cases, therefore, they became mediocre by comparison
with the " grace of heroism " ; in the worst, they were mediocre
even by peacetime standards.   In either case their followers had
little cause to be carried away by enthusiasm.   As a matter of
fact, many bits of evidence combine to show that rebellious
restlessness and even open disrespect for official leaders has been
cropping up increasingly since as early as 1939.

Once more, there is much evidence to show that the State
Youth system moved into even closer touch with the directly
martial machine almost as soon as the war began.   To-day, of
course, boys and girls who are merely in their 'teens engage in
the frantic and futile digging of trenches and bunkers, and
youngsters of sixteen and less are flung into the maw of the People's
Levy, the *Volkssturm*.   As early as 1942, however, mere children

The Man with the Whip.

had to stand guard, act as messengers, gather scrap metal, and beg for blankets, warm clothing, and skis for the use of the troops instead of jingling tin cups marked " Small Homes for Youth ". Unquestionably State Youth activities have come to seem more and more like fixed duties rather than spontaneous jamborees ; thousands of youngsters must seek elsewhere the carefree abandon of which even the pre-war State Youth managed to preserve some semblance.

Further, propaganda appeals either followed the stereotypes well established before the opening of the war, or played on fear in the hope of intensifying the will to victory. In both instances gratifying visions of a roseate, romantically irresponsible future for Germany's youth were lacking. Children underwent " education for death ", but many of them would doubtless have preferred a somewhat less forbidding albeit similarly exalted prospect. Indeed, it is entirely possible that some youngsters were in essentially the same frame of mind as the English curate who was questioned about the life after death. " When I die," he replied, " I shall of course enter into eternal bliss—but I do wish that you would not talk about such depressing subjects." Films extolling the martyrdom of Herbert Norkus (Hitler Junge Quex) and stories akin to the one about the Spartan youth who allowed the fox to gnaw out his vitals may have had much the same effect—" Death for Party and Fatherland is glorious, but let's talk about something else to-day."

Still further, it should be remembered that 1943 was the year in which the first batch of adolescents who knew the Youth Service only in its period of growing institutionalization, its stiffening ecclesiastical structure, passed on to the Labour Service and the army. For them the rousing adventures of the Hitler Youth in the days before the founding of the Eternal Reich formed the substance of epic tales almost as remote as those recounting the exploits of the Roamers. Odd as the analogy may sound, they found themselves in compulsory Sunday school memorizing sacred stories after their predecessors had witnessed all the fun of harrying and slaughtering the " inner enemies " of the Chosen People, of the Master Race. Some youngsters almost certainly began to become insurgent, to fall into the " fed-up " mood which seized upon so many boys and girls in the middle and late 'twenties, when cut-and-dried youth tutelage absorbed and stultified the erstwhile spontaneity of the youth movement.

What has been said is not wholly inferential ; let us look at some of the available evidence more directly. As early as 1939, when only the effects of six years of rigid institutionalization, salaried and place-seeking leadership, and waning of enthusiasm could be felt, eighty-eight German boys and girls from fifteen to twenty-one were tried *en masse* for high treason. The greater number of the youngsters received severe sentences ranging from three to eight years in prison or concentration camp. A political prisoner ran across one of the boys, Ernst by name, who got a three-year sentence, and by persistent questioning drew his story from him. The political prisoner eventually escaped and made his way to the world outside, where he recounted Ernst's astounding tale in a form fairly close to the way in which it was elicited :

" What were your activities, Ernst ? "

" We fought against the Hitler Youth."

" What are you fellows, anyway ? "

" We are the Pack. You see, about four years ago, fourteen or fifteen of us joined a football club ; it used to be tied up with one of the workers' sports societies. Then Hitler passed a law saying that all sports clubs had to join the Hitler Youth, so most of us resigned. We didn't want to go into the Hitler Youth."

" Why not ? "

" Who the devil wants to spend all his time drilling, marching, rattling tin cups, and running service errands—all the damned nonsense ? That's no life ! "

" What did you do then ? "

" All of us who left the football club stuck together. We had a hard time keeping clear of Hitler Youth spies and we had to meet with the idiots once in a while, anyway. Just the same, our crowd got together evenings, went roaming on Sundays, and managed to sneak away to our own summer camp. We wanted to keep people from thinking that we belonged to the Hitler Youth, so we fixed up a kind of uniform of our own : black shorts and a pirate's necktie."

" A pirate's necktie ? What do you mean ? "

" Oh, a big bright-coloured handkerchief we tied around our necks. When we were out camping we met lots of other boys who would sneak away from the Hitler Youth and get off by themselves too. There were Rhinelanders and Saxons and Holsteiners and Bavarians. When they saw our uniform, lots of them copied it, and by and by we all began to call ourselves the Pack. We got things all fixed up so we could meet again next summer in the Fichtelberg, or the Harz, or some other place where we wouldn't be bothered. And do you know that we held a regular convention of the Pack at the same time a big Nazi get-together was going on ? We were good."

" What did you fellows think about ? What did you try to do ? "

" Well, some of the Pack read books about history and things like that. I don't read much myself, and most of the time I didn't know what the older chaps were talking about—politics and all that rubbish, I suppose."

" Well, what on earth kept you together ? "

" That's easy. We hated the Hitler Youth. Do this and do that, drill, listen to speeches from those quack leaders—all they want is to make money and be big shots in the Party. And then they were always talking about getting ready for the war ; who wants to go to war for those fellows ? We wanted to do what we liked while we were young."

" Did the Hitler Youth let you get away with it ? "

" What could they do ? They were always being told where they had to be at one time or another ; they couldn't chase us. But we chased them when we got a chance ! And at night we used to throw rocks at their Small Homes and their hangouts. Once there was a fight ; they pulled their Blood and Honour daggers on us. But we had knives too, and one of their leaders—a bossy fellow about sixteen—was cut up so much that he bled to death. The police hushed it up because they thought he'd been fighting about one of those League girls that they run around with when their higher-ups aren't looking. That was a joke ! "

" Did they ever catch you before this ? "

" Just once. Last year they arrested a flock of us ; a Hitler Youth leader asked them to do it. But they couldn't get anything on us, and after two weeks they let us go. We got even in one way or another, and when I get out of here, some of those idiots are going to pay for this too." [1]

From other sources it is known that in the spring of 1939 the Élite Guard asked for a setting up of a special division of the Gestapo to run down and wipe out the Pack. Further, a Gestapo official who testified at Ernst's trial said that at least two thousand boys and girls were involved in this outlaw gang.

The evidence showed that the Pack was essentially unpolitical except for a few random notions here and there ; aimless rebellion against the regimentation of the Nazi equivalent of a State Church summed up their activities. The only superficially political note that did appear further demonstrates the inability of Pack members to think of themselves as other than mere opponents of the Hitler Youth, for when an especially daring or steadfast fellow-rebel was to be praised, he was called " a stout reactionary " That is to say, they had taken over the Nazi term for anyone— Communist, Junker, recalcitrant pastor or priest, pacifist—who did not subscribe to the Nazi gospel, and applied it to themselves with equal lack of discrimination.

The Pack was defined negatively, not positively. Hatred of cynical careerists who were moving up the leadership ladder, unimaginative discipline, lack of spontaneity, pressure of " service " to the folk community when actually the Party was the beneficiary, dinning in of catechism and creed which had meant much to their fathers and older brothers but which was increasingly meaningless to them—those hatreds gave the Pack whatever unity it possessed.

Note, now, that the first assault on Rimmon's House was spearheaded by lads from the comfortable middle class, and that the whole context of the society against which they revolted was strikingly different from that of Hitler Germany. Pack members seem to have been drawn from the very lowest levels of the middle class and from factory workers ; their schooling was vocational, not humanistic.[2] Consequently, their adolescent romanticism was perhaps of coarser fibre, and their heroes had what we might call a more directly criminal tinge. Nevertheless, the mood sweeping through these contrasting groups seems to have been surprisingly similar, and the absence of clearcut goals likewise runs parallel. Are the Nazis confronted by a fresh conflict of generations ? Is it once more true that " the fathers have eaten sour grapes, and the children's teeth are set on edge " ?

Two thousand members of the Pack in 1939 ; two thousand Roamers in 1900 . . .

Speculating further : Whatever may have been happening before the onset of the war, it is entirely possible that the smooth working of the Nazi indoctrinating machine has been notably hampered since the war began. Counteracting influences are at work. Mothers in factories, fathers at the front ; school and extra-curricular training broken into by frequent shifts of personnel ; unsettling change of living quarters forced by influx of foreign workers, migration of industries, and devastation wrought by bombs ; escapes from supervision made possible by blackouts and the helter-skelter of evacuation and taking refuge from air attack ; the continual interruption of radio propaganda by war news, good or bad ; part-time and even full-time work in strange surroundings where the customary controls are absent —all of these things have perhaps weakened the grasp of the Nazi dogmas.

Perhaps, perhaps . . . The United States is witnessing a wave of adolescent looseness that far surpasses anything hitherto known in our society. We have long been notorious, however, for our irresponsibility at all age levels ; embezzlement, homicide, family disintegration, and the glorification of the gangster (white-collared or otherwise) have long been characteristic of our way of life. A safer comparison may perhaps be found in British experience ; the inhabitants of the tight little island have for generations gazed in dismay—and sometimes with a dash of smugness—at our truly distressing conduct. No people, however, is immune to the effects of a world-shaking upheaval, and the British now have large-scale troubles of their own :

When civilization goes haywire through war or revolution, first to go savage are children. That Britain's children are no exceptions to this rule was made plain last week when Sir Alexander Maxwell, Permanent Under Secretary of the Home Office, gave out the first report on juvenile delinquency in Britain since World War II began.

Sir Alexander's figures, covering only the first four months of 1940, showed a 50 per cent. increase in crime committed by children under 18. Chief offences : stealing, breaking into homes and shops.

That these early figures did not tell the whole story became all too clear when the city of Manchester, in Britain's industrial Midlands, reported on child delinquency for the entire year. Manchester suffered a juvenile crime wave that set an all-time record, up 77 per cent. over 1939. Of 1,323 children indicted on criminal charges, 797 were boys and girls of 14 or less. The rest ranged in age from 15 to 17.

In London last week juvenile courts were sitting double their pre-war hours to hear the stories sullen juniors told them. One curious fact they had unearthed : poverty does not, as in peacetime, lead to crime. On the charge sheet 20 boys were listed in a day, eight of them only 16 years old. All were earning salaries big enough to support a respectable family before the war. Scores of one-time errand boys were doing demolition work at £4 : 5s. ($17) a week. They gave their mothers $6, squandered the rest on liquor, gambling, girls.

Principal cause of Britain's youthful crime wave was the relaxation of grown-up authority. Many a father had gone away to camp, or worked overtime in a war factory. At least half of London's compulsory grade schools had been destroyed by bombs, or converted to other uses. Parents had put their children to work (or taught them to beg) in order to bolster family earnings. With boys' clubs broken up by evacuation, social centres taken over for war work, high-spirited youngsters turned to crime out of sheer boredom.

Britain's Government and press racked their brains, wondered what to do with youthful criminals. Homes for delinquent children were overflowing, convicted moppets were being crowded in prisons with hardened felons.[3]

Granted, these are the results of chaos. But is it likely that contemporary Germany is any less chaotic ? And with the breakdown of the Nazi machine, now happily proceeding apace,

will not the turmoil and confusion of German life immeasurably
increase ?   May not bands of roving youngsters akin to the Pack
spring up here, there, and everywhere ?   May it not be remotely
possible, considering the completeness of the totalitarian collapse
that will almost inevitably come about, that gangs similar to the
" wild boys " of postwar Russia in the first years of the Revolution will run amuck, wreaking vengeance on everyone they
identify with the Nazi value-system and its works, and throwing
in other violent escapades for good measure ? [4]

To some extent, such questions can already be answered.
Whatever the reasons for their actions may be—and the foregoing pages have perhaps done something to make the possible
reasons less obscure—German youngsters are running wild *to-day*.
Gangs bearing the older label of the Pack are much in evidence,
and newer groups calling themselves the Anchors, Hambigos,
Vienna Prater Slicks, and other queer names abound on every
hand.   Neutral newspapers carry many items bearing witness to
the activities of these demoralized youngsters,[5] which in general
take the following forms :

There is much street-corner brawling with Hitler Youth, both
leaders and rank-and-file, frequently leading to cutting affrays.
On many occasions the police have been compelled to intervene,
and have themselves then become objects of assault.

Along with this goes general intimidation of parents and
youngsters ; there are many dire prophecies of what will happen
if active functioning in Nazi youth organizations is continued.
Quite often the prophecies are fulfilled : boys and girls have their
uniforms splattered with paint, torn or even ripped off, and bloody
noses and scratched faces occur with some frequency.

Less violent but nevertheless troublesome are the verbal
attacks.   Jeering, calling of derogatory and obscene names, and
otherwise spreading " dirt " is a frequent pastime.   The League
of German Girls is often called the League of Soldier's Mattresses
or the League of Silly Tarts, and the members of the Hitler Youth
are termed the Young Homos, the Rump Paraders, and the like.

Here and there, especially in the larger cities, boys have made
themselves conspicuous by wearing bizarre costume and long hair,
and by mimicking female mannerisms.   The Slicks, wearing a
bob or *Schlurf* of almost shoulder length, have been especially
notorious.   Actions of this kind seem to be in direct defiance of
the aggressive masculinity of the Hitler Youth—which, by the
way, can quite well co-exist with homosexuality.   The Slicks seem

merely to champion their own feminized variety of sexual inversion.

Sexual excesses of less striking type are also on the upswing. Roughly, juvenile delinquency involving sexual offences has increased by more than five-fold since the beginning of the war if one is to believe newspaper reports. As we have seen, there is no compelling reason why they should be disbelieved.

Vandalism is common, and often manifests itself in the breaking into and damaging of nests, small homes, and hostels. Thieving from such State Youth centres is likewise an everyday occurrence. Sometimes destructive conduct appears to take the form of planned sabotage ; small-scale industrial, communication, and traffic disruptions [6] have been attributed by the police to young apprentices, and several convictions have been secured.

A far more frequent kind of " sabotage " is the breaking up or hampering of Hitler Youth and LGG meetings by deliberate inattention, heckling, scuffling, and wilful misunderstanding of instructions. When this is too dangerous, boycotting of the meetings is resorted to ; the authorities have had to threaten the withholding of ration cards for all who cannot show a good attendance record.

Begging and fraudulent Youth Service collections are by no means unknown ; the public has been repeatedly warned by the Nazi officials against youthful solicitors without proper credentials.

In sum, one substantial section of contemporary German youth is significantly out of hand. The mere fact that the Nazis have been compelled to resort to fines and to threaten loss of ration cards, and to set up special bureaus to supervise errant juveniles and fight subversive youth propaganda and rumour-mongering is eloquent testimony to "German youth on the loose".

Just how many of these Dead End Kids are to be found in to-day's Germany is almost anybody's guess ; on purely inferential grounds I should hazard a figure of not less than fifteen per cent. of all those between ten and sixteen years of age. They represent the outcome of a system whereby youth has been brutalized by being robbed of those traditional foundations of conduct upon which stable personalities can be built. " Man is not born human ", and if the humanizing process breaks down or is perverted to cynically exploitative ends, there ensue vice and crime of the most revolting sorts. The Nazis have sowed the wind, and they are reaping the whirlwind.

There is some possibility, of course, that in the general chaos now appearing a considerable proportion of German youth will group around centres of allegiance deriving from pre-Hitler tradition and not yet perverted by the Nazis. Hard to imagine, for instance, is a situation so utterly disorganized that Catholic youth tutelage would not be able to re-establish itself in some way. Similarly, the Lutherans and other Evangelicals may be able to draw a number of disillusioned boys and girls to their standard. The likelihood that the Social Democratic Party will ever come back to anything distantly resembling its pre-Hitler shape is highly doubtful, but some party having traditional connections with it—such as the New Beginning organization—may get a foothold. If it does, youth tutelage not wholly foreign to the ideals of Western democracy may once more enlist thousands of working youth. If not, the Communist Youth will successfully claim the loyalty of proletarian youngsters—indeed, chances for substantial membership under almost any circumstances are exceedingly good.

Highly uncertain, however, is the *extent* to which youth tutelage will be able to exert its influence. Revulsion against everything smacking of adult guidance, to say nothing of regimentation, may be so strong that by far the greater portion of German boys and girls will remain aloof. By contrast with the rigours of Nazi control, of course, youth tutelage of even extremely adult-dominated type may seem like the very essence of liberty to those youngsters who have not succumbed to " wildness ". For them, then, youth tutelage will perhaps have something to offer. If as little as one-third or one-half of the membership totals of the 'twenties could be attained, that would still represent a million or more young Germans who had been brought back within the youth tutelage fold. If adult domination is not too extreme, this figure might be increased—always assuming that competition from more spontaneous groupings can be successfully surmounted.

Among the competitors there will almost certainly be a number of groups claiming to be the heirs of the alliance youth. As such, they will announce themselves as proponents of " youth for youth's sake ". Announcements, however, are one thing ; actual power to command allegiance is another. Can the alliance youth organizations, if they take forms approximating those characteristic of the late 'twenties, ever again enlist a large proportion of German boys and girls ? Most if not all of the traditional alliance youth moulds have been broken and their leadership decimated. Even if the alliances had not been weighed down by an undue quota of eternal adolescents, more than ten years have elapsed since they had any semblance of autonomy. Moreover, any leader who would now be able to hark back to pre-Hitler days would be well on his way towards thirty ; youth movements that so much as try to seem spontaneous are not headed by oldsters. True, it would be readily possible for the alliances to revive their literature, but they had advanced so far on the path towards denominationalism that their handbills and pamphlets would have little or no appeal to a generation accustomed to much more highly seasoned fare and facing an utterly different set of situations. In any case, the greater number of alliances, with their rabid nationalism and Chosen People ideology, were readily perverted by the Hitlerites. Admitting that the perversion was not complete, in that resigned passivity rather than whole-hearted espousal of Nazism was the chief effect of Hitler's machinations where alliance youth youngsters were concerned, it is still true that they slowly drifted into the Nazi harbour. If the alliances could revive, therefore, there is at least an even chance that many of them would be regarded as so nearly identical with the State Youth organizations that their members would be assailed and driven to cover by the " wild " youngsters who will unquestionably be milling about in droves.

It must be granted, of course, that a sizeable proportion of the alliance youth did not manifest near-Nazi features or, if they did, got rid of them with reasonable promptness and thoroughness. That is to say, there were some scores of thousands of pacifists, mystic democrats, devotees of mutual aid, advocates of reconciliation, and even aggressive supporters of the Weimar Republic. Many of them, like the unfortunate Zirker, tried to carry their ideals into adult life, and here and there achieved minor successes. Such persons, however, fled betimes or, if they did not, were hustled off to concentration camps, exiled, or executed ; the insignificant remainder who have escaped fates like these cannot possibly act as rallying-points for new groupings. Worst of all they are now far too old to play any effective part in youth activities as such. To repeat, the day of the eternal adolescent has passed.

Purely from the standpoint of the probabilities, therefore, it would be reasonable to expect a revival of little sects strikingly similar to those of Karl Fischer's day. If there was rebellion against the routines of the 1890's, how much more likely is there to be revolt against the regimentation of the 1940's !

Clear it is, from evidence and inferences already presented, that many thousands of disorganized German youngsters are on the loose. These youthful delinquents and criminals not infrequently give names to their gangs, but in spite of this—if one excepts earlier groups such as the Pack—they seem to have little if anything in the way of organization that goes beyond the confines of limited localities.

Are there other boys and girls who cluster together in escapist, romantic sects patterned along the lines of the early Roamers ? Are they lacking in the grossly delinquent and criminal traits of the hordes of " wild " youngsters ? Do they have symbols and social structure that transcend their everyday haunts and behaviour ?

Yes. For more than three years past reports circulated in neutral countries seem to bear witness to the fact that in some parts of Germany, particularly the Rhineland and the south-west, many Germans of twenty and under have linked up in a movement called the Edelweiss. This term applies to a small white flower often found in the higher mountains of Central Europe and traditionally regarded as a symbol of freedom.

The members of Edelweiss are anti-Nazi, but their opposition is not so much to the actual content of National Socialist doctrine as it is to the high degree of control to which the State Youth system has subjected them. In other words, their longing for liberty is just as vague and formless as was that of the would-be destroyers of Rimmon's House. Moreover, the social instruments they use are equally expressive of an ill-defined wish to be free. Uniforms of all sorts are cast aside in favour of leather shorts or *Kluft*, with accompanying loose shirts and knockabout jackets of the utmost variety. To this array is frequently added a neckerchief reminiscent of the " pirate's necktie " mentioned when describing the Pack. Concealed under a lapel or in some other " secret " part of the costume in most cases, but sometimes flaunted openly, is a little Edelweiss that serves as badge of fellowship. The lute or guitar with its fluttering ribbons plays its traditional part and, furthermore, songs that sound for all the world like those of the lads who fled from the ultra-conventional cónfines of Steglitz provide the core of the repertory. Here is one, dedicated to the mocking sprite of German folklore, Rübezahl, who serves as guardian of the Edelweiss :

The firs mount high and the stars are coldly gleaming
  Where the stormy floods of the Isar pour ;
There the camp of the Edelweiss lies a-dreaming
  And Rübezahl guards as in days of yore.

Hearken, O Rübezahl, to our dreary story :
  Robbed of freedom are hapless land and folk ;
Swing high the mace as in times of ancient glory,
  Shatter the wranglers, strike off discord's yoke ! *

The diffuse rebelliousness of songs of this kind is virtually identical with the adolescent *Sturm und Drang* of the supremely individualistic Roamers. Taking one thing with another, however, there is an all-pervasive difference between Karl Fischer's followers and the adherents of the Edelweiss, and this difference issues from the contrasting situations facing the two movements. The adult world of Wilhelmian days clamped fetters of many forms on its youthful inmates, but it never achieved the degree of efficient repression characteristic of the Nazi system. Parents, teachers, and pastors may have been despised and evaded, but there was little if any need for direct physical resistance or attack. To-day the devotee of Edelweiss freedom must be prepared to combat Hitler Youth who are still strong in the faith, grown-up leaders anxious for their careerist futures, and bloodthirsty agents of the Gestapo. The Roamers, then, were non-political, but the Edelweiss are political—here lies the essential difference.

To say that the Edelweiss movement is political runs counter to current opinion. Escapist romanticism, even in Nazi Germany, is held to have no political implications. Well, the Catharist heretics were not directly political in orientation, but they were nevertheless handed over to the tender mercies of the secular arm. A great ecclesia must exterminate heretics, root and branch, if it and its supporting political structure are to survive. Heretics who resist secular liquidation by the same token threaten the foundations of the sacred order. The Edelweiss movement should not be over-rated, true enough, but neither should it be

* Hohe Tannen, leuchtende Sterne,
  An der Isar mit stürmender Flut
Liegt das Lager der Edelweisspiraten,
  Doch du, Rübezahl, schützest es gut.

Höre, Rübezahl, was wir dir sagen :
  Volk und Heimat die sind nicht mehr frei ;
Schwinget die Keule wie in alten Tagen,
  Schlaget Hader und Zwietracht entzwei !

dismissed in quite so cavalier a way as the writer of the following passage seems inclined to do :

The stories of anti-Nazi youth movements called Edelweiss Pirates are mainly misleading. The truth is that Edelweiss is the name given, presumably because of its association with free mountain air, to the largest organization of young people in revolt against Hitler Jugend discipline. This organization, if it can be called such, exists all over Germany, but it is no more significant than is the existence of the Black Market. Boys and girls, ranging from 14 to 18 years old, in the intolerable war conditions in Germany, have banded themselves together . . . to oppose authority . . . They are not . . . capable of making a revolution which might end the war. . . .[7]

Waiving in this context the point that the black market may be of rather considerable significance, it is still fair to say that even a movement incapable of " making a revolution which might end the war " can nevertheless hamper the functioning of the war machine. And, to be trite, the adage about the straw that broke the camel's back is perhaps not altogether irrelevant. Granting that most Edelweiss activities represent sheer escapism, how do these youngsters have to act in order to get the feeling of having escaped ? What are the remoter consequences of their actions ?

To begin with, roaming and camping out in defiance of State Youth regulations not only engenders the habit of disobedience to a system that cannot maintain itself without blind acceptance of authority, but it also keeps supervisory officials and the Gestapo away from other tasks more directly contributory to the war effort.

Again, Hitler Youth leaders who find their compulsory meetings unattended and who then prowl about searching for stragglers get many unpleasant surprises. When a lapel is turned back and an Edelweiss disclosed, the youngster thus caught *in flagrante* does not always passively submit—indeed, he rarely does. More often than not he puts up a fight, some of his fellows come to his aid, and in the ensuing scuffle the leader may not come off with a whole skin. Many cases of knifeplay have occurred— after all, the wearing of Blood and Honour daggers is in conformity with Hitler Youth regulations—and in several the wounding or even killing of leaders has been reported.

Further, brawls between youthful heretics and the faithful of their own age are by no means uncommon, and on more than one occasion the heretics have come out on top. Such affrays have strong resemblance to those engaged in by the "wild" youngsters everywhere in evidence, but they show important differences : groups of more than local character are involved, and stories of the struggles have become part of the lore of the Edelweiss.

Once more, Edelweiss followers even when not openly and confessedly rebellious do much to obstruct the Nazi war effort. Long before Germany began to scrape the bottom of the man-power barrel by the People's Levy, the State Youth were used in all sorts of ways which would release men for the front. Recalci-trant youngsters naturally did not take the risk of direct opposition, but tardiness, feigned sickness, "forgetfulness", and "losing" and "misplacing" of messages, orders, and equipment were resorted to frequently. Attendance at meetings was kept up, but noise, inattention, and scores of other tricks known to every schoolboy helped to throw sand in the cogs. Occasionally hoots and catcalls traceable only to juvenile heretics disturbed adult Party gatherings. In many instances the official meetings of both youngsters and adults were used for the spreading of rumours and morale-sapping news.

Yet again, Edelweiss youngsters have been among the most frequent violators of the ban on listening to foreign broadcasts—usually the source of the morale-sapping news just mentioned. Severe penalties have been imposed, but the necessity for their re-imposition testifies to the continuance of the violations. Swiss and Swedish newspapers have carried items which indicate that B.B.C. information, for example, has often been spread by boys and girls who in all probability had Edelweiss affiliations.

Still further, bits of evidence here and there point towards these youthful heretics as responsible for the distribution of subversive leaflets, some of them apparently printed by them-selves, as well as for the chalking up of anti-Nazi slogans. Contact with foreign workers has doubtless played some part in this, and we may be reasonably sure that secret agents of the United Nations have also been involved. Nevertheless, Edelweiss members have probably displayed a good deal of initiative There has also been alteration of air raid protection and similar signs, and on occasion such signs have even been torn down or destroyed. Air raid wardens and others who have tried to prevent behaviour of this kind have been attacked to the accom-paniment of shouts of " Down with Hitler ! " or " End the war ! "

Finally, with conduct of the sort just noted, we encounter

political action *per se*. There have been several trials and convictions of juvenile rebels for spreading general defeatist propaganda, to say nothing of arranging for lectures and discussions
along democratic and pacifist lines. Here the example was
probably given by certain students at the University of Munich
who publicly protested against a speech by Gauleiter Giesler in
January, 1943. By March of that year these students were not
merely demonstrating against Nazi speech-makers but were
staging anti-Nazi meetings of their own.[8] The neutral sources
reporting these seemingly incredible activities made no mention
of the Edelweiss, but there are strong inferential grounds for
attributing to that organization at least the spreading of the news
of the student revolt. However this may be, Edelweiss youngsters
have been convicted for disseminating anti-Nazi propaganda ;
whether they got their ideas from Munich students is of secondary
importance. *They have engaged in direct political action*—that is the
significant point.

So much for what now seems to be going on among German
youth. What of the future ? The upshot of the evidence and
inferences thus far presented is that our occupying forces will be
confronted with at least four roughly distinguishable aggregates
of young Germans.

Our greatest immediate concern will be with the substantial
numbers of State Youth who, in spite of defeat, will cling desperately to their faith in the Nazi system and all its works.
Harmless-looking lads will zealously serve as agents for the Nazi
underground, and girls with braids and bland faces will help to
lead unwary sentries to sudden death. With such permanently
perverted youngsters, whether called " Werewolves " or not, the
prompt and unshrinking use of force will be the only means of
control, and at best such control will be partial. Not until the
Nazi underground has been entirely wiped out will its juvenile
aides and accomplices likewise be rendered harmless—and that
may take a long time. Our own kindliness and readiness to
believe the best of the enemy even when he is plainly hitting below
the belt will be our greatest handicap—that and sheer ignorance
of what is going on under our very noses. Surveillance of arms
factories and hideout sites will be of no use unless we are continually on the alert against fanatical Hitler Youth and the Nazi
criminals whom they will gladly protect and help.

Causing almost equal difficulty will be the " wild " youngsters.
Roving bands of demoralized, brutalized boys and girls, almost

Spying as a duty, from a Nazi book for children.

wholly free of any adult counsel and supervision, good or bad, will fight it out with the identifiable remnants of the State Youth, with rival factions of their own kind, with whatever youth tutelage groups may re-establish themselves, and with spontaneous bodies such as the Edelweiss. Devoid of the cultural ballast that lent the Roamers a measure of stability and desirable influence on Wilhelmian society, these youthful gangsters will long continue to manifest shockingly criminal traits. Granting that the premature establishment of law and order by the United Nations is inadvisable where it would check the self-purging that is so necessary if a long roster of spurious martyrs is to be avoided, such youngsters nevertheless cannot be permitted to run amuck indefinitely. The added load piled on top of the ordinary burden of occupation might well impose an intolerable strain. In our own interests we must take steps to domesticate Germany's " wild " youth.

Other difficulties would arise with the spontaneous sects of Edelweiss type if German chaos were prolonged or if United Nations administrators confused them with the more grossly delinquent and criminal gangs. They could then readily deteriorate into wandering packs of the sort to which reference has so often been made. If, however, they are properly handled —which means, amongst other things, if some measure of spontaneity is preserved—such groups need not degenerate at all. On the contrary, the Edelweiss can be made to serve the long-range purposes of the United Nations and, we may add, of Germany. But more of this later.

Youth tutelage of the old-fashioned type will probably succeed in regaining some of its membership, as already noted. The boys and girls who can thus be brought within the traditional folds will cause little if any trouble—but neither do they seem to offer any opportunities for the effective reshaping of German life along lines promising much for the future.

Explicitly stated or implied throughout all of the foregoing remarks is the proposition that continued United Nations control of the German younger generation will be necessary until such time as we can be assured that the danger of fresh aggression has passed. This control can take on two major forms. On the one hand are the ordinary repressive measures embodied in the firing squad, the concentration camp, and the prison ; on the other are measures designed to drain the foaming currents of youthful excess into socially acceptable channels.

Unquestionably repression of the first sort will and must be used, for even if no particular solicitude were felt for the Germans remaining after the liquidation of the Nazis, effective occupation would be hampered if it were not. Control, however, is always a more or less judicious mixture of force and consent ; in well-worn phrase, " You can do anything with bayonets but sit on them ". Something will have to be done with the hundreds of thousands or even millions of boys and girls who will be roving hither and yon. In any case, it will be impossible to confine any very large proportion of the youthful delinquents and criminals of less flagrant type, and if they can find suitable channels for their energies, confinement will be unnecessary. Among bodies such as the Edelweiss leaders of their own will emerge, but the Edelweiss as they now are have so many escapist traits that they cannot readily be fitted into the patterns of a stable society—and if Germany is to fulfil the obligations justly imposed on her, stability is a prime requisite. Moreover, the Edelweiss could not be trusted to carry on with their unchecked spontaneity in any case, for by now we know what disastrous conduct may follow in the wake of " grace-endowed " Pied Pipers, whether of major or minor dimensions. Spontaneity there must be, but it cannot be identified with complete " on-the-looseness ".

Youth tutelage in any of its old forms certainly offers no way out of the difficulty, that is clear. Too little spontaneity is as bad as too much. Is it over-optimistic to suggest that one of the possible alternatives may be the setting up of new youth tutelage organizations with United Nations' backing ?

Such backing certainly could not be widely advertised, for no matter whether a hard or a soft peace is imposed, " outside interference " with German affairs will be resented by a sub-stantial part of the population. No one need be tender about wounding German feelings as long as the achievement of United Nations' objectives is not thereby endangered—that we can take for granted. If, however, certain avoidable affronts to German sensibilities would militate against the achievement of our own ends, we can well dispense with such luxuries. Hence the youth tutelage that is sponsored should not be given too much fanfare by us ; if there are suitable German leaders who can launch, on their own initiative if possible, programmes which we regard as suitable for our own purposes, they should be discreetly aided —but discreetly !

Some suitable precedents may exist; I mention them with great hesitation and with keen awareness of the liabilities they unfortunately possess.

Members of the German Pathfinder groups, linked with the International Boy Scouts' and Girl Guides' organizations, numbered almost forty-six thousand in 1931. Nationalistic and even militaristic though they appeared to outsiders, the more extremist Germans regarded them as so strongly disposed towards internationalism as to be suspect.

Further, a British movement called the Kibbo Kift Kindred, strongly similar to the Scouts but with an even more definite international slant, had many sympathizers among the small proportion of alliance youth open to reconciliation efforts after the First World War.

Once more, the American Youth Hostel Association, headed by Isabel and Monroe Smith, has patterned itself along lines somewhat like those of German groups following the Roamer tradition, with the erotic emphasis fortunately absent and with heavy stress on internationalism.

It is barely possible that youth tutelage deriving directly from or in some way related to these precedents could have some effect on youngsters such as those of the Edelweiss, and perhaps on some of the less badly demoralized " wild " contingent. *Barely* possible—why? Because even the most adroitly managed youth tutelage, even when run by Germans, has tremendous liabilities. Personnel gets topheavy, mediocrities with no " personal grace " or at best a diluted " grace of office " rapidly infest the directive staffs, unwillingness to take risks alienates worthwhile leaders and followers, and finally the collecting of dues comes to loom larger than actual work with and for youth.

The recent history of the Boy Scouts of America gives melancholy confirmation of these misgivings; at present only a small fraction of the upper middle class is reached, and in the face of the rising tide of juvenile delinquency there is only the reiteration of the slogans of 1910. Expediency, efficiency, and conservative planning will not turn the trick here or elsewhere

Only if the German leadership—and it almost certainly must be German—of internationally-minded youth tutelage can minimize or eliminate such handicaps is there the remotest chance of success. To me the chance seems worth taking, but whether United Nations' representatives will be able to look beyond the confusing situation with which they will be confronted when they take over is in the highest degree doubtful. Too, it must be remembered that the necessary combination of genuine understanding and analytic detachment is not easy to achieve. There tends to be cleavage into " kiss and make up " and " kick 'em around " turns of mind. I tend to sympathize with the advocates of reasonably stern measures—but can highly emotionalized policies, tough or tender, be followed with confidence ? Is there not real danger of becoming just as intuitive as the Führer, with ultimate results on a par with those he has brought about ? Some crystal-gazing will be necessary in any case, but those who are suitably prepared may see something more than their own fatuous smiles or belligerent scowls.

If the vision of our policy-makers is to pierce the haze of the immediate future even a little way, it will have to be sharpened by knowledge of the basic patterns of German youth activities and tempered by detached calculation. To be sure, mere range of information and cold-blooded analysis are not enough, but neither are those good intentions with which the floors of the nether regions are presumably paved. Clever perversion for the sake of ends regarded as good by the United Nations and, we may perhaps assume, ultimately reconcilable with the welfare of Germany as part of a more or less peaceful world, must be practised.

It was said earlier that perversion as here used is a colourless term ; it refers only to the intentional substitution of goals differing from those originally followed by the members of the social grouping in question while at the same time preserving the outward semblance of their cherished social actions. Any American boys' worker, for example, who insinuates himself into a delinquent gang, gains the confidence of its members, and slowly directs their activities into what he calls " constructive " channels while at the same time permitting the youngsters to feel that they are just as devil-may-care and tough as they ever were, is a practitioner of perversion.

If organizations such as the Edelweiss et al. are to be successfully perverted, the substitute must not only be as good as the original—indeed, far better—but must actually appear to be so. In particular, this means that the social methods and instruments of the Roamers and alliance youth, so adroitly taken over by the youth tutelage organizations for their own ends and then skilfully adapted to Nazi purposes, must once more be given the subtle twist that in the long run makes all the difference.

There is no reason why roaming, cultivation of the sense of fusion, nesting, camping, and going on long expeditions should not be used for all they are worth—and that may be a great deal. Similarly, distinctive costume, even when uniform-like in character, song-books such as The Pluck or unobtrusively altered versions thereof, lutes and other romantic folderol, Small Homes, hostels, and other material symbols of primitivism, hard or soft as the case may be, must be lavishly utilized.

Even the specific organizational moulds can and should be perverted. " Grace-endowed " leaders and devoted followers must be tolerated and even encouraged as long as erotic patho- logies and excessively divisive cults do not appear. Sects may be permitted to develop if their differences give only a gratifying sense of distinctiveness and importance. Efforts to unite with this or that part of the German people regarded as worthy repre- sentatives of the ideal of the folk community can well be allowed and perhaps fostered.

Everything depends on the ultimate goal : as long as the sense of national uniqueness, dignity, and responsibility does not lead to mental and social isolation, with its accompanying delusions of grandeur and virulent hatreds, even German nationalism itself need not be tabooed. Reiterating an earlier conclusion : " The poorest way to be an internationalist is to begin by apologizing for your nationality ". The boy or girl, young man or young woman, forced perpetually to disavow differences from others which no disavowal, however vociferous, can ever wholly eradicate, falls prey to excessive self-awareness, aggressiveness, and deep-rooted although perhaps unconscious resentment.

Those called upon to carry out perversion of this kind must be social surgeons of great skill, no doubt of that. In most cases, moreover, they must be persons deeply immersed in and keenly aware of the swirls and eddies of German life concerning which very few outsiders are ever sufficiently cognizant. The broad outlines of schemes for perversion can perhaps be drawn with approximate exactitude by persons reared in one or another of the United Nations, always assuming that they have oppor- tunity to take counsel with native Germans.

When it comes to the directing of these scripts on location, as it were, the man who puts the actors through their paces must almost certainly be a German of the Germans. In addition, he must have initiative of his own, and moderate scope in exercising it. Whether or not it is possible to find a sufficient number of properly qualified Germans who also possess the necessary willingness to work with United Nations' representatives, to say nothing of the basic good will, is, to put it mildly, an open question. Scarcity of personnel may make the perversionary task a sheer impossibility ; only a determined effort to secure a suitable staff will supply the answer. If the requisite plans, persons, and backing are secured, some hope of success is perhaps permissible.

Everything that has been said thus far refers exclusively to youngsters in their 'teens and below. For the age group between twenty-one and thirty-five only faint hope, if that, is at all warranted. Clearly, the animosities of a titanic struggle are hard to shake off, and there is a strong likelihood that the pessimistic tone of my remarks conceals biases of which I am necessarily unaware. No student of things human can get more than one foot off the ground, however violently he tugs at his bootstraps. Nevertheless, I am tugging, and at the moment I am unsteadily poised on five toes. This much " detachment " taken for granted by the charitably disposed reader, I must still say that my pessimism is borne out by certain considerations which I now advance :

To-day's German soldier of twenty-one was a boy of twelve when Hitler was deified in 1933. At a highly impressionable part of his life he passed through a revival experience which, for a time at least, closely joined him in the Nazi value-system. Exceptions ? Of course. Every religion has its backsliders, and even when open lapses from the faith do not occur, the corrosion of indifference frequently eats to the very core of belief. Moreover, the demonstrated shortcomings of a leader once devoutly followed often produce revulsion—no doubt of that. Nevertheless, I strongly feel that the rank-and-filers geared into the military machine have not yet notably weakened in adherence to their fanatical creed. Apparently spontaneous surrenders of whole regiments to the Russians there have been, but on the Western front few instances of the kind have occurred, and the confidence and even arrogance of German prisoners quartered in the United States is already a well-known fact. Always admitting the possibility of surprising shifts in the near future, I should be inclined to say that not more than a dozen or two out of every hundred Germans in their middle or even early twenties are significantly lacking in zeal for the Nazi value-system and all its works.

Over and above this, I cannot avoid the conviction that if

and when the Nazi belief is cast aside it may well be replaced by espousal of a Germanized Communism, differing in important respects from the present Russian variety, that will retain fundamental elements of Hitlerian dogma. Guarding against the overlooking or ignoring of counteracting influences, it should be noted that some well-knit Social Democratic families have doubtless resisted Nazism, and would resist its Communist substitute. Where Nazism is concerned, however, it is notorious that a very large proportion of Social Democrats did not stand together, and that in many families the younger generation betrayed the older.

Continuing in the same vein : Devout Lutherans and Catholics hold out in little centres of refuge, and will probably continue to do so, but taking it for all in all most of their fellow-religionists have been able to reconcile Nazism with their private beliefs. Visitors to prison camps in this country are often struck by the number of Germans who wend their way to services on Sunday morning, and with naïveté which is unfortunately typical of most Americans, they conclude that Nazism is only skin deep. It is nevertheless regrettably true that it can penetrate to the innermost fibres of political thought and action without touching the walled-off sanctities of faiths that yield all of man's outward life to the sway of Caesar.

Still dealing with the same age group, but focusing on the contingents approaching the upper limit of thirty-five, let us remind ourselves that they were men and women in the early or middle twenties when Hitler seized power, and that they were several years short of the 'teens when Germany collapsed at the close of the First World War.

This means that their late childhood, adolescence, and young adulthood suffered the shattering impact of the Tumult of the 'Twenties. They witnessed revolution that reached few of its desirable objectives, small-scale but bitter civil war, passive resistance that began with impotence and ended with hatred, inflation, unemployment, and a Babel of fantastically impractical, decadent, and brutal ideologies.

. As if this were not enough, those who clung to youth movement spontaneity saw the creeping paralysis of routine and self-seeking officialdom cripple their alliances, with the result that disillusioned cynicism plus the necessities of livelihood made Philistines of many. " Yes, I used to belong to a youth movement group, but that nonsense leaves me cold nowadays " was more and

I

more widely heard. In fact, the very intensity with which high-flown precepts and practices were followed operated to produce ambivalent reactions of the most crassly blasé and grossly self-indulgent type. Abstainers not infrequently became drunkards, advocates of mutual aid leaped into the fire of " Devil take the hindmost ", pacifists espoused aggressive nationalism.

Greater numbers were of course simply confused and bewildered ; they continued to mouth the old maxims and to make half-hearted gestures toward their realization, but the vital push had vanished. Thus becalmed, their idly flapping sails hesitantly filled with the winds of Nazi doctrine, and by many a devious route they slowly steered towards landmarks so subtly transposed by the Nazis that when they finally cast anchor it seemed that familiar havens had been reached. Manifold misgivings there unquestionably were, but for those who did not become thoroughly Nazified such doubts were seldom expressed in action ; loss of faith in any and all compass bearings and beacons was the most usual outcome.

The advent of the Second World War did not change matters essentially ; tame acceptance of the seemingly inevitable ; blind but dogged grappling for survival ; mute acquiescence to the whinings of fear ; fluttering hope of eventual victory—these and many more compulsives still hold thirty-year-olds on the path to destruction. Even when those on the outskirts of the mad rush waver momentarily, it is still true that their potential confidence in any proposals looking toward Germany's restitution of the debt she owes the world and, it may be, toward her eventual regeneration, is at so low and fluctuating a level that they must be almost wholly discounted as significant factors.

With Germans of forty and above these dark forebodings have slighter justification. Many oldsters, particularly those whose social and economic status has long been lowly, dimly remember times which for all their mingled pettiness and strained ambition, their spurious progress and delusive optimism, their arrogant expansiveness and ruthless exploitation, granted far more scope to humble decency and parochial good-will than the brave new world of the Nazis permits. Shreds and tatters of elementary fellow-feeling and simple justice still clothe many middle-aged and elderly Germans ; indeed—Rex Stout and Lord Vansittart to the contrary—" shreds and tatters " may well be too great a concession to the prejudices of wartime.

It is now fashionable to throw all Germans into one pot, to

assert the utter and total depravity of everyone between the Rhine and the Oder, to clamour for serfdom, starvation, sterilization, slow torture, and extermination. Confessing in advance that my gorge rises at revengeful and sadistic gutter-crawling of which the net effect is to smear us with Nazi filth, may I also say that such demands border on the impossible? Whatever our conceptions of justifiable punishment may be—and some kinds of punishment are certainly justifiable—why furnish grist for the Goebbels mill by emitting programmes which sober second thought among all but a baker's dozen of "Nazis in reverse" will unhesitatingly reject? War degrades both victor and vanquished, but we know, do we not, that when Germany lies prostrate we will not deliberately trample upon her?

Few if any of us are or can be Christian in any fundamental sense, and it is perhaps just as well that we remain of the earth earthy. Still, the Christian ethic in diluted and secularized form still governs some of our conduct and interweaves with the most profound layers of our personalities. Short of mass insanity, there is little likelihood that we will attempt to perpetrate the callous crimes for which the bestial Heydrich has already paid and for which Himmler and many others among Hitler's infamous henchmen, let us be determined, will pay to the last man.

Indeed, German fathers and grandfathers who lost the props of their declining years at Stalingrad and other glorious demonstrations of the Führer's intuition will do much to exact that payment if we ourselves are not so obsessed by the desire immediately to establish law and order that we prevent "the night of the long knives". If we should find that the process of German-initiated liquidation of the betrayers of their own people does not proceed far or fast enough, as may well be the case, we shall have plenty of opportunity for formal trials and executions. By letting the Germans who are so minded do a fair amount of their own blood-letting, the shorter the list of martyrs we shall create and the lighter the task of occupation.

The risk of saying that some Germans are not wholly Satanic is no small one in view of the frenzies of some of our doughty knights of the pen: "Hell hath no fury like a civilian". Possible denunciation as "pro-German" can never be calmly envisaged by a responsible American, but there are higher responsibilities than the whipping up of insensate and indiscriminate rage. The words spoken by Spencer when considering the task of him who concerns himself with the study of man and his doings are still true :

> The highest truth he sees he will fearlessly utter ; knowing that, let what come of it, he is thus playing his right part in the world—knowing that if he can effect the change he aims at—well : if not—well also : though not *so* well.[9]

Therefore, I deliberately assert that for the older German generation a few gleams of light may relieve the sombre shadows—light that issues from the possible killing off or hamstringing of quantities of Nazis who might otherwise profit by our bungling intervention and ill-adapted " due process of law ", but not from that source alone. Why ? Because, beyond assistance in the purge of the body politic, ageing Germans may also aid in diminishing the turmoil among German youngsters. The conflict of generations is unhappily an old story throughout all of Central Europe, but in the erstwhile domain of the Nazis it may be most intensely evident and bitter between parents and children. Dare we entertain the hope that grandparents will be able to reach steadying hands across the gulf ? Can older value-systems, sadly inadequate in their heyday and badly crumbled or even almost demolished as they now are, ever be bolstered up and eventually rebuilt in altered but effective guise ? Who knows ? Can the myth of The Linden Tree be revived so as to allay rebellion and unite old and young ? Can it ever lose its present ambivalence and body forth its reassuring outlines against a cold grey sky ?

Speculation so remote seems futile. To the man of forlorn good-will it may appear that our hapless world faces a return of Hesiod's Age of Iron, that even Hope has taken flight, forsaking the creatures of earth, to the tribe of the Immortals. But we are not ancient Greeks ; in spite of the shortcomings for which the Papacy can well be condemned, Pius XII spoke truly and nobly when he proclaimed the fact that " In spirit we are Semites ". Hence the call from Seir in Edom, for all its mystery, evokes tremulous anticipations of a future, far away though it be, when the brand of remorseless enmity may not mark mankind—if only we remain steadfast to the best that is in us :

> Watchman, what of the night ? Watchman, what of the night ? The watchman said, The morning cometh, and also the night : if ye will inquire, inquire ye : turn ye, come.

NOTES

1. This is an account recast from the dialogue given in Jon B. Jansen (pseudonym) and Stefan Weyl, *The Silent War* (Philadelphia, 1943), pp. 254 ff.

2. *Ibid.*

3. *Time* (March 24th, 1941), p. 27.

4. Numerous newspaper stories tell of roving gangs of German youngsters who loot, destroy, burn, and kill. These are perhaps to be taken with a grain of salt, but there is nothing inherently improbable about them—*on the contrary !*

I should like to add that in 1940 I wrote a chapter, " After the Deluge ", for Henry P. Jordan's symposium, *Problems of Postwar Reconstruction*, published (Washington, D.C.) in 1942. In this chapter I forecast the present wave of wartime delinquency in the U.S. It was speculation, yes, but speculation not wholly fantastic.

5. One among the many which might be cited is an article on " Deutsche Kriegsjugend " in *Die Weltwoche*, Zürich, March 19th, 1943.

6. *Hamburger Fremdenblatt*, July 20th, 1944.

7. *The New Statesman and Nation*, vol. 29, no. 724, Saturday, January 6th, 1945, p. 1.

8. *Die Nation*, Berne, July 8th, 1943.

9. Herbert Spencer, *First Principles* (London, 1861), end of Part I, " The Unknowable ".

EPILOGUE : AFTERMATH, OMENS, AND PORTENTS

Menenius. You know neither me, yourselves, nor any thing . . . you wear out a good wholesome forenoon in hearing a cause between an orange-wife and a fosset-seller, and then rejourn the controversy of threepence to a second day of audience.—When you are hearing a matter between party and party, if you chance to be pinched with the colic, you make faces like mummers, set up the bloody flag against all patience, and, in roaring for a chamber-pot, dismiss the controversy bleeding, the more entangled by your hearing : all the peace you make in their cause is calling both the parties knaves.

—SHAKESPEARE, " Coriolanus ".

The bedraggled prisoners in the dock at Nürnberg represent only the demi-gods of the great Nazi ecclesia ; Hitler and Goebbels shuffled off mortality in an operatic grand finale worthy of Wagner, and Himmler swallowed poison in the best traditions of melodrama. For them, then, the Twilight of the Gods was a reality.

But what of the rubble heap they left behind on the stage ? Who would have thought, in the summer of 1944, that the Gestapo was still so efficient that over five thousand participants in the July 20th conspiracy against Hitler's life would be wiped out ? Who realized, in spite of the long years of terror known to the whole world after 1933, that Dachau and the other horror camps had so thoroughly decimated even the potential " Aryan " leaders of a German revolt ? Who imagined that responsible Allied leaders like Roosevelt and Churchill would have furnished grist for the Goebbels propaganda mill by their ill-considered proclamations about unconditional surrender ? Who guessed that the nonsensical legend about a Jewish world conspiracy to exterminate all Germans without distinction would have been lent the semblance of actuality by endless public chatter, with the usual Goebbels echoes, about the Morgenthau plan ? Who foresaw the consequent last-minute stiffening of German morale which, together with Pearl-Harbourish ignoring of intelligence reports, conjured up the Battle of the Bulge ? Who reckoned with the frenzied determination of the People's Levy, the *Volkssturm* ? Who supposed that, in the face of the greatest mass bombing of civilians ever perpetrated, rank-and-file Germans would mutely and doggedly hold out until May ? And who dreamed that the Allies·would so soon begin to throw away the fruits of victory ?

Germany is a rubble heap, material and mental. But although we have organized work squads for the clearing away of bricks and twisted steel, we have done little to clear the muddled minds of the people we have undertaken to rule until they can rule themselves. Indeed, we have notably increased the confusion.

Perhaps part of this was inevitable ; people who plunge from fantasies of world domination to realities of abject defeat are necessarily befuddled. But note that I have said " people ", not " a people ". There were many Germans who thought clearly and felt humanely in spite of the ceaseless pounding of the Goebbels drums, and it is these people, our actual or potential friends, whom we have succeeded in bewildering along with the others. If we are ever to be free of the unwelcome burden of occupation, we must find Germans whom we can trust and who can trust us—and before they trust us, they must understand us. But do we understand ourselves ?

In the Tumult of the 'Twenties, it will be recalled, " the name of Germany became a synonym for Babel " (page 109). That Tower of Babel is now a rubble heap, a heap that our perpetual organizing and planning at cross-purposes has made even more chaotic than bombs alone could ever make it. In the sketches that follow, the one persistent motif is " organized chaos " ! First we listen to the mouthings of a German youngster who, following the Hitlerian pattern, uses " fanaticism " as a word of self-praise but at the same time displays uncanny knowledge of our stupidities. Next comes a country parson who in his naïveté and complete prostration before the powers that be shows the appallingly weak side of certain " religious " youth tutelage activities on which we nevertheless rely. Following him there speaks a *Wehrmacht* officer, who obviously will indoctrinate with rampant nationalism the groups entrusted to him as an exponent of " cultural and non-political " youth leadership. After him in the sequence appears a worker who risked his life in anti-Nazi effort during the war, but who to-day has been so thoroughly disillusioned by " military government bungling " that he is reluctant to aid us in any way. Immediately following him speaks his son, a member of the Edelweiss movement, now so " all mixed up " that he could perhaps be pushed into revolt against an occupation régime " almost as bad as the Nazis ". Then we come to a lad whose older brother was killed in the famous Munich student outbreak of 1943, and as we listen to him we gain some conception of what anti-Nazi Germany might have been and, with wise treatment which we unfortunately show no signs of applying, could still be. Last, we hear from a man in his early thirties, a former member of the German Boy Scouts, who held a key position in a determined revolt against the Nazis in the closing days of the war, and who represents the kind of person from whom successful youth tutelage leadership in the interests of Germany and the United Nations might be expected—if it were not for our present penchant for " organized chaos ".

I

" Yes, you caught me stringing the piano-wire across the road, and two drunken soldiers careering along in a jeep last night struck a similar wire and had their filthy necks slashed through. What of it ? I don't care what you can prove or can't prove. No, I won't say whether I'm a Werewolf or whether I'm not. Try and find out from me, that's all—just try it !

" Oh, so you know that I am the leader of the illegal youth group in Mordnacht ? Well and good ; does meeting illegally twice a week make us Werewolves ? You can't prove anything.

" I know that you'll probably shoot me because I was caught with that wire. It serves me right ; the clumsy conspirator endangers his cause. What ? Admissions like that will be used against me in the trial ? You're giving me a trial ? What fools you are ! But I don't care ; you'll shoot me, anyway, and the trial publicity will make me a martyr to our cause. I'm satisfied.

" You can't shake me ; even if I am only seventeen, I'm hard as steel and tough as leather. That is what the Führer demanded of us. I have been a leader from the days when I was in the Junior Boys, for I had faith and the will to action. I still have it. You'll see.

" I don't care if you did find a copy of the speech I have been making to my followers. I am like the Führer ; I don't need written copies. I just kept that one to give to my deputies when they wanted something to read aloud when I'm not there. I am a real orator, like the Führer ; I can talk so that my followers come flocking around me shouting for me to lead them into action. And the time will come ! I shall not be there to lead, but others with the same gift of sacred fanaticism will appear.

" Germany will win this war-in-peace, you may be sure—if not gloriously and immediately, at least in the long run. Whatever stretches of land you occupy in Germany, you will never conquer or defeat the German nation. Though outwardly we may smile and bend under the Allied yoke, we shall resort remorselessly to ambushes and tricks of guerrilla warfare until in the end every inch of sacred German soil is freed from the hated invader.

" A Master Race born to govern cannot be held down eternally. Do not underestimate us Germans. We have learned to hate a world of nations that denies us living space. Great deeds inspired by this immortal and sacred hatred have been performed in the past ; in the future it will give birth to new ruses and new ways of fighting. Militarism and mastery are the two callings of the German, and we shall not rest until our mission is fulfilled. With this mission is bound up the destiny of National Socialism ; if you want to destroy National Socialism you must exterminate the German people. We shall never really capitulate. A Master Race may be temporarily checked in the completion of its mission, but it does not capitulate.

" There are thousands of fanatical German youths who are willing to sacrifice everything for the liberation of a defeated Fatherland and who, posing as friends, will infiltrate the military governments set up by the Allies. They will collect information about German traitors and see to it that these traitors are wiped out. They will risk their nameless lives in the sabotaging of every Allied effort. They will act as informants and contact men for the Nazi underground all over the world.

" One man and the spirit he evoked will always be the guide of our youth : our Führer. Hitler united us as a nation. Hitler awakened Germany to her mission and strength. Hitler may be dead, but the ideals he called forth will always live in the hearts and deeds of the German people. Stronger than any intellectualistic philosophy, Hitler's National Socialism has the power of myth. It does not appeal to cold reason, but plumbs the warm depths of emotion ; it overwhelms us with its misty power. We do not think. We feel, we believe, we act. We have faith in our Fatherland, and this faith will give us the strength to hold out, no matter how long Germany may be occupied. We shall never cease to fight back, with deception and ruse, with ambush and open assault, until the last wearied invader is killed or driven from Germany. *Sieg Heil !* " [1]

II

" Oh . . . I haven't done anything. Oh . . . so you want to see Pastor Steck ? He isn't here any more ; he hasn't been here for ten years. I took his place in 1935.

" Come right in, honoured sirs, come right in. I am glad to welcome you to this humble parsonage, for it has always been my conviction that we should obey the government in all its lawful demands. As officers of the occupying army, you represent the responsible authorities.

" To Germany ? What do I think should happen to Germany ? Why, I want a Kaiser, of course, and so do hundreds of thousands like me. The German people need a Kaiser, for they have to have someone to look up to. If we only knew what is going to happen to us . . .

" We don't have any real newspapers ; it's the way it was when we had the Nazis. We're just a little village of three hundred souls here, of course, but we used to get the paper from nearby Schafskopf. Now there is only the paper from Unding, where you have so many occupation troops. Right at the top it says that it's issued by the occupation corps for the civilian population. We know that you wouldn't tell us any lies—no, no—but we're afraid of propaganda. All through the war we were warned not to listen to propaganda. Oh . . . yes. Maybe that was propaganda too. The fact is, we think that your officials are good to us, but that they may be tempted to keep the bitter truth from us. Maybe they wouldn't want to hurt our feelings—yes, that's it, that's it.

" The result is that people just talk a lot, and nine-tenths of it is lies. Most of the talk is that the Russians are coming or that there will be no fertilizer for the fields this Spring—*Gott in Himmel*, is that true ?—and—and things like that.

" Imprison people ? Did the Nazis imprison our people ? Yes, to be sure, that's why we just had to adapt ourselves to everything. Yes, to adapt ourselves. Yes. We didn't dare open our mouths ; as your great leader said, ' The Germans have locks on their lips.' Even the teachers told the children in the schools that if they didn't give the Hitler greeting they would be arrested and never let come back home again. That's what they told them, indeed they did.

" But even though we couldn't talk, we knew that things weren't coming out right. We knew that the war would be lost after those officers like Witzleben and the others helping him tried to kill the Führer on July 20th, and when the invasion got bigger and bigger. In the end, though, we lost because God didn't want it that way. We must bow to His inscrutable will, and the fear of the Lord is the beginning of wisdom.

"Started? How do my people think the war started? Oh, I can tell you that exactly; there were just three things. First, it was 'Home to the Reich'; next it was the Jewish question; and last it was the church problem. When Hitler tried to bring back all the Germanic peoples into a Greater Germany, all the peoples from the Tyrol and the Sudetenland and Memel (no, I'm not quite sure about Memel), that was a big mistake. He made all our neighbours jealous. Then the Jews: they burned the little synagogue here in Hude, even the beautiful tapestries. That synagogue looked just like a church; they shouldn't have burned it. But it wasn't any of our people; it was those *Gesindel* from Buchste. And when they held up the scrolls of the Law and tried to burn them, the scrolls wouldn't light. That shows what God's will was. And some of our people well know that they wouldn't have lived through the First World War if it hadn't been for the kindly gifts of Mr. Busshelm, a Jew whose relatives had that great retail store in Unding—ten show-windows at least. I know too that Frau Busshelm, whose three sons were lost in this war, helped several families with money and food. Finally, the Nazis should never have interfered with our good Christian people; they should have kept their filthy hands out of church affairs. 'Render unto Caesar the things that are Caesar's, and unto God the things that are God's.' That's what I'll always say. Yes, they should have kept their filthy hands out of church affairs. The Führer should have acted more wisely. Yes, indeed.

"Yes, he should have acted more wisely. He was mistaken in many things, I know. Home to the Reich? Why did he start the war in the West when he had already brought so many Germans home to the Reich? Well, we were told that our enemies were planning to invade Germany by coming in through Holland and Denmark and Norway. Many of our people thought that he couldn't do anything else. And about the East? To be sure, we did have a non-aggression pact for ten years with Poland, and another with Russia. I must confess that I don't quite know how that whole business in the East got started, but I do think that we shouldn't have got in so deeply. We couldn't avoid defeat. If I had been with the Führer, I would have told him, ' You should act more wisely.'

" But when you think about defeat—and I think about it a lot —you know that the attempted assassination of July 20th had a lot to do with it. There was betrayal of the Führer in high places, many high places, and not only on July 20th. Then there was the material superiority of the Allies, especially of the Americans. How can you defeat an army where every soldier has his own jeep ? Our soldiers, however brave, couldn't fight those masses of machines. In the end they became war-weary, and so did all of us. We just couldn't become enthusiastic any more. Of course, we didn't say much ; we might have been sent to concentration camp.

" What do I know ? Know about concentration camps ? Oh, nothing directly, nothing directly. But—but at least I was personally acquainted with two people who were persecuted in them. I'll tell you about the most important, the case of Pastor Alteglaube. At the burial of a Hitler Youth, one of his comrades who made a funeral oration said that the departed had entered into the eternal Storm Troop of Horst Wessel, and Pastor Alteglaube said that in Heaven there is no Horst Wessel Storm Troop. After long persecution in a camp near Kaltblut he died, or was killed, and when his wife came to see the body they wouldn't let her come near ; only the head of the corpse was visible. She was permitted to bring home the body, or at least the coffin. That way ? Why do I say it that way ? Because the coffin was sealed with seven seals, and they do say—mind you, I didn't witness this myself—that a while ago they dug it up and it was filled with stones ! Later on I had to bury a Nazi myself, and somebody at the funeral made the offhand remark that he too had entered the Horst Wessel Storm Troop. But I didn't reply, for what good would it have done my family or the Church of God which I serve if I had been dragged off to concentration camp as poor Pastor Alteglaube was ? No, I didn't go to his funeral. No.

" Question ? The Jewish question ? It was solved far too crudely, in my opinion. They should have cleaned the Jews out of governmental circles, certainly ; there was too much of a Jewish streak there. But once that was done, then they should have left the others in peace. They didn't do any particular harm, and sometimes did good, like our Busshelm here. Can I name any Jews aside from Rathenau who stood high in the government ? Well, I can't say that I can—no, I really can't. There must have been some, but I don't know. I don't know the names of many people in the ministries ; I don't know what race they belonged to.

" Goebbels told us that the Jews would rule us if Germany failed, but I'm glad to say that I haven't noticed any Jews among the occupation officers. What officers ? Why, you, of course, gentlemen. Yes, and some others who have come to see me. Who ? Why, the ones who told me that I could have religious youth gatherings here in Hude and also in Buchste. Major Flock and another officer—a captain—whose name I can't remember.

" Major Flock was very nice. He said that his new directive permitted almost all kinds of youth groups except political ones.[2] That's good ; youngsters shouldn't have anything to do with politics. In fact, most grownups shouldn't—at least that's what I think. He said that if religion couldn't save Germany, what could ? That's what I think, too. He told me about that big camp near Komm—Komm-something-or-other in France, where they've got so many boys who were in the People's Levy and even in the *Wehrmacht*. They have lots of teachers—they found lots among the grownup German prisoners—who teach the lads religion and German literature and English, and things like that. All the teachers are anti-Nazis—just like me, Major Flock said. And he told me that one of the boys right here from Hude had made a lovely hymn for the choir ; he called it ' Lord, to Thee '.[3] Isn't that wonderful ? When that boy was here—Karl Zweideut, his name was—he was in the Hitler Youth and made trouble all the time ; I was glad to see him go with the People's Levy. And now he becomes famous, and tells Major Flock to call on his old pastor. Isn't that wonderful ? I can hardly wait until Karl is released ; he'll make a fine deputy leader for our Lutheran tutelage group. And a lad who writes hymns won't get us into trouble about politics ; he'll let politics alone, I'm sure. We've got too many youngsters who chatter about democracy and all those things they don't understand ; they should leave things to the responsible authorities.

" I've told you a great deal, haven't I ? Now that I've shown you that I am always willing to co-operate with the responsible authorities, perhaps you can do me a favour. When your troops first came through here and asked us to give up our cameras I surrendered both of mine faithfully. We should obey the government in all its lawful demands. One camera was for small-size film, the other was a plate camera. Do you suppose that you could get the plate camera back for me? I need it to take pictures of people who have the silver and golden and diamond anniversaries of confirmation; I need it the worst way. I don't mind if they keep the film camera; I want the plate camera.

" Quiet, quiet, my treasure . . . Gentlemen, my wife wants me to ask you about something else. When the Germans came through here, just a few days before your splendidly victorious army arrived, a German lieutenant confiscated my car. It was a 1936 model, and wasn't streamlined, but it was still a very nice car. I asked about it in Unding three months ago, but nobody could tell me anything. Could you help us to get it back? I need it for pastoral visitation, and especially for the blessed task of supervising the youth tutelage group in Buchste.

" Good-bye, gentlemen. God be with you."

III

" To be sure I have been meeting with the youngsters of Weissnichtwo; our gatherings are of purely cultural character, and those are permitted under the terms of your directive. My hobby is German history, and I am free to talk about it, your chaplain said, as long as I don't deal with anything later than 1910. I can't imagine why he set that date, but he said to me, ' History is mostly nonsense, anyway; you may not do much good, but you can't do any harm. Kids won't listen to that stuff.'

" I am proud to say, however, that they do listen to me. They respect me; they know that my artificial forearm and hand represent sacrifice for the welfare of Germany. I was an officer of the *Wehrmacht*, the regular army. Yes, indeed! Oh, you thought I had been a private? Hm-m. You know that I am Colonel *Rupprecht* Stramm? Yes, Rupprecht, not Eugen. That question explains it: you have confused me with my brother, the man who openly broke with National Socialism after an initial period of enthusiastic acceptance. The confusion is quite pardonable, quite pardonable. After all, we are a large family. If you intend to see my brother, please remember that he married a Jewish wife and still has her. Further, he was imprisoned by our government for eight months, and when released he lost his officer's rank. At forty-nine he saw out the war as a private drilling other privates. We are not on good terms. I should prefer not to comment on his case.

" Not only as a former officer but also as a member of a defeated nation, gentlemen, I have a certain amount of pride. I do not feel myself inferior to the representatives of any other nation, in spite of the critical remarks about Nazi interference with the *Wehrmacht* which I have sometimes made. After all, the German nation has a long and glorious history ; the recent past is only an episode. I feel myself to be the spokesman of a justifiably proud people ; please understand this.

" The outlook for the future, where Germany is concerned, is not a rosy one. After all, we have lost a war, and we must accept the consequences. Regrettable, true enough, but wars are either won or lost, and the loser must know how to lose. I am perfectly clear on that point ; I see it plainly.

" We have had hard times before, but they did not wipe out that dream of a Greater Germany which has been the guiding star of our great statesmen through all the centuries. We must not give up hope of a better day. You would like to have me talk about the more recent developments ? Very well, gentlemen ; you wear officers' uniforms, even though no insignia of rank are visible, and I trust you to hear me out. Please understand this.

" National Socialism, as an economic-political-social system, has not been discredited by the fact that we have lost a war. The years 1933–9 saw a tremendous upswing in Germany ; for example, you should have seen the contrast between the do-nothing tactics of the Austrians and the hum of activity in nearby Bavaria. Anyone could see that National Socialism was inherently more dynamic ; without capital, with only the will to work and a near-perfect system for realizing that will, great things were accomplished that will stand for ever in history. History is a great comfort, gentlemen : who would have thought, seeing the devastation of the Thirty Years' War, that Germany would have almost conquered the world three centuries later ?

" Naturally, the remarkable results of the National Socialist system were by no means indifferent to Germany's neighbours. Britain and France could not look on without uneasiness. Their standard of living was higher than ours, and they feared that we would force them to compete so strenuously that their business men could no longer take Friday-to-Tuesday week-ends or retire at forty. Further, we are certainly not an inferior people ; our

history shows that. We have our natural pride, and we want
to be recognized for our legitimate achievements. We did not
need a war to make our power felt ; the others did. Still, as
history shows, that is the way of the world—to be jealous, I mean
—and I am perfectly clear on that point. War had to be the
outcome ; I see it plainly.

"The Treaty of Versailles did not lay down the European
system for all eternity. It had to be changed some time or
other ; we wished to change it by peaceful means. All we
wanted of Poland was the return of Danzig and an automobile
highway across the Corridor, and the Chauvinistic Poles refused
to grant our request. The result was that we had to denounce
the ten-year non-aggression pact, for the Poles had already broken
it by persecuting the German minority in Poland. I will grant
that our campaign against Poland was unleashed rather suddenly,
but please take account of the fact that the campaign lasted only
eighteen days. Certainly the end justified the means !

"Ever since our recovery from the Thirty Years' War we
have been a people without sufficient living space. That is
especially true in modern times ; we acquired no suitable colonies,
no worthwhile dominions overseas, even when Africa was divided.
It may be our own fault, for at the time when we should have
been laying hold of a great empire we were wasting our strength
and substance in religious wars. Oh, the lessons history can
teach us ! When we finally achieved the unity we had so long
sought the world was already parcelled out ; we could get what
we needed only by taking something away from other nations,
and that meant war. I see it plainly, and I do not protest. We
must learn to lose as well as win. The course of history is not
over.

"Naturally, I do not approve of all the methods which
National Socialism used to keep itself in power. You call attention to the exaggerations and discrepancies in *Mein Kampf.*
Well, you must recognize the fact that revolutions—and the
advent of National Socialism represented a genuine revolution—
are not made without certain, shall we say, regrettable occurrences ? Ordinary people can be moved to action only by
strong measures. Perhaps the results of the measures constituted
too rapid an upswing, perhaps even an eruption. Some of the
methods, however, were not of the worst kind imaginable. Take
the great economic results brought about by making little use of
capital and much of the German power to work, to work intelli-

gently and unceasingly ! The majesty, the grandeur, of the National Socialist system, as system, must be granted. Hitler merely gave expression to the most fruitful ideas of his time ; the system can survive without him. We are an intelligent people, in no way inferior to any other ; we are not taken in by any bluff that happens to be made. History shows that. But we needed no war, and wanted none ; if the others had recognized our just claims, we could have remained in the path of peace.

" But let me repeat, I do not sanction all the methods which were used by people such as Himmler, the most hated man in Germany. As an officer of the *Wehrmacht*, I always maintained a certain inner distance, a certain aloofness, with regard to the concentration camps and the methods by which they were filled and operated. Yes, a certain aloofness. Moreover, there was a clique around the Führer which kept him from knowing what was going on. It is certain that the affair of July 20th would never have occurred if the high *Wehrmacht* officers had not despaired of overcoming the machinations that kept the Führer in the dark about the real course of the war.

" The *Wehrmacht* was always ' correct '. In France and elsewhere the civilian population was treated with the greatest consideration. I dismiss as mere propaganda the charges that our troops committed atrocities. During my whole stay in France I never witnessed one single inconsiderate act by the German military. You say that there were atrocities, chiefly but not exclusively attributable to the Elite Guard and the Gestapo ? That there were brutal massacres of the populations of entire villages ? Yes, I am willing to listen . . . That is a vivid description of what you say you personally witnessed. There were many more such happenings ? So ? Well, as the war went on, longer and longer, year after year, harsher and harsher practices crept in. And I will grant that Himmler was a truly frightful person ; when I first saw him I immediately despised him. But *Wehrmacht* officers always maintained a certain aloofness with regard to such excrescences on the truly imposing structure of National Socialism. Methods such as those Himmler represented were not necessarily bound up with National Socialism as a system. If I think so much of National Socialism, why wasn't I member of the Party ? I see nothing inconsistent about that. We officers of the *Wehrmacht* ordinarily kept ourselves aloof from political matters ; we regard ourselves as instruments of the State. History shows that an officers' corps is most efficient when it concentrates on its military business exclusively.

" It's fortunate that I knew that, isn't it ?　I let others busy· themselves with Party affairs, with the result that I wasn't at all troubled when I had to fill out your official questionnaire. If I had been a Party member, I would have replied to that effect, of course, and then I should have been put on the black list.　Then I could not have taken charge of this cultural youth group, and our youngsters would never have been duly impressed with the lessons that history can teach us about the destiny of Germany.　The study of the past is a marvellous thing !

" But to return to the present : we of the *Wehrmacht* knew that the war was lost as soon as the invasion beachheads were firmly established.　It was a crime against Germany, against National Socialism, to continue the war after that one day longer than was necessary. Yes, that was a crime ; I am perfectly clear on that point—I see it plainly.　We should have been ready to lose in time in order to prevent the final catastrophe we now witness.　But I do not protest ; my knowledge of history enables me to see why other nations banded together to put us down.　It is quite understandable.　Now it will be many years— many years indeed—before the imperishable ideas embodied in National Socialism are fully realized.　We have lost a war, and we must take the consequences.　But we are a proud people, and are in no way inferior to any other.　The great role we should have played in the world is denied us—for how long one cannot say.　One cannot say.

" No, during the war I did not listen to radio news coming from outside Germany.　It was all propaganda.　Even if it had not been, I am too much the soldier, and much too proud as a person, to demean myself by sneak-thief listening.　I would not stoop to such unsoldierly practices.　The soldierly virtues are Germanic virtues.　Now, of course, I have no radio, but even without it I read the newspapers as little as possible.　After all, they are published, I am told, by what you call the Information *Control* Commission.　I don't need to read propaganda, even if it is up-to-date ; I prefer to rely on my history books. Moreover, your newspapers are written in pedestrian, uninspired German ; they have no vim, no swing, no emotional pull.

" No, I'm not necessarily comparing your newspapers with Goebbels' flamboyant style of writing.　You must realize that you all think too much in terms of specific persons.　National

Socialism was not dependent on the historical accident of a
Goebbels ; it could have come into being without him.   Greater
Germany, gentlemen, will some day be realized, and when it is,
National Socialism, whether bearing that name or not, will also
be realized.   The stream of history flows on unceasingly.   But,
I admit, for a long, long time we shall not be able to play the
role which rightfully belongs to us.   We have lost a war and we
must bear the consequences.   I am perfectly clear on that point ;
I see it plainly.

" So, you must go ?   Oh, let me ask you to tell your chaplain
that I am rigidly following his rule that I am to make no references
to history later than 1910.   I very much cherish my cultural
meetings with the youth of Weissnichtwo, and I am sure that
the occupying authorities will not be able to find anyone else
who was not a Party member and at the same time is competent
to impart the inspiration which the history of earlier Germany
can give to youngsters.   Tell him that whatever I may have said
to you about the more recent history of Germany was entirely at
your request, will you, please ?   After all, the German nation
has a long and glorious history ;   no matter how far back we go,
we can learn many lessons.   Please pardon this last-minute
delay ;   I know that you have other matters to attend to this
afternoon.   Good-bye, gentlemen."

IV

" I haven't got over it yet, for it was the first time in my
life that I'd been in gaol, the first time.   Well, maybe I have
been a fighter, but I've had to fight hard all my life.   Yes,
I had trouble with the Catholic clericals here in black Fernseits ;
I stood up for the free trade union movement.   Then, as you can
imagine, I had a lot more trouble with the Nazi scoundrels ;
I'll tell you more about that later.   But it remained for you
people to put me in gaol.   I know it was all a big mistake ;
you came as our liberators, and I believe what Eisenhower told
us.   It's a little hard to believe that this winter, but I know
what a rubble heap the Nazis left behind.   You can't do everything overnight, and some of our own people don't try to help
themselves as they should.   But I still haven't got over that
time I was in gaol ;   it was the first time in my life, the first time.

" I learned the plumber's trade when I was a boy, and from
the time I was sixteen I was an organizer for the free trade unions.
From 1911 until the Nazis kicked me out I was employed by the

city administration of Fernseits. Just about the time I got the job with the city I was chosen as the leader of our local ; I was only twenty-three then, but I had worked like the devil as apprentice and journeyman and had read a great deal. Maybe I shouldn't say so, but I knew my job as plumber and I was really interested in trade union affairs. By the way : if this gets too long-winded just tell me to stick to the points you want to get cleared up. I've sat in the chair at meetings often enough to know how much of a damned nuisance a man who doesn't know how to turn off his jaw can be. You want me to talk away ? All right ; I'll try to siphon everything out as fast as I can.

" I've had to fight hard all my life. Of course I was pulled into the army in World War I, and I had one hell of a time, like everybody else. What a pot of slop that was ! When I finally got back home I went back on the job for the city, and in a little while—perhaps because I fought for the workers all the time—I was elected leader of all the trade unionists who worked for the city. I went to trade union congresses every so often, too ; once I was sent to a meeting of the Second International at Amsterdam. Maybe I had all these chances because, although I was a Social Democrat, and stuck close to the official ideology, I was always more interested in trade union affairs than in politics. Workers like to hear about big ideas, you see, but they also want somebody on the job who asks when the next rise is coming, and how much it's going to be. You have to be a fighter, not just a platform speaker, I can tell you. I've had to fight hard all my life.

" My biggest fight, I guess, was the Jehima business. The Jehima was a Polish-Jewish acting troupe with a lot of new artistic ideas that people talked about—I didn't understand them—and that made trips all over Europe. It was one of the best play-acting organizations in Europe, people said, during the 'twenties and the early 'thirties. I worked at extra jobs in my spare time, for I had a family to support, and I was chief janitor at the theatre where the Jehima played in Fernseits. It was a night job, you see. At first there was no Nazi opposition, but after a little while the local muscle men did their part in breaking up the performance. The police were called in because the theatre help couldn't face up to the Nazi bullies alone. The police finally got order, but the performance was ruined, and the Nazis were arrested for breach of the peace.

"Who, me? Why, I was called as chief witness, and my evidence was damaging, I can tell you. The Nazis couldn't bluff me. The trial took over half a year, for the defence lawyers and their clients hoped that they could 'convert' me to the Nazi cause. They tried to get me to perjure myself, but I didn't budge. I've had to fight hard all my life. The result was that the biggest Nazis involved were convicted, and I had to take the blame. 'The Jehima affair' made headlines in all the newspapers, and my name was mixed up with the whole mess.

"The end of it all was that I was kicked out of the Workers' Front, and the end of that was that I was thrown out of my flat, but somehow, gentlemen, I managed to keep out of Dachau. Those Nazi bastards threw more than a hundred thousand workers into concentration camps, I'm told. If I'd known what was going on, I might have kept my mouth shut, but I didn't. I was entitled to job compensation of 110 marks, but they wouldn't give it to me, the bastards. I got a lawyer, and won the case, and the Nazi officials were ordered to pay me the 110 marks I had coming. Well, the mayor called me in, and he told me that if I kept on yelling about my rights I'd be thrown into a concentration camp to be educated. Well, I sort of quieted down. It was pretty hard, when you consider that I'd been fighting that case for five years! But I've had to fight hard all my life.

"I even had to fight in the People's Levy during the last days of this war, but when I knew that your army would soon be here I threw my rifle in the Schlauch and hid out in the country. I didn't want to run away altogether like the yellow Nazis, who were always yelling about the welfare of the people but who never really took any risks with their own dirty hides. When your troops marched in—and how they marched!—I worked with them for five weeks putting their barracks in shape. Here is the slip from the colonel to show what I did. Look at it; I'm proud of it.

"Proud of it, yes—but for over six months after you came here the Nazis were still in power. What's more, you didn't appoint understudies who could learn the Nazis' jobs, and then some of your officers said the Nazis were indispensable! They fixed it so the Nazis would be indispensable. We were under the heel of those Nazi bastards. Lots of them could speak English and your officers couldn't speak German. That was nice for the Nazis! They could keep on diddling us without interference.

"Well, I wouldn't stand still to be diddled. The workers kept on asking me to do something about those Nazis, and at last I got permission to set up an organization. I asked the workers in all the different trades and industries to delegate representatives to take part, and I wrote a letter to the mayor telling him that we, the workers, were ready to co-operate in flushing out the Nazis. What do you think? That letter was sent six weeks before we finally held our meeting, but we got no answer. We got no answer, so we went ahead.

"I did take matters in my own hands in one way, I'll admit : I insisted that no Communists should be delegated. I've got nothing against Communists as Communists, for I've always been more of a trade union man than an orthodox Social Democrat—although I won't permit anyone to challenge my Social-Democratic orthodoxy—but I can't have them around because they always make trouble. They're mostly to blame for the splits among the workers that made the Nazi pushover of the trade unions possible. If the Communist rats hadn't gnawed away at the foundations of our movement, no Hitler could have seized power.

"Yes, I know this is a long story. Yes, I'll try to make it short. Although the mayor didn't reply to our letter, he had previously given us permission to set up our anti-Nazi organization. We met in the Brahms school, and said in advance that we were going to meet there. I set up the agenda ; first, minutes and announcements ; second, attitude toward trade union organization ; third, protective clothing and other safety measures for workers in dangerous trades ; fourth, payment of wages ; and fifth, suggestions to your military government as to which Nazis could be kicked out without loss in efficiency.

"Now, I didn't have the scratch of an idea that special permission was required, for I didn't think that a delegates' meeting of this kind, dealing with economic matters, would be regarded as a public assembly, much less as a political one. But in came the military police and arrested all of us. As chairman, however, I took all the blame, and the others were let go. And there I was in gaol for the first time in my life. The first time in my life, under our liberators. They let me out after two weeks, with twenty marks fine.

"What was the offence? Don't you know? Under the regulations of MG, public assemblies of no more than six could be permitted ; we numbered seventeen. There'd have been nineteen, but two Nazis were shut out of the meeting—on my initiative. What a good laugh they must have had, the bastards !

" My family had suffered hunger and shame because of my convictions, and under our liberators they had to suffer again.. I know what the occupying authorities are up against, I think. They want to avoid chaos, and they insist on law and order. Right enough ! I'm for law and order, too. But does law and order mean that the Nazis, the lovely ' gentlemen-Nazis ', are to decide who is to be punished and who is to go free ? Just because Eisenhower's order got rid of the Party members who were holding jobs under military government, that doesn't mean that the Nazis have lost all their influence. Far from it ! Are they to furnish all the ' lady interpreters '—the damned tarts !— to your officers ? And what about those secretaries who were leaders in the League of German Girls one short year ago ? League of Officers' Mattresses !

" Why don't you trust the workers ? One of your officers said that I was a ' Socialist agitator '. Do you suppose he gets Social Democrats mixed up with National Socialists ? But surely nobody could be that stupid ? All I want is to see Fernseits happy and free of Nazis. I'm no idler—why, when I was in gaol I went right to work to wash up our filthy cell, and I got the Nazis I was caged with to work right alongside me. I was in a cell with four Nazis, you know. I tried to agitate them into democracy.

" Of course I'm a great believer in democracy ; I'm a Social Democrat. I'm fifty-five, as you know, so the only job the Nazis forced on me before they got that brainstorm of the People's Levy was air-raid warden up there in the old tower on the hill. Yes, I watched for enemy planes—who wants to be bombed ?— but I was also a ' black listener '. I listened to Allied broadcasts, especially the broadcasts of Thomas Mann from New York. I had no radio of my own ; I had to listen while I was on the job as air-raid warden. That was risky ; people were beheaded for doing that. But I listened, and I spread the good words that Thomas Mann spoke far and wide among my friends. It was counter-propaganda ; somebody had to do something against that devilish Goebbels. But I've had to fight hard all my life, and Thomas Mann is a fighter, too. Still, I can't help but remember that I was thrown in gaol for the first time in my life under liberators who said they were bringing us democracy.

" I suppose I do think about what's past and done too much—

I suppose I do. But things don't look any too good. Some of our young fellows around Fernseits want to organize a youth group, but they've been told that they can't engage in politics or choose a leader who is likely to talk politics. They had been planning to ask me, and I'd like to help them get started, but I don't want to take a chance of sitting in gaol again. I never did think much of this youth tutelage, anyway ; I think youngsters should have leaders of their own age. But I would help out if I thought that I wouldn't get into trouble right away. I've been a fighter all my life, and it's hard for me to keep my mouth shut. *Verboten* never meant much to me. But now it's beginning to ; maybe I'm getting old. Or maybe I've just been liberated.

"What I can't understand is the way you let all kinds of people spread all kinds of poison in these ' cultural ' and ' religious ' youth organizations. But maybe you know what you're doing. Maybe. I think I'd better stick to plumbing. I've been a fighter all my life, but maybe I'd better be a plumber."

V

"That's odd ; I thought everyone knew how the Edelweiss got its name. You see, when we were first getting together to fight the Hitler Youth, we had to have some way of knowing who was who. You couldn't always use catchwords, sometimes it would have been awkward to try secret grips, and anything halfway looking like a uniform was out of the question—the ' pirate's necktie ' and black shorts that some of our members wore soon drew suspicion, and was therefore practical only when we could get out into the woods or hills. You know, don't you, that the Hitler Youth had a patrol service—they called it a *Streifendienst*—that roved around just for the purpose of picking up rebels like us ? We had to think faster than those fellows. What was the answer ?

"Well, the answer was easier than you'd think. When the war was on there were still lots of the ordinary peacetime ' fun fairs '—you call them carnivals in America ? Oh, but ' carnival ' has quite a different meaning with us ; they're like what the Frenchmen call Mardi Gras. Our fun fairs have merry-go-rounds and coco-nut shies and crazy houses—crooked mirrors and all that, you know—and strength machines. It was the strength machines that gave us the idea. You know, you squeeze on spring handles or hit a lever with a sledgehammer, and things like that. If you squeeze the handles together or knock the sliding marker 'way up to the top of the column with the hammer you get a prize. Most of the time the prizes don't amount to anything that has cash value ; the fellows who run those strength machines know that people like to show off, so they just give them a little badge to show how strong they are.

"Now, the people up in the mountains in Bavaria and the Tyrol and Switzerland are supposed to be real outdoorsmen— work-hardened and with big muscles. You'd like to be like them, so what do the fun fair barkers do ? Why, they just give you something that comes from the mountains and is easily recognized and is cheap. Good, and what's that ? Well, everybody knows that the Edelweiss is a little white flower that grows high up in the mountains and is real hard to get—at least, people think it's hard to get. Good, wear an Edelweiss and you're a rough and tough *Knab' vom Berge*, a real hillsman with iron sinews.

"The Edelweiss is really cheap, of course. In Thuringia— that was one of the places where the Edelweiss movement got the strongest start—they grow lots of Edelweiss in those green-houses near Erfurt. The fun fair crowd could hand out lots of Edelweiss without letting much real cash slip through their fingers. Oh, sure, sometimes they gave away little jewellery Edelweiss instead of the real flower, and sometimes they passed out little posies made of coloured leather. Of course, they didn't give away too many ; that would have kept people from trying to beat each other.

"All this gave us our cue. We just started to wear the Edelweiss ourselves. We could do it, for the competitions were for different ages and weights ; there was nothing queer about having an Edelweiss even if you were only twelve or thirteen, and us older fellows of sixteen or seventeen (remember we got started four or five years ago) were pretty husky, anyway. The big idea, though, was to wear the Edelweiss so that it was a signal. Sometimes we put it under the right or left lapel of our coats so that you had to turn back the lapel to discover a fellow-rebel, or we wore two, one outside and one concealed, and lots of other ways. We changed the way we did it every so often ; we knew that the Hitler Youth would catch on after a while. But we made fools of them most of the time, and when we caught them when all the odds weren't on their side, we rattled their teeth for them.

"Yes, most of the Edelweiss were from workers' families. Just the same, we had lawyers' sons and officials' sons and quite a sprinkling of university students. We had some Catholics and some Communists, even, but most of us just wanted to get rid of Hitler and his big shots. Otherwise we didn't care much about politics. We just had our noses full of the Hitler Youth, that's all.[4]

" Yes, there's quite a bit of the Edelweiss spirit left, but things aren't like they were. When you fellows won, we thought you'd clean out the Nazis first thing, and here it is January, 1946, and lots of them are still running around as though nothing had happened. Sure, you threw a good many of them out of jobs in the government, but my father says that you haven't touched some of these ' recreational ' and ' cultural ' and ' religious ' clusters that give them a good chance to boss other people and spread more of their poison. And a man didn't have to be a Party member to be a complete Nazi fanatic ; my father says he knew lots of them. And, on the other hand, some people joined the Nazis just to get on the inside and mess things up when they got a chance. My father says that you've got to quit relying on this fill-out-blanks business ; use the advice of some of the known anti-Nazis about who the real *Schiesskerle*, the genuine stinkers, are. That's what he says, anyway.

" Why, of course we like the way your soldiers treat the youngsters ! They give them chocolate and fix up Christmas trees and show them pictures. That's a lot right now, with everything we used to have in rubble heaps. But why do the soldiers act so mean to us ? Even when those chaplains and special services officers fix something for us older fellows—the girls get taken care of well enough without any official plans !— the soldiers who have the job of getting the hall ready or running the motion picture machine or bossing us while we clear the rubble off playing fields give us grim looks and swear at us and tell us that we ought to have been shot. They don't seem to realize that there's a big bunch of us who hate the Nazis just as much as they do, and another big bunch that is still undecided about democracy and all that stuff. Even some of the officers don't seem to know enough to treat anti-Nazis different from Nazis ; they either hate all the Krauts, as they call us, or they like them all, especially the women, whether they're Nazi spies or not. Young fellows like me feel all mixed up, and even some of the Edelweisses are getting pretty sullen. I don't know what's going to happen.

" Please don't get the wrong twist here ; I think it's great that you're letting us have youth committees and that here and

there a nest or youth home has been started up. I heard the
other day that over in Blauhimmel they're printing a weekly
youth paper with volunteer help ; that's good, very good. Oh,
really ? There's a big youth organization in Schneewittchen,
with hundreds of dues-paying members ? Wonderful ! How
I wish we had one here, with a few of our good Edelweiss trusties
in the right places ! We'd soon see to it that democracy was
more than just a word, the way it is now. No, we don't know
much about democracy, I suppose, but I don't see what was
wrong in saying that. How are you going to get democracy
without help from young Germans who want to give it a trial,
at least ? After all, we've got to get started really doing things
sometime, haven't we ? And what if we do kick a few Hitler
Youth around ?

" Father says it's good that you're letting people get together
now to talk politics and do a little organization. You threw
him in gaol, you know, last June. In gaol for the first time in his
life, under our liberators. He'd been trying to get the municipal
employees to get together ; he wanted to get rid of the two Nazis
heading up the workers at the power plant and the gas works.
But he made a mistake ; he called seventeen people into a committee meeting—there'd have been nineteen if they'd have let
the two Nazis in—and the military police clamped down on him.
What ? Why, there weren't to be any groups of more than six.
Yes, six, and even though the meeting was a trade union affair,
your military government officers said it was political. That's
right ; at that time politics was absolutely *verboten*. Now it's
better, he says. And, after all, he was only in gaol two weeks,
and he got off with a twenty-mark fine. Two special check-up
officers from Eisenhower's headquarters came to town, and they
got a lot of pressure in the boiler when they discovered him in
gaol with Nazi criminals. Yes, it's better now. Of course, it's
better. Of course. That's what he says, anyway. After all,
he was in gaol last June. The first time in his life.

" But why won't you let the trade unions organize youth
groups ? Ye-es, I suppose that ideological talks and discussions
are enough. But my father says, ' How can you get young
fellows to flail wind ? They want to do as well as talk.' Anyway, we know too damned well what the Nazi ideology is like
and what stinking nonsense it is ; we don't need to talk about
that. We've got to be able to decide what we can really do in
politics, and what Germany can do to get democracy—not in

words or on paper, but right where we live every day. If we can't get together with the old trade unionists who fought political battles against the Nazis and know what's chalked up behind the door and can teach us how to keep those stinkers from getting on top again, what's the use?

" That's what we all keep asking, ' What's the use ? ' We're all mixed up, like I told you. Look at me, now. I didn't want to follow my father's trade, even if he is head of the town plumbers' union here ; I wanted to be a machinist. I just got started with my trade training when the war came, and I got shoved into a mass-production factory job where I didn't really learn anything about machinery. I just had to do the same little trick over and over, from daylight to dark. Then they put me in the army, and I just learned to run machine-guns—that's the kind of a machinist I was ! Now I don't really know how to do anything that amounts to much ; as we say, I've got a twenty-litre backside and a one-litre head. Some of the fellows I know say that the British and Americans want to use us in a war against Russia, that's why they won't open the trade schools and the factories. I don't believe those rumours, but lots of the fellows do. They just hang around and twiddle their thumbs when they're not on work squads clearing up rubble.

" I suppose we could do worse than clear up rubble. When I have to sit around I think too much. Sometimes I get away from everybody and think by myself. I don't know which is worse—getting off by yourself or being where you hear the other fellows grumble and talk about what they'd do if they could catch the occupation troops off guard. They don't mean a mass uprising—although once in a while some braying donkey makes that kind of a noise, too !—they just talk about beating up the soldiers who take their girls or their sisters. Listening to that gets me all mixed up. That's right, I've got a girl myself, and I'm worried. What do you mean, a sickly grin ?

" Of course I've got a girl. Well, if you get right down to it, she isn't the one I used to have. But she's all right ! What about the other one ? I'd just as soon not talk about her. All right, all right, if you want to know. It don't make any differ-ence, I guess. She's—her name is Augustine Schrott—laying up with one of these occupation heroes. Oh, I suppose he treats her all right ; she gets cans full of beef stew and chopped-up chicken and all that, and I've seen some of those cardboard packages, too, with all those fancy inside wrappings and canned eggs and cheese. But I don't mean she's a tart ; she likes him, I think. Her little brother told me that she got busy with her needle and sewed creases into all his shirts and pants ; he doesn't have to keep pressing them all the time. She acts as if she was his wife, the poor fool. We-e-ell, he might marry her, maybe. Yes, I know that lots of occupation heroes are borrowing civvies from Germans and getting married against orders. Will those be legal weddings ? No, I don't suppose anybody knows much about it.

"Anyway, I don't give a damn. I can't get married ; I haven't got any job, and there's no place to live. Hildegarde— that's the girl I've got now—doesn't seem to want to get married. Anyway, we don't talk about it, and if we don't, why should you ? Pardon me, I forgot myself. I'm all mixed up. Anyway, I'm still too young to talk about getting married. When you don't know what you're going to do to earn a living, and your father is getting old, why should you think about getting married ? Why should anybody get married ? You don't have to nowadays. Oh, well, I'm all mixed up."

VI

" How did you get my father's address here in Neuss ? Our house is still standing, I know, even if it does have one side blown off, but how would anyone know that we were still living in that rickety box ? Just luck ? Yes, but how did you know our name ? No, I'm not afraid of asking so many questions ; we're treated all right here. What should I be afraid of ?

"So, so. You actually worked as an engineer with my father in the International Harvester G.m.b.H. ? When ? In 1927 ? What were you doing in Germany then ? That's a little hard to believe—a university student in philosophy and sociology. What were you doing in Neuss, then, if you were studying at the University of Cologne ? Oh, you came back and forth on the train during the long Spring vacation ? I still think it's pretty queer ; how could anybody studying philosophy and sociology know enough about practical things to be a machine designer ? Well, I suppose you're right ; you don't have all eternity to answer questions.

"You want to ask some ? All right, go ahead. What should I be afraid of ? But wait a minute : where did you hear about the Kittelbach Pirates ? From *The Central European Observer* ?[5] What's that ? Oh, a British journal. I suppose

the British do know a lot about us.   But we're treated all right
here.   Yes, we're half starved, but I suppose we've got to stand
at the end of the queue.   The Greeks and the Norwegians and
all those people will have to be fed first, that's clear.

   " Oh, yes, the Kittelbach Pirates.   No, we had no tie-up
with the sea ; the Kittelbach is just a little stream that flows into
the Rhine near here.   Hans—he's my older brother who was
killed by the Nazis—I'll tell you about that if you want to hear—
told me that the name of our alliance was taken from the Nerother
Roamers.   The Nerothers had a summer camp at Moers—that's
just a little way from here.   They had a secret ' Order of Pirates '
in their alliance ; maybe they'd been reading Cooper or Karl
May.   Of course Cooper has a pirate story !   Why, he wrote
The Pilot and *The Red Rover* and *Jack Tier* !   I've read them
myself—translations, of course.   But I can read English.   I wish
I had some books like that to read now.   You don't have any
with you, I suppose ?   Yes ?   Are pocket-size books like this
printed for the American soldiers ?   That's a good idea ; I wish
I'd been an American.   I think I'll like this book ; it's a fat one.
Is it the only one you've got with you ?   You think it may be
too old for me ?   Well, after all, I'm nearly sixteen.   I'm not
very husky, I know, but I know a lot.   *The History of Rome Hanks*
is a queer title ; what's it about ?   The Civil War ?   I guess
I'll like it, but we're fed up with war.   My brother Hans was
killed by the Nazis because he tried to stop the war.

   " Shall I tell you about Hans ?   Good ; maybe you'll tell
other people, *gelt* ?   They ought to know about fellows like
Hans.   He was a wonder, my father used to tell us.   Yes, he's
dead, too.   People's Levy.   Just before the end.   Well, about
Hans : he was a wonder.   He hadn't had much education, but
he managed to pass a lot of special examinations the Nazis set
up, and by keeping his mouth shut and going to Storm Trooper
meetings once in a while he got a chance to get into the university.
Our family were Independent Socialist Party, and Hans never
really believed that Nazi stuff, but he kept his mouth shut
I guess he was just waiting for a good chance.

   " He had already finished three semesters at Münster when
the war started.   They dragged him into the army, and he fought
in Poland and lots of other places, but he finally got into that
awful Stalingrad campaign.   That was awful, that was !   His
letters would just make your hair stand on end !   Those Russians
fought like wild beasts, like—like tigers.   Anyway, we didn't

take Stalingrad, but Hans had a little luck. He was in one of the detachments that was almost ground to pieces months before the final collapse, and he managed to get back to Germany while troops could still get back.

" He wasn't supposed to, but he sneaked home without a furlough. It was before they began shooting all the *Wehrmacht* AWOLs as deserters, and he only lost his sergeant's stripes. No, there was another punishment : he couldn't do active duty any longer, but instead of letting him stay in a unit near home here, they sent him to Bavaria. After he'd been there a couple of weeks an army doctor found out that Hans had tuberculosis and might not live long, so they gave him an army discharge.

" But he didn't come home ; he'd met a nice Munich girl there, and she was going to the university. Hans, I guess, thought that he'd go to the university too and finish up—how he managed to get the money father never knew. He didn't tell us much. Klärchen—that was Hans' girl—had never been enthusiastic about the war, and maybe what had happened to Hans made her like it even less. Anyway, she did typing over in the *Landesregierung* in her spare time, and from what Hans wrote, Gauleiter Giesler began to flirt with her right away. You know. That must have made Hans wild. Anyway, both Hans and Klärchen got into an anti-Nazi student organization that was doing all sorts of underground work in the university. I guess they were in pretty deep.

" Then came the news of the final defeat at Stalingrad. Even the anti-Nazis were upset ; nobody felt good around here— even my father was upset. I don't know exactly what happened among those Munich students, but one day we got word that Hans, along with a big lot of other students, had been executed for treason. It seems that Hans had made a speech or something —he was always a kind of ringleader wherever he was—and that later somebody had made a lot of typed copies and passed them out among the students right in one of the big lecture-rooms. Maybe it was Klärchen—we never knew. But we never heard from her again either.

" That was in 1943. Then, only this year, one of the older Kittelbach alliance who came through here after we were driven out of the Ardennes—he was in the *Wehrmacht* then—gave my father a piece of paper all wadded up. He was pretty secret about it. After he'd slipped away and we got the creases all smoothed out we could see why : it was Hans' speech ! That was in February, I think—anyway, my father didn't seem to care any longer about anything. My mother was half crazy from the bombing, and maybe—maybe my father knew that he would be killed in the People's Levy. Anyway, he gave me Hans' speech, and said that the Kittelbachers should make lots of copies and go out at night and stick them on advertising kiosks and every place else we could. We did, and we had the Gestapo and the regular police snuffing around like bloodhounds, and they never caught us!

"Look, I have a copy of that speech right here; I keep it folded up and use it for a bookmark. Shall I read it to you? You seem to have a little Cologne accent, but your German really isn't very good. Shall I?

"'Fellow-students: Our people, our folk, stand appalled; the men of Stalingrad have succumbed. Three hundred and thirty thousand German men have been thrust into death and destruction by the strategy of a genius, the irresponsible, senseless corporal of World War I. Führer, we thank thee!

"'The German folk seethes in indignation. Do we want to go on trusting the fate of our armies to a dilettante? Do we want to sacrifice the remnants of Germany's youth to the debased instincts of a power-lustful Party clique? Never again! The day of reckoning has come, the reckoning of our German youth with the most despicable tyranny that our people has ever suffered. In the name of German youth we demand the return of personal freedom from the State set up by Adolf Hitler— personal freedom, the most treasured value of the Germans, which Hitler has swindled from us in the most contemptible way.

"'We have grown up in a State where every free expression is remorselessly bludgeoned. The Hitler Youth, the Storm Troops, and the Élite Guard have tried to regiment us, to drug us, to pervert us. "Ideological training" is the name given to the perfidious method which stifles in a fog of meaningless phrases every impulse to think and judge for ourselves. The selection of leaders is almost unimaginably diabolical and cynical; future Party high-priests are trained, at the "castles of the order", to become conscienceless exploiters and murderers, to be blind, stupid tools of the Führer. We, devoted to the things of the mind in the highest sense, are thought to be exactly suited for bludgeoning by this new caste of masters. Front-line soldiers who have returned to the university are herded about

K

the halls by student imitations of a shabby Führer, by would-be Gauleiters, as though they were schoolboys, while at the same time the real Gauleiters attack the honour of women students with their lustful buffooneries. German women students at the University of Munich have given a dignified answer to those who would stain their honour, and the men students, with a few scoundrelly exceptions, have taken up and manfully defended the cause of their respected comrades. Here is a worthy beginning of the fight for our self-determination as students—without which self-determination the values of the mind cannot be created. Our thanks to the brave comrades of both sexes who have set us so splendid an example !

" ' For us there is only one slogan : Fight the Party ! Leave the Party squads set up to make us still more politically impotent than we already are. Leave the lecture rooms of the Élite Guard leaders, big and little ; refuse to listen to Party toadies and lickspittles. Our only interest is in true science and genuine freedom of thought. We cannot be frightened by threats ; not even the closing of the University can deter us. We must fight for our future, for our freedom and honour in a State mindful of its moral responsibilities. Freedom and honour ! For ten long years Hitler and his henchmen have befouled and twisted these two splendid German words in ways possible only to charlatans who throw the highest values of a nation before swine. What they think of freedom and honour can be seen in ten years of destruction of material and mental freedom, of all moral substance in the German people. Even the most stupid German has had his eyes opened by the sight of the frightful bloodbath in which they have drenched Europe and in which they daily plunge afresh—all in the name of the honour and freedom of the German nation ! The very name of German will remain for ever besmirched if German young men and women do not finally arise, exact revenge and manifest remorse alike, exterminate our oppressors, and rebuild Europe on new spiritual foundations.

" ' Students, the German people look to us. From us our fellows await, in this year 1943, the breaking of the National Socialist terror by the power of the spirit even as 1813 saw the shattering of the Napoleonic yoke. Beresina and Stalingrad flame up in the East ; the dead of Stalingrad invoke us.

" ' Awake, my people ; the fiery signals beckon. Our people stand in revolt against the enslavement of Europe by National

Socialism ; faith shatters all fetters in the surge towards freedom and honour.' [6]

" Yes, that was Hans all right . . .

" Is that a jeep ? Is that driver a private ? Are you driving back to-night ? I'd like to tell you more, and ask some more questions, but I suppose you must go. If I ever find any of the other Kittelbachers I'll tell them that you knew the name of the alliance before you got here. Were we really in print ? "

VII

" You know that we anti-Nazis in and around Nirgends had a far-reaching organization, don't you ? No, we weren't tightly tied together ; if we had been, we'd have been too easily detected by the Gestapo. Our organization was shrewdly built ; after all, we had to have something out of the ordinary to stage an uprising against the Nazis in the closing days of the war. Not even so-called ' Red Vienna ' had an uprising ; Nirgends did.

" One of our first steps was to seize the radio station and send out our code word ' timber ', announcing the start of the putsch. Before that, through several go-betweens, we told the advancing ' enemy ' of what was under way, and asked that air attacks be stopped as they would only ruin our preparations for rebellion. They did stop, but this may not have been the result of our appeal—we don't know.

" Then we got one of the local figureheads, Aberwitz, in front of the microphone. Although we had a gun at his head, he nevertheless refused to send a surrender order to the German troops defending Nirgends. We should have shot him at once, I suppose, but we shrank from using Nazi methods. We've had enough ruthlessness.

" Although we failed with Aberwitz, we did succeed in getting the People's Levy, that collection of schoolboys, grand-fathers, lame, halt, and blind, pretty thoroughly torn to pieces. Freisinn here was out and around the night of April 14th when the People's Levy was supposed to throw itself heart and soul into the defence of the city, and he managed to mix its leaders up so completely that it never did get pulled together effectively. Some leaders, seeing what they were up against, just told their men to throw their rifles in the river and go home. Anyway, the planned last-ditch resistance didn't come off ; both sides were spared the loss of many lives.

" Too, you must realize that we tore up the whole web of communications by means of which the Nazis were running the city and the region around it.　And by ' running ' I mean running military operations, not just ordinary government.　The rapid collapse of resistance, the failure to blow up bridges, and many other things that helped the entry of the ' enemy ' army was the result of this and similar actions by our organization. We can honestly say that we have deserved well of our supposed enemies, and that our action was taken because we believed in the cause of the United Nations.　Not one of us has tried to get a position in the administration of Nirgends under MG ; our cause could readily be misunderstood if it was thought that we were merely trying to act like Vichy collaborators or Norwegian quislings.

" Now, gentlemen, perhaps I have told you enough ; moreover, I have been forbidden to engage in political activity of any kind.　I really think that we should now end our discussion.

" Oh, these are your credentials from headquarters ? Are you really empowered to let me talk as freely as I wish ? In that case I am willing to give you my present point of view, even though the giving of it might be construed as passing the bounds of purely ' private ' activities.

" Gentlemen, I feel somewhat reassured, for when you first came in here you introduced yourselves, and now you show me your credentials.　Do you know that you are the first representatives of our conquerors who have done that ?　These things may seem like very little, but to those of us who are dealing with a victorious power they mean much.

" To be sure I'll tell you about the attempt on Hitler's life on July 20th, for where our organization—which we'll call Freedom and Honour—is concerned, there isn't much to tell. We knew some of those involved personally, and suspected that something was afoot, but we weren't on the inside in any sense. Moreover, news of the attempt came too late and in too garbled a form to warrant any risk-taking action by us.　Over and above this, we probably wouldn't have taken any action if we had been on the inside, for we have little or no confidence in German generals and the putsches they stage.　Revolutions must come from the people if they are to be anything but an exchange of one evil for another.　What's more, we know a lot about the exchange of one evil for another !

" No, I wasn't aware that my tone had suddenly become

bitter, but I think that I know why.   I won't say that I am disillusioned by what the occupation government is doing, for I
know a good deal about 'military necessity' and about human
nature as it is moulded in bureaucracies, civilian or military,
and I therefore don't expect too much.   But many other members
of Freedom and Honour are disillusioned—terrifically so.   And
it was all so unnecessary !

"Examples?   Many, but one will suffice.   When a high-
ranking officer strikes with his riding-crop the table to which
we have been called for consultation, and shouts, 'You are all
German swine.   Listen to what I have to tell you', there is
justified resentment among men who took their lives in their
hands, and the lives of their families as well, to make the triumphal
entry of such officers possible, I can tell you !   We have been
treated like common criminals.   Yes, I know that there is a rule
of military government against meeting in groups of more than
six.   The Nazis get around that by forming in those long waiting
lines outside the offices of MG, conducting very efficient meetings
by whispering back and forth.   We can't even form anti-Nazi
committees such as the Russians actively sponsor in their zone.
Can you call the forming of such committees 'political activity'
in any strict sense?   We're now under city arrest, but some of
the less fortunate are in gaol.   At this rate you'll have all the
active anti-Nazis locked up with Nazis standing guard over them.

"We could understand all this when you were first learning
the occupation job, as it were, but here it is December, seven
months after you came, and the same nonsense goes on in
Nirgends even though your general has said that anti-Nazi
activities are to be given a little leeway.   Further, we find that
people who were granted high honours by the Nazis still occupy
positions of trust under you.   Simply because they weren't Party
members doesn't mean that they were not helpful and sympathetic to the Nazi cause.   Filling out questionnaires by officials
who know little or nothing of German conditions under Nazi
rule doesn't really help things much, does it?   To me, it only
seems to muddy up the waters still more.   Two or three men
who really know German conditions could do more to clear
things up than fifteen or twenty of these ignoramuses who collect
great sheaves of almost meaningless forms and then fuss around
'adding up the score'.

"Yes, I know that you have been compelled to improvise
a great deal, and that this half-crazy desire to run back home,

on the part of both officers and men, hasn't helped matters
much. But are you going to go on improvising? Worthwhile
forces that might rally to your aid are dissipated when no consistent plan for using them is followed, and Germans, in particular,
just can't understand officers who shrug their shoulders and say,
' That's the Army for you ! ' Mistakes made now will have
a fateful way of perpetuating themselves, I fear. What is done,
alas, often cannot be undone, no matter how much good-will
is exhibited.

" What would be the first thing the Freedom and Honour
organization would do if it had the power to act? Well, if you
put it that general way, it's hard to answer. Since you ask,
however, I'll try to give some kind of a reply. It seems to us,
I think, that a good beginning would be the appointment of
a kind of semi-independent governor, or whatever, from among
well-disposed Germans. He should have a definite anti-Nazi
record but, if you will excuse my saying so, should not be
a Communist. Why? Because Communists are thought to be
irresponsible, except where Russia is concerned. Oh, I beg your
pardon ; I did not realize that you would regard the toleration
of references of this kind as committing you to unfriendliness
with your former comrades-in-arms. And after all, we hear
some of your officers talking almost every day about going to
war with Russia. So? Well, if they are irresponsible and in
no way representative either of your army or of established
governmental policy, why are they tolerated? Well and good,
I'll be more careful in my remaining remarks. About this
semi-independent governor, again : he shouldn't be an aggressive
clerical, either. All over Germany the Catholic Church, which
I revere from the strictly religious standpoint, has been earning
disfavour even among its own communicants because of its undue
activity in dispensing favours and influence. Oh, I mustn't talk
in this vein either ! But you said that I could talk freely. I see :
you can't listen freely. Right, I'll confine my comments to less
embarrassing topics.

" We talk too much, I suppose, but you who have lived in
freedom cannot imagine what a relief it is to be able to speak
one's mind—within limits, of course—without fear of rotting in
a concentration camp. The other day I said to one of your
officers, ' Your tactics are as bad as those of the Gestapo '—but
I was wrong. Had I said the equivalent of that to a Gestapo
officer I would have been liquidated—promptly. Your people

simply smile tolerantly, and here I am, still speaking my mind—within limits, of course.

" For long years we lived like those hermit communities on Mount Athos, cut off from the outside world. Still, we got great comfort through listening to forbidden radio broadcasts. Our group had access to a good radio (unfortunately, it was confiscated seven months ago and has not yet been returned), and we risked our lives to listen to B.B.C., ABSIE, Luxembourg, *Soldatensender West*,[7] and several German underground stations. Yes, we really did risk our lives in listening to them. Many Germans were summarily beheaded for doing exactly that. The Nazis were much too efficient.

" Speaking of efficiency, do you suppose that there will be any change in the regional government now that the army setup in Nirgends is being shifted ? I assume that there will be none, and we'll be gratified if there isn't. At the same time, I imagine that some people in Nirgends will breathe a sigh of relief when the new army unit replaces the old. We have already heard that the new one is more rigidly disciplined. The officers of the old unit say, ' You are now being dealt with more humanely and casually than the new unit is likely to deal with you ', but many of us think, ' We'd like to be handled a little less casually by men and officers more mindful of military discipline. We'll run the risk of the " humanely ".'

" As things now stand, you know, you can't count on anything. In the part of town where I live we have a good deal of trouble with drunken soldiers who come into our homes and demand bottles of wine and the like. Most of us don't have any, and that can be embarrassing, to say the least. The other night two soldiers hammered on the door at about one o'clock until I was forced to let them in, and on ransacking the house, they found an old bottle nearly full of mineral oil. You know, the digestive lubricant. One of the soldiers insisted that it was wine, in spite of all I could tell him, and stubbornly drank it. Would you believe it ? He drained the whole bottle ! It's best not even to imagine the consequences the next day.

" That's a good joke, but it's not a joke when such fellows demand intercourse with my wife. Fortunately, I've picked up a little English since your troops have come here and, more fortunately still, long experience has taught me how to avoid quarrels with drunkards. Beyond this, I can truthfully tell them that Mrs. Nimmer is pregnant, although sometimes they cursingly proclaim that they won't give her any consideration because of that. Usually, though, their humane feelings come to the top, even when they're very drunk. With no police near by, and of course no telephone, I'll admit that I'm sometimes a little anxious. There are signs on most of the houses near my home, and on mine as well, indicating that as trustworthy civilians we are not to be disturbed, but soldiers don't seem to believe in signs.

" Most of the time, of course, your soldiers make use of the safety-valve available in the numerous German girls who roam around waiting to be ' fraternized '. It would be a mistake, however, to think that these girls have always been—well, common whores. I'm reasonably well-off and, more than that, I have secreted many articles that I can use for barter in this terrible winter, but I shudder to think of what my wife might do if she were not pregnant and saw our children wasting away. Many a girl or woman who accepts food as the price of her favours loathes herself and the man involved, but nevertheless goes on prostituting herself for the sake of her loved ones. That sounds like cheap melodrama, but it's true. It's too damned true.

" Sometimes I wonder whether we of the Freedom and Honour organization—ironical name ?—would have acted as we did had we foreseen this winter. And when we who took such risks have such doubts about the value of it all, what are those who were merely non-Nazi instead of actively anti-Nazi thinking ? They will soon be fuel for the fanatical Nazis who are still at large, if this goes on much longer. And the fanatical Nazis ? From all I can learn, they're not only busy among those Germans who were old enough to be in the armed forces, but they're also working on the minds of youngsters not yet in their 'teens—the very ones, except for the people of fifty and over, who have been least tainted by the Nazi poison until now. The Nazis not only spread rumours about quarrels among the United Nations—quarrels ? open warfare !—but also take pains to point out to these innocent youngsters how their sisters and aunts and even mothers are being corrupted by the hated invader. The Nazis say that German women are being starved in order to force them into the arms of Senegalese and American Negroes and Gurkhas and whatnot, and many of their little victims believe it. And after all, they do see a great deal that is not altogether savoury, don't they ?

" Some of us have been trying to take the minds of the youngsters off the filth and hatred that threatens to engulf them by taking advantage of the recent directive permitting youth activities—you know, the one that was issued by the occupation authorities late in 1945. Nirgends, like other cities, once had youth activities of all sorts and descriptions. So far only the traditional youth tutelage organizations have been permitted to function, and then only when they are of religious, recreational, or cultural character. That's a joke! Why? Because the Russians set up a Youth Committee in their zone in Berlin, I'm told, and after a little while this Committee became the only active youth organization in all four zones. It's in charge of a veteran Communist leader. And we of the Freedom and Honour organization, who want actively to sponsor the cause of the democracies, are told that we mustn't permit political discussion in our youth groups. Moreover, the Boy Scouts—we call them Pathfinders—are frowned upon by your authorities. I can't imagine why ; after all, we were persecuted by the Nazis because of our international affiliations. Perhaps your authorities are simply uninformed or misled. Their interpreters and secretaries—yes, and their mistresses !—are so often in sympathy with the Nazis that the current confusion is understandable. But the confusion shows no signs of clearing up—in fact, it's getting worse. If we had foreseen this ' organized chaos ', would we have risked our lives ? That question tortures me.

" Well, I know that I shouldn't talk in this way, but at times I become almost desperate. If it weren't for the fact that I have friends abroad—yes, in Britain and France and America—whose messages get through to me in spite of the cutting off of mail, I'd lose hope altogether. I met those friends when I was in the Pathfinders. Will you do me the favour of telling them—I'll give you their addresses—that the Nimmers didn't yield to Hitler, and that they won't yield to despair ? And tell them that we have faith in a better day for Germany and the world, and that we hope that the war hasn't been too hard for them. But before that better day comes, we'll have to make amends, we know, that almost stagger the imagination. The greater the crime, the greater the guilt and the greater the need for untiring effort by men of good-will.

" Yes, I'll be more discreet hereafter. Good-bye, and may we meet again under happier circumstances. It's decent of you to shake hands with me. Good-bye once more. Good-bye."

"Organized chaos!" What will it be like by June, 1946, when military government as such finally abdicates entirely and a civilian régime takes over?

Questions of this kind are futile; only resolute leadership and a definite policy administered by men who know what Germany is like can answer them—by making them superfluous. In spite of everything, it is not yet too late. We can still save our own prestige, our own potential world influence, our own strategic positions as Central European powers, our own importance in the United Nations Organization. We can save much more than this : children's lives, goodwill, man's faith in his fellows, the hope of a world which atom bombs will not blast out of unworthy existence—but why go beyond the immediate? Let us meet the blatant cynic and the crass materialist, the arrogant nationalist and the irresponsible isolationist, on grounds of their own choosing. The cold fact is that these self-seeking, narrow-hearted creatures cannot achieve even their miserably limited goals unless we act intelligently, and act *now*. "Five minutes past midnight" does not yet loom before us, but time is getting desperately short. The Control Commission has some able men on its staff, but there are far too few of them and they are hampered at every turn. They can do nothing without an aroused public opinion in Britain and America. That arousing must take place now, not next year or next war. This Epilogue ends, then, with a shout of warning : The sands are running out![8,9]

NOTES

1. This sounds like a passage from *To-morrow the World* or *Education for Death*, but actually follows the pattern of a great many tirades made by a certain type of Hitler Youth prisoner when first captured, as I have been repeatedly assured by U.S. Army interviewers with whom I have been closely associated.

2. I am informed that a directive of this kind was issued to MG and tactical units by USFET (United States Forces, European Theatre) late in 1945. Extensive comment on the consequences of this directive appeared, I am told, in a report on the German Youth Movement made by the ICD (Information Control Division) on December 27th, 1945.

3. Some of the details of this come from the account by Quentin Reynolds, "Children behind Barbed Wire", *Collier's*, 116, 17 (October 27th, 1945), pp. 18–19, 32. The implicit interpretation, however, is wholly my own. One additional matter should perhaps be called to the reader's attention : the man in charge of the re-education programme in the Compiegne camp as of October was *Private* Francis Tourtellot, formerly Assistant Professor of German, Brown University, Providence, Rhode Island. Does the U.S. Army value even the security features of the re-education of thousands of present

and potential future enemies so lightly that it places so far-reaching a programme in the hampered hands of a private, or is there good reason why he
should be a private? I have run across many motor pools containing no
more than a few jeeps, three or four command cars, and a couple of trucks,
for which the dignity and authority of at least a major were deemed necessary.
There seems to be more here than meets the eye. Is this educator's rank
a gross injustice—or what?

4. Hans Ebeling, "Youth and Democracy in Germany", *The Central
European Observer*, October 19th, 1945, pp. 306–7.

5. *Ibid.*

6. Of course, the foregoing is a direct translation of a genuine text. One
of the active leaders, if not *the* leader, of the revolt was Hans Scholl, and the
speech, which circulated from hand to hand in Munich, may be one he
made—I have been unable to check thoroughly. The Hans of this "synthetic" case, however, is *not* Hans Scholl, nor do any of the details about
family, war experience, etc., refer to Hans Scholl.

7. The British themselves released security on *Soldatensender* shortly after
V-E Day.

8. The reader has undoubtedly become well aware of the fact that there
is a considerable gap between the time when the earlier part of the book
was completed and the writing of this Epilogue in early February, 1946.

More precisely: Knowing that severe security restrictions would be
placed upon me when I joined the Office of Strategic Services, everything
but the Preface and the Epilogue was completed, in all essentials, *before the
fateful date of August 21st, 1944.* The reason for the qualification "in all
essentials" is this: two or three references to Swiss and British journals were
added in February, 1945, when the book was placed in the publisher's hands.
These references, however, were to publicly accessible sources.

Rigid observance of security restrictions proved to be of no great hindrance,
however, for in spite of increased knowledge of details I saw no reason, even
in the early Spring of 1945, for changing anything that I had written at the
time when I could freely present my evidence and conclusions. As I look
back, I can say that I did a workmanlike bit of prediction—or prophecy.
Whatever it may be called, for every practical purpose the last chapter,
"Premonitions: What of the Night?" is the stuff of to-day's headlines—
and to-morrow's.

Not even a confirmed addict of the crystal ball, however, sees all the
details. The chance to observe, on the ground, the mental and material
rubble heap that is to-day's Germany necessarily added much that I had only
dimly envisaged or had not foreseen at all. I was able to move freely
throughout the entirety of both British and American zones from V-E Day
on, and before that time I had not only been on the fringes of Germany but also
had many opportunities for conferring with anti-Nazis who were in the
closest possible touch, to put it discreetly, with affairs inside Fortress *Deutschland.*
Further, as a civilian with the assimilated rank of lieutenant-colonel, I was
neither fish nor fowl, and therefore may have preserved a certain detachment
that sharpened observation of both the enemy and our own forces during
combat and occupation.

Nowhere in the Epilogue, however, have I recorded any "personal
experiences of a military character". My work as leader of the Morale
Operations Unit attached to Secret Intelligence had nothing to do with
German youth as such, and my earlier work in OSS had only remote and
incidental connections wholly unmentioned here. At the same time, it is
impossible to wipe out accumulated impressions even though these are
by-products. All the cases contained in the Epilogue maintain the "illusion
of fiction" mentioned in the notes of Chapters I and VI, but there is a great

deal of empirical basis for them in every instance. Moreover, since my return to the United States in September, 1945, I have followed closely the accounts by foreign correspondents in reputable journals here and abroad, and have received several personal letters from informants on or near the spot. It is therefore possible to say that although the Epilogue violates no security regulations, it also contains no " pure fiction ".

As an American, it is obvious that many of my comments and the details of my " synthetic " cases would refer primarily, although perhaps involuntarily, to happenings in the American zone. Nevertheless, I have tried to present my materials in such a way that the British zone is taken into account—and, as already noted, I did a good deal of work there on matters not directly related to the Epilogue.

In closing this long-winded but necessary explanation, let me quote from page 141 :

" The reader can therefore be reasonably certain that in spite of the form of presentation no liberties have been taken with essential truth—at least, truth as I then saw it and, with minor qualifications, as I still see it."

9. The tone of the Epilogue, and of many parts of the book proper—especially Chapter IX—should make it clearly apparent that I do not write these pages as a professional sociologist. My conception of professional sociology is that of a scientific specialism from which moral and like value-judgments are strictly excluded—in so far as they can be excluded at all. (For this and related points see my " Supreme Values and the Sociologist " in the *American Sociological Review*, 6 : 155–72, April, 1941.)

Here, however, I write as a whole man, not as a specialist. No one can engage in planned social action, or recommend such action in terms of the kind I have used at various crucial points, and at the same time pose as a detached analyst. For better or for worse, this is the voice of Howard Becker warbling his native woodnotes wild.

Further, nothing I say here in any way represents *any* official organization, much less the Office of Strategic Services. I am not attached to that agency by any bonds save those of pleasant memories of brave and loyal associates. Now, as the immortal Rob Roy exclaimed, " My foot is on my native heath, and my name is MacGregor ! "

BIBLIOGRAPHY

I. GENERAL REFERENCES : BACKGROUND, METHOD, SOCIAL-PSYCHOLOGICAL AND
SOCIOLOGICAL PRINCIPLES, YOUTH MOVEMENTS IN NON-GERMAN COUNTRIES, ETC.

ABEL, THEODORE, " The Pattern of a Successful Political Movement "
American Sociological Review, 2, 3 (June, 1937).
ALEWYN, RICHARD, " Das Problem der Generation in der Geschichte ", in
Zeitschrift für deutsche Bildung, Heft 10 (Frankfurt am Main, 1929).
ALLPORT, G. W., " Attitudes ", in *A Handbook of Social Psychology*, ed. by
Murchison, Carl (Worcester [Mass.] and London, 1935).
ANDERSON, J. E., " The Genesis of Social Reaction in the Young Child ",
in *The Unconscious*, ed. by Dummer, E. (New York, 1937).
BAIN, READ, " Personality Development and Marriage ", in *Marriage and the
Family*, Becker, Howard, and Hill, Reuben, eds. (Boston, 1942).
——, " Sociology and Psychoanalysis ", *American Sociological Review*, 1, 2
(April, 1936).
BARKER, ERNEST, " The Development of Administration, Conscription, Taxa-
tion, Social Services, and Education ", in *European Civilization*, vol. 5,
ed. by Eyre, E. (London, 1937).
BARNES, HARRY ELMER, and BECKER, HOWARD, *Social Thought from Lore to Science*,
vols. 1 and 2 (Boston, 1938), *passim* for " sacred ", " charismatic leader-
ship ", etc. A very full and systematic topical index is provided.
BARNES, HARRY ELMER ; BECKER, FRANCES BENNETT ; and BECKER, HOWARD,
eds., *Contemporary Social Theory* (New York, 1940), *passim* for " constructive
typology ", " historical sociology ", etc. A very full and systematic
topical index is provided.
BECKER, HOWARD, " Interpretive Sociology and Constructive Typology ", in
Twentieth-century Sociology, Gurvitch, G., and Moore, W. E., eds. (New
York, 1945).
——, " Peoples of Germany ", in *Problems of the Post-War World*, McCormick,
T. C. T., ed. (New York, 1945).
——, " Changing Societies as Family Contexts ", in *Marriage and the Family*,
Becker and Hill, eds. (Boston, 1942).
——, *Systematic Sociology on the Basis of the* Beziehungslehre *and* Gebildelehre
of Leopold von Wiese (New York, 1932), *passim* for " perversion ", " youth-
age conflict ", etc. A very full and systematic topical index is provided.
——, ed., *The Student Challenge* (Chicago, 1924–5). Contains numerous
articles and editorials on youth movement matters.
BELL, E. H., " Age Group Conflict and Our Changing Culture ", *Social
Forces*, 12, 1933.
BELL, HOWARD, *Youth Tell Their Story*. The American Youth Commission
(Washington, D.C., 1938).
BITHELL, JETHRO, *Germany : A Companion to German Studies* (London, 1932).
BLONDEL, CHARLES, *Introduction à la psychologie collective* (Paris, 1928).
BOLL, FRANZ, *Die Lebensalter* (Leipzig : Teubner, 1913).
BOSCH, B., " Massenführer und Gruppenführer ", *Zeitschrift für pädagog.
Psych.*, 30, 6 (1929).
CANTRIL, HADLEY, *The Psychology of Social Movements* (New York, 1941).
CARPENTER, J., and EISENBERG, P., " Some Relations between Family Back-
ground and Personality ", *Journal of Psychology*, 6 (1938).
DAVIS, KINGSLEY, " The Sociology of Parent-Youth Conflict ", *American
Sociological Review*, 5, 4 (August, 1940).

DAWSON, W. H., *The Evolution of Modern Germany* (London, 1908).

DOLLARD, JOHN, *Criteria for the Life History* (New Haven, 1935).

EXTON, E., *Youth : A Contemporary Bibliography with Annotations.* Committee on Youth Problems, U.S. Office of Education, Circular 152 (Washington, 1935).

FREYTAG, GUSTAV, *Bilder aus der deutschen Vergangenheit*, in the translation by Mrs. Malcolm, *Pictures of German Life in the XVIIIth and XIXth Centuries*, second series (London, 1863).

GLUECK, B., " The Significance of Parental Attitudes for the Destiny of the Individual ", *Mental Hygiene*, 12 (1928).

GOLDHAMER, H., and SHILS, E. A., " Types of Power and Status ", *American Journal of Sociology*, 45 (1939).

GÜNTHER, HANS F. K., *Das Bauerntum als Lebens- und Gemeinschaftsform* (Leipzig, 1939).

HADFIELD, J. A., *The Psychology of Power* (London, 1933).

HARTMANN, HANS, *Die junge Generation in Europa* (Berlin, 1930).

HERRMANN, GERTRUD, *Formen des Gemeinschaftslebens jugendlicher Mädchen*, supplement 2 of *Zeitschrift für angewandte Psychologie*, 44 (1929).

HIGH, STANLEY, *The Revolt of Youth* (Cincinnati, 1923).

HOFSTÄTTER, WALTHER, and PETERS, ULRICH, eds., *Sachwörterbuch der Deutschkunde*, 2 vols. (Leipzig, 1930).

HORNEY, KAREN, *New Ways in Psychoanalysis* (New York, 1939).

KARDINER, ABRAM, *The Individual and His Society* (New York, 1939).

——, " Security and Cultural Restraints ", *The Family*, October, 1937.

KNOPPERS, B. A., *Die Jugendbewegung in den Niederlanden* (Emsdetten, 1931).

KOHN, HANS, *Geschichte der nationalen Bewegung im Orient* (Berlin, 1928), trans. by M. M. Green (London, 1929).

KOSOK, PAUL, *Modern Germany* (Chicago, 1933).

LASSWELL, HAROLD, *World Politics and Personal Insecurity* (Chicago, 1935).

LEOPOLD, L., *Prestige : A Psychological Study of Social Estimates* (London, 1913).

LICHTENBERGER, HENRI, *Germany and Its Evolution in Modern Times* (New York, 1913).

LÜDTKE, GERHARDT, and MACKENSEN, LUTZ, eds., *Deutscher Kulturatlas* (Berlin, 1928–38).

LUITHLEN, W. F., " Zur Psychologie der Initiative und der Führereigenschaften ", *Zeitschrift für angewandte Psychologie*, 39, 1931.

McDOUGALL, WILLIAM, " Organization of the Affective Life : A Critical Survey ", *Acta Psychologica*, 2 (1937).

McGILL, NETTIE, and MATTHEWS, ELLEN, *The Youth of New York City* (New York, 1940).

MANNHEIM, KARL, *Diagnosis of Our Time*, especially Chapter 3, " The Problem of Youth in Modern Society " (London, 1943). The whole book, however, is of the highest relevance.

——, *Man and Society in an Age of Reconstruction* (London, 1940). This has an elaborate seventy-page bibliography that should be used to supplement the somewhat abridged list given here.

——, " Mass Education and Group Analysis ", in *Educating for Democracy*, ed. by Cohen, J. I., and Traver, R. M. W. (London, 1939).

MEHNERT, KLAUS, *Die Jugend in Sowjetrussland* (Berlin, 1932), trans .by Michael Davidson (London, 1933).

MENTRÉ, FRANÇOIS, *Les générations sociales* (Paris : Bossard, 1920).

MERRIAM, C. E., *The Making of Citizens : A Comparative Study of Methods of Civic Training* (Chicago, 1931).

PARSONS, TALCOTT, *The Structure of Social Action* (New York, 1937).

PINDER, WILHELM, *Das Problem der Generation* (Berlin : Frankfurter Verlagsanstalt, 1926).

PLANT, J. S., *Personality and the Cultural Pattern* (New York, 1937).

REUTER, E. B., " The Sociology of Adolescence ", *American Journal of Sociology*, 43 (1937).

REUTER, E. B., MEAD, M., and FOSTER, R. G., " Sociological Research in Adolescence ", *American Journal of Sociology*, 42 (1936).

ROTH, HEINRICH, *Psychologie der Jugendgruppe* (Berlin, 1938).

SCHAIRER, R., *Not, Kampf, Ziel der Jugend in sieben Ländern* (Frankfurt, 1935).

SCHETTLER, CLARENCE, " Topical Summaries of Current Literature : Personality Traits ", *American Journal of Sociology*, 45 (1939).

SCHMALENBACH, HERMANN, " Die soziologische Kategorie des Bundes ", *Die Dioskuren, Jahrbuch für Geisteswissenschaften* (Munich, 1922).

SCHURTZ, HEINRICH, *Altersklassen und Männerbünde : Eine Darstellung der Grundformen der Gesellschaft* (Berlin, 1902).

SIKORSKI, HANS, " Die Auswahl und soziale Zusammensetzung des Führernachwuchses ", *Volk und Reich*, 8 (2), 1932.

SMITH, H. L., and KRUEGER, L. M., " A Brief Summary of the Literature on Leadership ", *Bulletin of the School of Education* (Bureau of Co-operative Research), Indiana University, Bloomington, Ind., 9, 4 (September, 1933).

SPEIER, HANS, " Honor and Social Structure ", *Social Research*, 2 (1935).

STEINHAUSEN, GEORG, *Geschichte der deutschen Kultur*, 3rd ed. (Leipzig, 1929).

STERN, L., " The Sociology of Authority ", *Publications of the American Sociological Society*, 18 (1923).

STRICH, W., *Der irrationale Mensch : Studium zur Systematik der Geschichte* (Berlin, 1928).

THOMAS, W. I., " The Behaviour Pattern and the Situation ", in *Personality and the Group*, ed. by Burgess, E. W. (Chicago, 1929).

THRASHER, FREDERICK, *The Gang* (Chicago, 1927).

THRUM, G., *Der Typ des Zerrissenen : Ein Vergleich mit dem romantischen Problematiker.* " Von deutscher Poeterey " Series, 10 (Leipzig, 1931).

TÖNNIES, FERDINAND, *Gemeinschaft und Gesellschaft*, 8th ed. (Leipzig, 1935), trans. by C. P. Loomis as *Fundamental Concepts of Sociology* (New York, 1940).

TROELTSCH, ERNST, *Die Soziallehren der christlichen Kirchen und Gruppen*, Wyon trans. (New York, 1931).

TRUHEL, K., *Sozialbeamte : Ein Beitrag zur Sozioanalyse der Bürokratie.* A Thesis. Frankfurt am Main, 1933. Sagan (Benjamin Krause) 1934.

VAERTING, M., " Der Korpsgeist bei Herrschenden und Beherrschten ", *Archiv. für systematischen Philosophie und Soziologie*, 31 (1928).

VAUGHAN, W., *The Lure of Superiority : A Study in the Psychology of Motives* (New York, 1928).

WÄHLER, MARTIN, ed., *Der deutsche Volkscharakter* (Jena, 1937).

WEBER, MAX, *Wirtschaft und Gesellschaft* (Tübingen, 1922), esp. pp. 140–5, 227–363, 753–78.

——, *Gesammelte Aufsätze zur Wissenschaftslehre* (Tübingen, 1920).

——, *Gesammelte Aufsätze zur Religionssoziologie* (Tübingen, 1920).

WECHSSLER, EDUARD, *Die Generation als Jugendreihe und ihr Kampf um die Denkform* (Leipzig : Quelle und Meyer, 1930).

——, " Die Generation als Jugendgemeinschaft ", in *Festschrift für Kurt Breysig*, I, Geschichtsphilosophie und Soziologie (Breslau, 1927).

WENDEL, HERMANN, *Aus dem südslavischen Risorgimento* (Gotha, 1921).

WIESER, M., *Der sentimentale Mensch* (Gotha-Stuttgart, 1924).

WINSLOW, THACHER, and DAVIDSON, FRANK, eds., *American Youth* (Cambridge, Mass., 1940).

WINSLOW, THACHER, *Youth : A World Problem* (U.S. Printing Office, Washington, D.C., 1937).

II. SPECIFIC REFERENCES : GERMAN YOUTH MOVEMENTS AND RELATED MATTERS

ABEL, THEODORE, *How Hitler Came into Power* (New York, 1938).
American Friends of German Freedom, *Inside Germany Reports*, 25 (August, 1943). Contains a complete translation of the leaflet distributed by German students in Munich after the student riots there in 1943.
Anti-Nazi Germans, a group of, *The Next Germany* (New York, 1943). See especially Chapter 7, " Education for a New Society ".
BECKER, HOWARD, " The Chance of Youth ", *The Student Challenge*, Walter Mueller, ed. (Chicago, 1924), 2, 2, pp. 2, 14.
BECKMANN, EMMY, *Die Entwicklung der höheren Mädchenbildung in Deutschland von 1870 bis 1914, dargestellt in Dokumenten* (Berlin, 1936).
BIESANZ, JOHN, " Nazi Influence on German Youth Hostels ", *Social Forces* 19, 4 (May, 1941), pp. 554–9.
BLÜHER, HANS, *Der Charakter der Jugendbewegung* (Lauenburg, 1921).
——, *Werke und Tage* (Jena, 1920).
——, *Führer und Volk in der Jugendbewegung* (Jena, 1919).
——, *Gesammelte Aufsätze* (Jena, 1919).
——, *Die Rolle der Erotik in der männlichen Gesellschaft*, two vols. (Jena, 1919).
——, *Wandervogel, Geschichte einer Bewegung*, two vols. (Jena, 1912).
——, *Die deutsche Wandervogelbewegung als erotisches Phänomen* (Berlin, 1912).
——, and von Prosch, Milla, *Mehrehe und Mutterschaft* (Jena, 1918).
BREUER, HANS, ed., *Der Zupfgeigenhansl*, many editions, see text. Last ed. available to me, Leipzig, 1938.
BROSSMER, KARL, *Wanderheime der Jugend* (Freiburg, 1920).
BUSSE-WILSON, ELISABETH, *Die Frau und die Jugendbewegung* (Hamburg, 1920).
Christian Century, " German Youth Is Not All Nazified ", 60, 27 (July 7th, 1943).
DÖRNER, CLAUS, *Freude, Zucht, Glaube* (Potsdam, 1937).
EBELING, HANS, *The German Youth Movement*, with a Preface by Barclay Baron, O.B.E. (London : New Europe Publishing Company, Ltd., 1945).
    This pamphlet is an excellent brief presentation of the case for the alliance or *bündische* youth of Germany. It is definitely partial to the alliance youth, but contains some evidence that would have led me to alter my interpretation somewhat had it come to my hands earlier.
——, " Youth and Democracy in Germany ", *The Central European Observer* (October 19th, 1945), pp. 306–7.
EHRENTHAL, GÜNTHER, *Die deutschen Jugendbünde* (Berlin, 1929).
FRÄNKEL, H., " Is Hitler Youth Curable? " *New Republic*, 111 (September 18th, 1944), pp. 335–7.
FRIEDLANDER, WALTER, and MYERS, KARL, *Child Welfare in Germany before and after Nazism* (Chicago, 1940).
FRÖBEL, FRIEDRICH, *Brief an die Frauen in Keilhau* (Weimar, 1935).
FRUCHT, LOTTE, and SCHNEEHAGEN, CHRISTIAN, *Unsere Kleidung* (Hamburg, 1914).
Germany. This is a confidential handbook, the precise title of which I cannot give, which was issued by British PID for general guidance during war time. Chapter XV, dealing with youth movements, is the best brief compilation to be found anywhere, to my knowledge. Administrative officers undoubtedly have access to this volume, and perhaps security on it has already been released. At any rate, it *must* be mentioned.
GOETSCH, GEORG, *Die deutsche Jugendbewegung* (Leipzig, 1928).
GRAY, H. D., " What To Do with German Youth ", *New Republic*, 111 (July 24th, 1944), p. 105.
GRÜNDEL, GÜNTHER, *Die Sendung der jungen Generation* (Munich, 1932).
GÜNTHER, ALBRECHT, *Geist der Jungmannschaft* (Hamburg, 1934).

GURIAN, WALDEMAR, *Die deutsche Jugendbewegung* (Habelschwerdt, 1924).

HALL, M., "German Youth : A Lost Generation?" *Christian Century*, 61 (September 27th, 1944), pp. 1098–1100.

HÄNSEL, LUDWIG, *Die Jugend und die leibliche Liebe* (Munich, 1938).

HARTSHORNE, E. Y., *German Youth and the Nazi Dream of Victory* (Farrar and Rinehart, 1941).

HAUSER, ERNEST O., "The Dead-End Kids of Cologne", *The Saturday Evening Post*, 217, 51 (June 16th, 1945), pp. 18–19, 84.

HEIMANN, EDUARD, *Das Sexualproblem der Jugend* (Jena, 1913).

HERMAN, STUART P., Jr., *It's Your Souls We Want* (New York, 1942).

HERRLE, THEO, *Die deutsche Jugendbewegung* (Gotha, 1924).

HILLER, R. L. H., "German Youth Will Gladly Die", *Survey Graphic*, 30 (February, 1941), pp. 68–71.

HÖCKNER, HILMAR, *Die Musik in der deutschen Jugendbewegung* (Wolfenbüttel, 1927).

HODANN, MAX, and KOCH, WALTHER, *Die Urburschenschaft als Jugendbewegung* (Jena, 1917).

HOFFMANN, ROLF JOSEF, *Fug und Unfug der Jugendkultur* (Greiz, 1914).

JACOBY, H., "Die Befreiung der schöpferischen Kräfte dargestellt am Beispiel der Musik", *Das werdende Zeitalter*, 4, 4 (Gotha, 1925).

KANDEL, I. L., *The Making of Nazis* (New York, 1934).

KIRKPATRICK, CLIFFORD, *Women in Nazi Germany* (Indianapolis, 1937).

KNELLER, GEORGE FREDERICK, *The Educational Philosophy of National Socialism* (New Haven, 1941).

KOTSCHNIG, WALTER M., *Slaves Need No Leaders* (New York, 1943).

KRIECK, ERNST, *Nationalpolitische Erziehung*, 22nd ed. (Leipzig, 1938).

——, *Nationalsozialistische Erziehung* (Osterwieck : Zickfeldt, 1937).

——, *Wissenschaft, Weltanschauung, Hochschulreform* (Leipzig, 1934).

KURELLA, ALFRED, *Die Geschlechterfrage der Jugend* (Hamburg, 1920).

LEHMANN, ERNST, *Erziehung im Volke : Darstellung der volkhaften Erziehung auf volkskundlicher Grundlage* (Langensalza, Berlin, Leipzig, 1936).

Life, "Boy Comes Home : Parents Get Back a Startling Product of Hitler's Education", 12 (June 22nd, 1942), pp. 31–4.

Living Age, "Triumph of German Youth : All Europe Is Now Ready for the Nazi Revolution in the Storm Trooper View", 358 (August, 1940), pp. 520–4.

LÜTKENS, CHARLOTTE, *Die deutsche Jugendbewegung* (Frankfurt am Main, 1925).

MASON, JOHN BROWN, "Academic Freedom under Nazism", *Social Science* (October, 1940).

MASSMAN, KURT, *Hitlerjugend—neue Jugend !* (Breslau, 1938).

MESSNER, A., "Die freideutsche Jugendbewegung", *Pädagogisches Magazin*, no. 597. Also as brochure, 5th ed. (Langensalza, 1915), and in *Die neue Jugend*, vol. 5 of *Forschungen zur Völkerpsychologie und Soziologie*, Richard Thurnwald, ed. (Leipzig, 1937).

MÖLLER, ALBRECHT, *Wir Werden das Volk* (Breslau, 1935).

Monthly Labour Review, "Employment of Young People in Germany" (tabulation), 55 (August, 1942), pp. 234–7.

MUCKLE, *Friedrich Gustav Wyneken* (Lauenburg, 1924).

MUNSKE, HILDE, *Mädel in aller Welt* (Berlin, 1936).

NEUMANN, S., "Conflict of Generations in Contemporary Europe", *Vital Speeches*, 5 (August 1st, 1939), pp. 623–8.

PAETEL, K. O., "Nazis under Twenty-One", *Nation*, 158 (April 1st–8th), pp. 391–2, 419–21.

PEISER, WERNER, "Educational Failure of the Weimar Republic", *School and Society*, 58, 1503 (October 16th, 1943), pp. 289–92.

PEISER, WERNER, "Goethe's Educational Philosophy and the Re-education of German Youth", *Education*, 65 (September, 1944), pp. 3–8.

PLENGE, JOHANNES, *Anti-Blüher : Affenbund oder Männerbund?* (Hartenstein, 1921).

Reichsjugendführung der NSDAP, eds., *Aufbau, Gliederung, und Anschriften der Hitlerjugend* (Berlin, 1934).

——, *Das Kleinheim der Hitlerjugend* (Berlin, 1939).

——, *Das Landdienstheim der Hitlerjugend* (Berlin, 1939).

——, *Youth Activities in Modern Germany* (Berlin, 1936).

REYNOLDS, QUENTIN, "Children behind Barbed Wire", *Collier's*, 116, 17 (October 27th, 1945), pp. 18–19, 32.

ROCHOLL, ARNOLD, *Deutsche Jugend im Beruf* (Hamburg, 1937).

RODATZ, JOHANNES, *Erziehung durch Erleben* (Berlin, 1936).

SCHNABEL, REIMUND, *Das Führerschulungswerk der Hitlerjugend* (Berlin, 1938).

SCHOMBURG, H. E., *Der Wandervogel, seine Freunde und seine Gegner* (Wolfenbüttel, 1917).

SIEMERING, HERTHA, *Die deutschen Jugendpflegeverbände* (Berlin, 1918).

——, *Die deutschen Jugendverbände* (Berlin, 1931).

SOFFNER, H., "Can Europe's Youth Be Salvaged?" *Survey Graphic*, 32 (January, 1943), pp. 15–19.

STAHLIN, O., *Die deutsche Jugendbewegung*, 2nd ed. (Leipzig, 1930).

STÄHLIN, WILHELM, *Fieber und Heil in der Jugendbewegung* (Hamburg, 1924).

STERN, W., *Die Inversionswelle, ein zeitgeschichtlicher Beitrag zur Jugendpsychologie* (Stuttgart, 1922).

STRASSER, O., "German Youth as a Postwar Problem", *Catholic World*, 156 (February, 1943), pp. 530–2.

TAYLOR, JOHN WILKINSON, *Youth Welfare in Germany* (Nashville, Tennessee, 1936).

TEPP, MAX, *Vom Sinn des Körpers* (Hamburg, 1919).

THIELE, GUNAR, *Geschichte der preussischen Lehrerseminare* (Berlin, 1938).

THOMSON, GEORGE, *The Influence of the Youth Movement on German Education.* Unpublished Ph.D. Thesis at the University of Glasgow, Dept. of Education, 1934.

Times Educational Supplement, "From Hitler Movement to Hitlerjugend", London, May 31st, 1941.

——, "Schools in Germany : Reorganisation in Theory and in Fact", London, February 20th, 1943.

UFFRECHT, BERNHARD, *Dr. Gustav Wyneken, eine Abwehr und Abrechnung* (Jena, 1917).

ULICH, ROBERT, "Germany", *Educational Yearbook* (New York, 1936), pp. 339–61.

VAGTS, ALFRED, *Hitler's Second Army* (Washington, D.C., 1943). See Chapter 12, "Hitler Youth : Hitler Jugend or HJ", pp. 190–220.

VESPER, WILL, *Deutsche Jugend* (Berlin, 1934).

VON SCHIRACH, BALDUR, *Revolution der Erziehung* (Munich, 1938).

WUNDERLICH, FRIEDA, "Education in Nazi Germany", *Social Research*, 4 (1937), pp. 346–60.

WYNEKEN, GUSTAV, *Eros* (Lauenburg, 1921).

——, *Der Kampf für die Jugend* (Jena, 1919).

——, *Der Gedankenkreis der freien Schulgemeinde* (Jena, 1919).

——, *Schule und Jugendkultur* (Jena, 1919).

ZAUGG, E., "German Youth Is Disillusioned", *Christian Science Monitor Magazine*, June 24th, 1944, p. 3.

ZIEMER, GREGOR, *Education for Death* (New York, 1941).

III.   YOUTH MOVEMENT PERIODICALS, CHIEFLY FROM THE HITLER PERIOD

Das deutsche Mädel (Berlin).
Das Jugendgelände (Berlin).
Das junge Deutschland (Berlin).
Der Altherrenbund (Grossenhain).
Der Pimpf (Berlin).
Die Bewegung (Berlin).
Die Heime der Hitlerjugend (Berlin).
Die Jungenschaft (Berlin).
Die Jungmädelschaft (Berlin).
Die Kameradschaft (Berlin).
Die Mädelschaft (Berlin).
Die Spielschar (Berlin).
Freideutsche Jugend (Hamburg).
Hitler-Jugend Jahrbuch (Berlin).
Illustrierte Hitler-Jugend (Berlin).
Jugend und Heimat (Berlin).
Kameradschaft (Brussels, 1937–40).
Wandervogel (Leipzig, 1907–12).
Wandervogel in Hessen und am Rhein (Giessen, 1912–15).
Wille und Macht (Berlin).

INDEX

(Epilogue and Bibliography are not included)